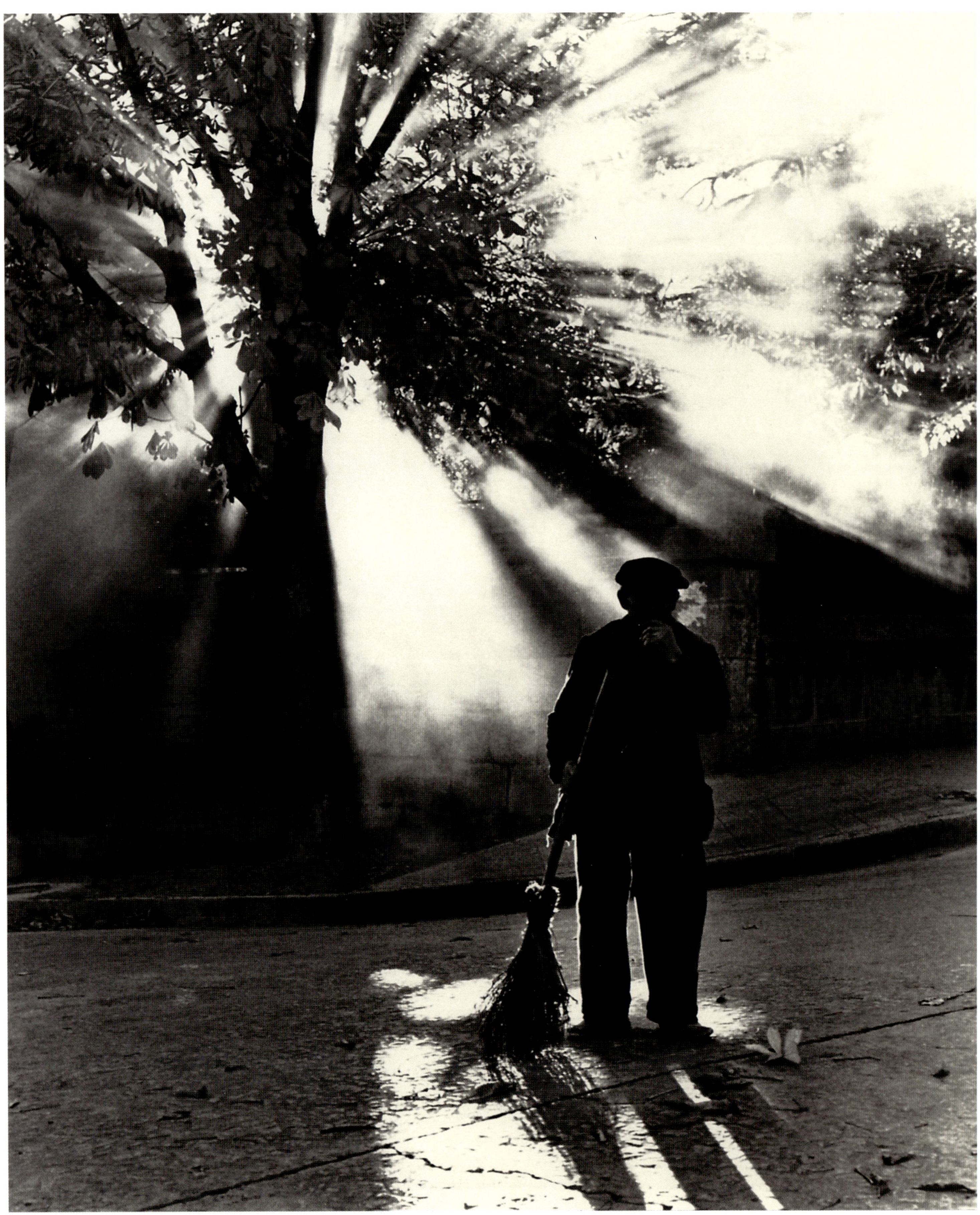

The Street Sweeper, Spain, 1966

THE EYES OF HIS SOUL
The Visual Legacy of Barry M. Goldwater, Master Photographer

Text by Evelyn S. Cooper
Michael P. Goldwater, Photo Editor

Foreword by Mary Dell Pritzloff

Arizona Historical Foundation
Hayden Library, Arizona State University, Tempe, Arizona 85287-1006

Library of Congress Catalog Card Number:
2002106313

ISBN: 0910152195

The Eyes of His Soul:
The Visual Legacy of Barry M. Goldwater, Master Photographer

Published by the Arizona Historical Foundation
Box 871006
Tempe, Arizona 85287-1006
U.S.A.

Printed in the U.S.A.

Respectfully Dedicated
to the
Spirit and Legacy
of
Barry Morris Goldwater
(January 1, 1909 – May 29, 1998)
and
Margaret "Peggy" Johnson Goldwater
(July 8, 1909 – December 11, 1985)

TABLE OF CONTENTS

Foreword   11

Prelude   13

The Family Birthright   14
Talking the Talk, Walking the Walk   31
Endnotes   50

About the Photographs   53

PORTFOLIO   55

FAMILY   57

Peggy, 1941   60
Joanne Goldwater, 1939   60
The Goldwater Girls, 1948   62
Barry Jr. Giving Michael a Haircut, Middle Fork
    of the Salmon River, 1960   64
Family Outing, 1950   66
Impromptu Family Portrait, 1948   68
Peggy the Fisherwoman, Middle Fork
    of the Salmon River, 1950   70
Self-Portrait, 1948   72

HOMELAND   75

Canyon Snow, 1951   76
The Valley, 1967   78
Big Country, 1953   80
Basaltic Schist, 1965   82
Hole In the Rock, 1938   84
Totem Pole and Yei-Be-Chai, 1967   86
The Fence, 1967   88
Desert Sentinel, 1968   90
The Mitten, 1967   92
Valley of The Monuments, 1967   94
Snowbank, 1965   96
Children On A Hill, 1950   98
Margaret Arch, White Mesa, 1954   100
Deer Creek Falls, August 15, 1940   102
Verde, 1951   104
Westward Ho, c. 1938   106
Navajo Pony, c. 1938   108
The Desert Corsage, 1936   110

Snow Fence Near Flagstaff, 1936   112
The Navajo, 1938   114
Pipe Springs, Wolf Hole, 1938   116
The Shepherdess, 1946   118
Road to Rainbow, 1938   120
Driftwood, 1965   122
Fallen Friend, 1965   124
Old Hualapai Indian Scout, 1938   126
Forest Lake, 1937   128
Hell Roaring Canyon, July 12, 1940   130
Spires, White Mesa, 1936   132
Cochise Stronghold, 1965   134
Church Rock, 1938   136
The Old One, 1938   138
Cabin At Old Mine in Glen Canyon,
    July 24, 1940   140
Bedroom, Dark Canyon, July 18, 1940   142
Journey's End, Separation Canyon at the Head of
    Lake Mead August 22, 1940   144
Bowknot Bend, Labyrinth Canyon,
    July 12, 1940   146
Navajo Elder, 1967   148
Chemehuevi Woman, 1938   150
Century Plant, 1948   152
Hopi Child, 1959   154
Sundust Family Portrait, 1959   156
The Chief, 1948   158
Navajo Maidens, 1956   160
Waterway, 1954   162
White Mesa, 1967   164
San Francisco Peaks from Mormon Lake, 1967
    166
Snowfall, San Francisco Peaks, 1957   168
Jegini Yazzie Begay, 1949   170
The Power of Advertising, 1948   172
The Hopi, 1949   174
Windmill, 1938   176
Maurice and Rosemary Knee,
    Informal Portrait, 1967   178
Navajo Man at Spring, 1959   180
Weaver's Needle, Superstition Mountains, 1938   182

Roosevelt Dam, 1936   184

Landscape, 1959   186

Saguaro Symphony, 1938   188

Middlefork of the Salmon River, 1950   190

Mount Borah, Idaho, 1950   192

Ocean, Monterey, California, 1940   194

STATESMAN ABROAD   197

Santiago, c. 1930   198

Acapulco, 1955   200

El Viejo, Mexico City, 1952   202

The Net Mender, 1952   204

Young Girl In Spain, 1965   206

Desert Architecture, 1938   208

Marcos De Niza Manuscript, 1965   210

Spanish Maiden, 1965   212

Caribbean, 1960   214

A Caribbean Native, 1960   216

Grass Huts, 1960   218

Nile River Washerwomen, 1965   220

Afterword   223

Index   225

About the Author/About the Photo Editor   231

Mary Dell Pritzloff enjoyed a friendship with
Senator Barry M. Goldwater richly textured
by the hands of time. She is a revered
community leader and timeless witness to
the mind, manner, and methods of a political
legend, who remained at his essence—
an artist with a cause.

FOREWORD

It is an honor to be asked to write the Foreword to this wonderful collection of Barry Goldwater's photographs that have not been seen before. I knew the Senator for thirty-five years. He was a great man and a master photographer. His camera became the eyes of his soul. The ability that Barry had to use his camera in such a variety of ways was remarkable. As the photographs show, his eye for all phases of Arizona—the land he deeply loved, and its people are a collection of master works, which are a treasure to own.

This album is a visual legacy to one of the greatest Americans. Barry and I traveled many roads together, both politically, and socially. He indeed was one of a kind.

Mary Dell Pritzloff
Phoenix, Arizona

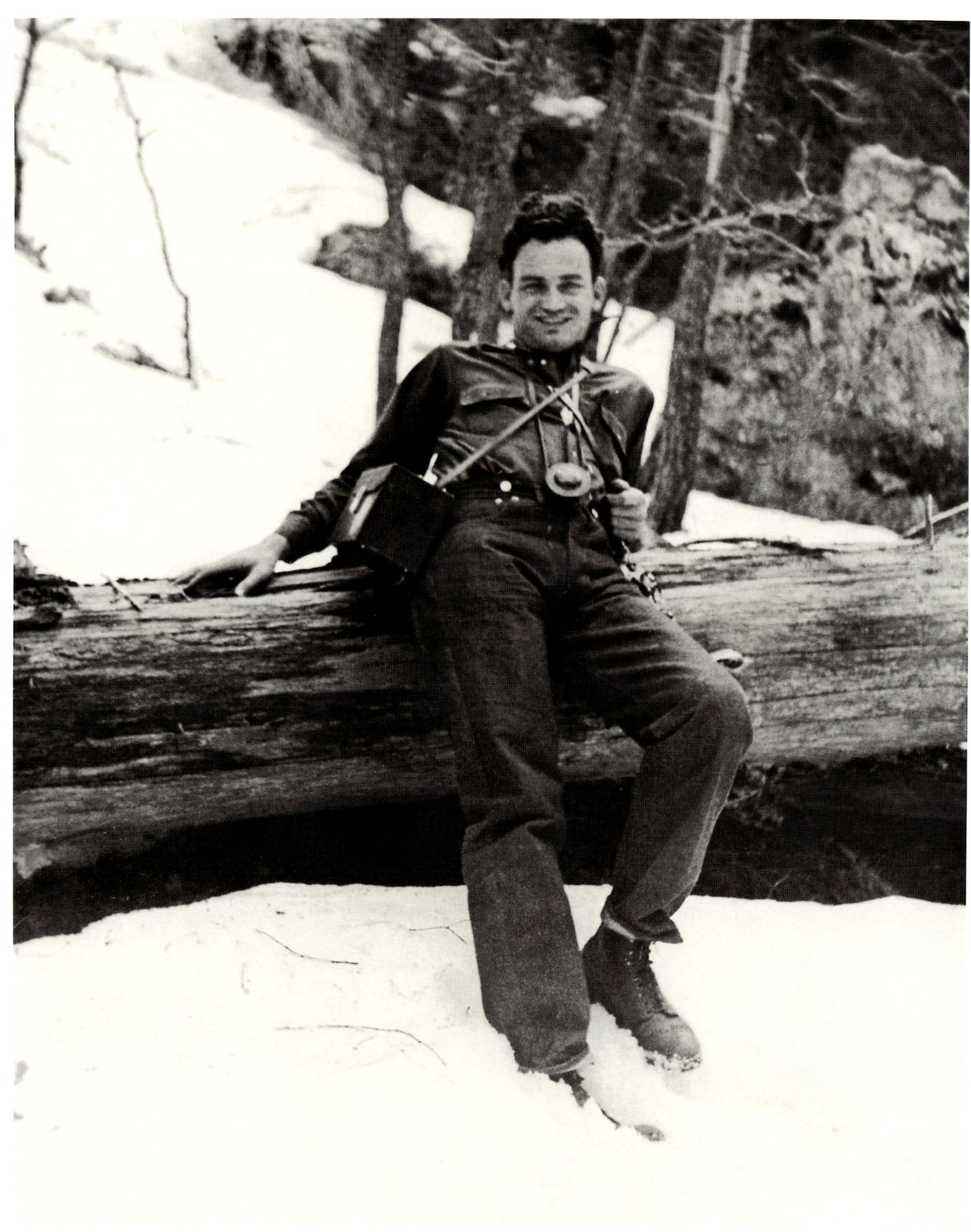

Portrait of the Artist as a Young Man, Mt. Lemmon near Tucson, 1925

PRELUDE

Barry Morris Goldwater was born with an artist's eye, a mechanic's brain and a warrior's heart. Nature mantled him with a powerful second sight that enabled him to instantaneously intuit nuance, spectrum and the peculiar glamour exclusive to oddity. A perpetual student of Mother Nature, he was also a hands-on tinkerer with a childlike fascination for the intricacies of mechanism. As principled as he was proud, he lived in a world of capital letter truths, where right and might commonly stood arm to arm. The tempering agents were always his well-oiled conscience and restless spirit, which thrived on lofty aspirations, fateful new discoveries and character building challenges. Impatient, ambitious and roguishly willful, Goldwater was marked by both destiny and disposition to be a fine arts photographer, whose focus extended far beyond the realm of churlish self-interest.

Cameras gave him power and he used it both widely and wisely, originally more out of curiosity than calculation. The initial awareness of the untold potentials of light in a controlled setting came during his youth, when he slyly experimented with his mother's Kodak, despite her explicit instructions to the contrary. By the time her son's insubordination became apparent, his photographic skills were such that she answered his cheek with unconditional support tempered only by the balm of experienced counsel. She kept him stocked in film and fed his fancy with enough excursions into the hinterlands to turn him into a full-fledged, wilderness addict long before he reached his majority. When he advanced to the point of awareness that photographic skill is relative to knowledge base, the woman he called "Mun" posited that everything he needed to know could be found at the library, a pivotal snatch of parental wisdom that led him to the work of photographer Edward Weston, the California master credited with heralding the modern Straight Tradition, or stark, direct representational prints empowered by the shadowy nuances of light as it falls across form.

Goldwater felt there was a special dignity in gutsy photographs that acted as mirror images of their subjects, but lacked the technical expertise to see the process through to fruition. He read and experimented widely with darkroom techniques, before seeking the aid of local portrait photographer Claude Bate, who graciously agreed to ad lib as darkroom mentor. Through trial, error and sound instruction, the self-taught adventurer mastered the basics, then spent the rest of his life testing the bounds of technical limitations. This was particularly the case after a haphazard encounter in the wilderness netted him an introduction to Weston's contemporary Ansel Adams, who quickly became both mentor and friend to Goldwater's photographic ambition.

Through the trauma and travail of learning photography full scope, Goldwater's staunchest ally and sharpest critic remained his mother. She was familiar with many of the scenes he captured through his lens and provided commentary that he later credited as beneficial in honing his conceptualization skills. Ever the proud parent, she displayed his photographs around her heavily trafficked home, essentially hosting the first public exhibition of his work.

With his maternal mentor solidly in his corner, Goldwater set his sights on his friends. A to-the-manor-born aristocrat more at home in the wilderness than he was the parlor, he delighted in taunting his acquaintances with seductive images of Arizona captured from vantage points guaranteed to strike terror into the hearts of the timid. As word of his growing collection spread through the tight knit community of Phoenix, queues of curious spectators appeared at his door and, in typical Goldwater fashion, he generously granted them quarter. As he later recalled, one youthful visitor's questions inadvertently spurred an epiphany that led to a portentous mission, which helped set the stage for the rise of a statesman:

*One day a student browsing through my
library of Arizona asked me if I had a picture of 'Peach Springs.' The answer was no,
but the purpose was born. To photograph
and record Arizona and its people—particularly its early settlers—was a project to which
I could willingly devote my life and I did, so
that I could leave an indexed library of negatives and prints to those who will follow.*[1]

Goldwater's self-ascribed mission to record
Arizona as it existed in his lifetime was greatly
aided by a pleasant encounter with a fresh-faced
maiden named Margaret Johnson, an Indiana born,
professionally trained artist, who earned her spurs
in the New York art world prior to the time Goldwater
spied her perusing the merchandise in the family
store in 1932. A child of parlor room privilege (her
family owned the Warner Gear Company in Muncie),
she was blessed with both the good taste to recognize
a diamond in the rough and the talent to further his
aesthetic aspirations, since she had both studied and
worked as an artist in what was arguably the most
competitive art market in the nation at the time.
After a spirited two-year courtship, the couple married on 22 September 1934 at Muncie's Grace
Episcopal Church. Aside from personal instruction
in the principles of line, balance and form, she gave
him his first, fully modern professional camera outfit, a first anniversary gift that proved a critical ally
in his quest to steal moments from time.

Across three quarters of a century and a full sea
change in photographic technology, Goldwater systematically built a stunning visual opus conserva-
tively estimated at 15,000 negatives and untold
miles of moving film, including Arizona's first color
feature, a masterful feat that later proved an unexpected boon to his political ambitions. Although his
remaining footage was set aside and used primarily
for the entertainment and edification of his family
and closest friends, his photographs toured the international circuit, ultimately earning him twin inductions into the Royal Photographic Society of Great
Britain and the Professional Photographers of
America, the oldest, most prestigious organizations
in the profession.

Learned and lay audiences alike are characteristi-
cally awestruck by the timeless nature of his compositions, which span the spectrum from character
studies of the human face to intricate depictions of
the landscape. Captured on fine-grained films and
printed on fiber-based papers, the photographs have
appeared in renown galleries and salons worldwide,
graced the pages of numerous magazines and journals and commanded center stage in nearly half of
the seventeen books that carry his byline.

Plaudits and peer praise aside, Goldwater forever
remained a man wedded to his mission. He kept his
subject fields diverse and his spectrum of interest
dynamic. No face was too insignificant, no place too
obscure and no terrain too treacherous to deter him
from his quest. As the self-taught adventurer later
revealed, the only limitations on his perspective
were strictly self-imposed:

*My photography has taken me over literally,
every mile of the Southwest, over both poles
and every major country on the globe. But it
is to Arizona that I turn for my inspiration
and what I think has been my best work.*[2]

The decision to remain faithful to his roots was
as natural to Goldwater as the kaleidoscope of
colors accompanying an Arizona sunset. He viewed
the state as nothing less than "114,000 square miles
of heaven" and its polyglot inhabitants none short
of divinely blessed. His was a proprietary stance
premised upon his profound belief that Arizona *en
toto* constituted a magical kingdom worthy of both
sound scholastic scrutiny and joyous celebration.
Critics have been quick to label his beliefs ethnocen-
tric, but the adjective is off the mark. Goldwater was
as he felt—entitled, initially as a matter of bloodline
and ultimately as just recompense for nearly nine
decades of peerless behavior.

The Family Birthright

The Goldwater story in Arizona began behind
the smoke screen of the Civil War, when a pair of
intrepid brothers crossed the Colorado River and
established quarters at La Paz. With little beyond
their dreams to sustain them, Michel and Joseph
Goldwater plotted, planned, struggled and stumbled,
ultimately building one of the largest private fortunes in the Southwest. Although the famous states-

man never knew the pioneer grandfather to whom he bore an uncanny likeness, he steadfastly credited his legacy as proof positive that Arizona was indeed the 'promised land,' for those with the guts and grit to parley with fate.

The evidence was a matter of family history, particularly those pages written by his Hollywood handsome, renegade grandfather, whose great height and personal bearing earned him the descriptive moniker of Big Mike. Born in October of 1821, he entered the world in the upper echelon of the twenty-two children born to Hirsh and Elizabeth Goldwasser, residents of the Jewish section of Kronin, a picturesque hamlet located in central Poland, which was then under the suzerainty of Russia.

Although Big Mike was not given toward sharing descriptive details of his Old World past with this children, the few tales he told suggested that the triple tyrannies of humble circumstances, familial disaster and a prejudiced society jointly conspired to make his early years hardscrabble and uncertain. Two of his siblings were evidently crippled, thus reducing the number of able-bodied contributors to the family purse. Around the time of his twelfth-year, a mysterious fire destroyed both the homestead and what remained of Big Mike's innocence. The daring pubescent boy who charged the fiery flames to bring his grandmother to safety was compelled by economic necessity to enter the adult world of commerce as an apprentice to a local tailor.

During the exacting quest to master the skills of his assigned trade, Big Mike stood direct witness to the nightmarish pogroms and rampant prejudice designed to keep the Jewish population in a perpetual state of peonage. Unwilling to bend the knee to an unjust system that deprived him of the right to own land, attain a higher education or practice a profession of his own choosing, he joined ranks with other like minded dissidents intent upon challenging the status quo. When word of the growing movement spread to Russian authorities, draconian measures were enacted to check its progress. Dragnets were conducted to root out the principals and the draft vigorously enforced as a means of limiting the available pool of potential converts to the cause.

Faced with the threat of serving as either target practice or cannon fodder for the Russian army, fourteen-year-old Michel's choices were limited to fight or flight and he pragmatically opted for the latter. He bid his parents an unknowing final farewell and fled his homeland for Germany for a brief stint, before relocating to Paris, where he practiced his trade, learned to speak French and built the first of many nest eggs he was destined to forfeit at the altar of hard times.

The proverbial first ax fell on February 24, 1848, when the conflict between liberals and socialists led to the collapse of the government of King Louis Phillippe, which set the stage for the advent of France's Second Republic. Along with the usual handmaidens of economic hard times and other associated dislocations implicit in class warfare, the revolutionaries introduced a virulent form of violence that quickly spread to other European capitols. By the time Louis Napoleon (he later took the name Napoleon III) was elected president and some semblance of order was restored, Big Mike had elected to cut his losses and relocate to London, where he used his savings to establish himself as a tailor, mastered English and Anglicized his name to Goldwater.

During a routine stroll along Petticoat Lane a few months after his arrival in London, Big Mike met the extraordinary woman who was destined to share his future. Small, dark eyed and self assured beyond her twenty-two years, Sarah Nathan was the middle daughter of Hannah and Moses Nathan, a successful furrier who contracted tuberculosis during a trip to Canada during the 1830s and ultimately succumbed to the disease in 1842. Although Sarah was only sixteen at the time and devoid of any business skills beyond her self-taught ability to read, she successfully assumed the responsibility of managing the family's fur processing plant, despite the fact that she was without the basic literary skills to even sign her name. By the time she crossed paths with Big Mike, she had also mastered the art of dressmaking. Although it would be a year before she saw him again, she would later tell her children that the face of the handsome stranger remained a steady fixture in her mind.

The established Jewish custom during Sarah's time and place required elders to serve as matchmakers for marriage age daughters. During the year after Sarah's casual introduction to Big Mike, a steady queue of potential suitors came to her door to be interviewed by her relatives to no avail. Consequently, Sarah was apathetic when her older sister Esther Tash, who had been with her at the time of her encounter with Big Mike, informed her that she had invited a young man to dinner. When Sarah entered the drawing room and discovered that the guest was the handsome stranger from Petticoat Lane, her indifference gave way to thoughts of romance.

Big Mike was evidently suffering from a similar fever, for he immediately opened negotiations with her relatives to establish the terms of their 'ketubah,' or marriage contract. Along with the customary pledge regarding honor, support and maintenance, twenty-nine year old Michel promised to give Sarah two hundred pieces of silver, with half remitted at the time of the marriage and the remainder to be paid at some unspecified future date.

On March 6, 1850, Chief Rabbi Nathan Adler joined the couple in marriage at the Great Synagogue of London. They set up housekeeping in a comfortable cottage located at 27 St. Mary Avenue. The following year brought the twin boons of the couple's first child (a daughter named Carolyn) and Big Mike's twenty-one year old brother Joseph, who had himself recently fled Poland one jump ahead of the conscription agent for the Russian Army.

Joseph moved in with his brother's family and commenced the information gathering canvas that netted him knowledge of the California Gold Rush and the bounty awaiting those willing to bet on chance. After nearly a year of concerted arguments and the birth of his nephew Morris, he finally persuaded his older brother that a better life awaited them on the other side of the Atlantic. Despite Sarah's objections to the contrary, Big Mike floated a loan from his in-laws, left the comforts of hearth and home and sailed with his brother to New York in 1852. After a brief respite under the hospitality of a Nathan family friend, the brothers paid one hundred and eighty dollars each for passage on a ship that took them to Grey Town, Nicaragua, then across the two hundred and twelve mile isthmus via a combination of native yawl, mule, steamboat and foot power to the port city of San Juan del Sur, where they caught a steamer bound for San Francisco.

Over the next eight years, the Goldwater brothers tested their mettle against the speculative, uncertain odds of Gold Rush California. San Francisco was in the throes of recovery from two devastating fires and struggling under the weight of a burgeoning population comprised largely of itinerant fortune seekers in the process of being deceived by their dreams. Deterred by the rough streets and hovel-like appearance of the urban landscape, the brothers headed eastward to Sonora, a bustling hamlet situated in the foothills of the high Sierras. Through circumstances that remain mysterious, they had the good fortune to encounter a group of European Jews willing to grant them a $200.00 stake, which they used to open a combination saloon and sporting house. Their eyes ever on the horizon in search of new opportunities, they soon expanded their operation to include mercantile goods such as thread, needles, soap, combs and other sundries.

Once the business began to post steady profits, Big Mike sent for his family albeit not without resistance from Sarah, who steadfastly refused to join him unless he paid passage for her sister Esther and her young son Marcos. Desperate to be rejoined with his wife and children, he relented to her demands and dispatched the princely sum of seventy-five dollars to cover the cost of a second-class cabin on the *Sierra Nevada*. A few days prior to the ship's slated arrival, he returned to San Francisco and used the intervening time to replenish and extend existing stock to encompass luxury items such as candy, notions, gifts and a billiard table.

When the six hundred plus passenger steamer sailed into San Francisco on the early Sunday morning of July 2, 1854, Big Mike was waiting on the docks anxiously anticipating a joyous reunion with the family he had not seen in close to two years. To his chagrin, he was greeted by children that did not remember him and a wife in a fury for a full battery of reasons, not the least of which was the lengthy separation that essentially relegated her to the role of single parent. When she spotted her husband waving from the dock, she refused to return the courtesy. Once they stood face to face, she vented her rage in systematic fashion, beginning with the ship's mean accommodations rounded out by choice words about the poor grooming habits and crude manners of the other passengers.

Big Mike suffered her wrath stoically, then set

about redeeming himself by treating his family to a holiday that extended across several days. Along with comfortable and commodious accommodations in a modern hotel, good food and a passel of pleasant sightseeing excursions around San Francisco, the family experienced their first Fourth of July celebration, complete with fireworks and drunken revelers in the street. Sarah was sufficiently appalled by the noisy and boisterous crowd to deem the entire proceeding proof positive that American culture was little more than a thin veneer laid across a barbarism as wild as the landscape. Rather than jeopardize the domestic harmony that enabled him to renew his acquaintance with his children, Big Mike suffered his fiery wife's anti-Yankee prejudices with the silent fortitude of a man resigned to his fate. He suspected that Sarah's newfound bliss was a timed engagement destined to expire in a matter of days and events soon confirmed the astuteness of his nervous conjecture.

Sonora, with its mean streets and rough inhabitants, chaffed the spirit of an English girl raised on parlor room fineries. The sparsely furnished, clapboard house Big Mike rented constituted cramped quarters for four adults and three growing children, while the town itself lacked even the most remedial cultural amenities. More exasperating was the presence of the bordello and the lawless element it inevitably attracted. With no other option open to her beyond that of leaving her husband and returning to England, Sarah did what came naturally. She complained to Big Mike, but saved her most malefic ire for his brother, if for no other reason than the role he played in instigating the relocation.

When it became apparent that Esther shared her sister's hostility, Joseph set up sleeping quarters in the back of the saloon and limited his presence in his brother's house to mealtimes, where he was treated like an unwelcome interloper. A few weeks into Sarah's residency, he decided to leave Sonora for the more hospitable reaches of the neighboring mining camp of Shasta. The brothers dissolved their partnership and parted amicably, with Joseph granting Big Mike open-ended terms with regard to compensation for his half.

During the aftermath of Joseph's departure, the resourceful sisters determined to make the best of a grim situation. They established a division of labor whereby Esther kept the family fed and Sarah kept them clothed. Social life was limited to family picnics, frequent trips to a nearby bookstore and an occasional performance or lecture provided by touring companies sponsored by a local theatre group. Within a month of their residency, Sarah became pregnant with the couple's third child, daughter Elizabeth, who was born on April 11, 1855.

Late the following year, Joseph returned to Sonora penniless and without prospects. In a fashion destined to repeat itself in cyclical fashion throughout their colorful lives, Big Mike floated his brother a loan to open a rival saloon and general store down the street. Joseph failed to pay his bills, a liquor dealer sued him for back debt and received a default judgment due to Joseph's failure to answer the summons. By the time the notice arrived, the audacious adventurer had already left Sonora to seek his fortune in the southern California village of Los Angeles.

In the midst of the crisis, Big Mike personally suffered a series of reverses that jeopardized both his business and his life. The first occurred when the Adams and Company banking office in Sonora failed to open for business. Desperate for funds to pay his creditors, Big Mike joined with a group of vigilantes and stormed the defunct institution, doling out dollars and gold to customers who could produce deposit slips to justify their claims. The next near disaster occurred a few days later, when Big Mike happened by a saloon just as a drunken patron discharged a shotgun through the front door. Although his injuries were not serious, the buckshot Big Mike carried home in his body sent Sarah into a fury reminiscent of her early days in Sonora. When she learned she was pregnant for the fourth time in 1856, she informed her husband that her patience had expired. Within a matter of days, Big Mike placed his wife, children, sister-in-law and nephew on a stage bound for San Francisco, where Sarah gave birth to their second son Samuel on July 15, 1857.

Sarah's departure from Sonora proved a critical watershed in both a personal and professional sense. For the next thirty years, family life would be a split proposition, with Sarah living comfortably in an urban setting, while her itinerant husband sought his fortune in the rugged reaches of the western frontier. Despite separations that ranged in duration from weeks to months, the couple held fast to their wedding vows and the great love that instilled the words with meaning. Reunions were much anticipated, joyous occasions, because somewhere amidst the trials and tribulations of their first seven years they discovered that longevity in relationships has less to do with the romantic illusion of two souls merged as one and more to do with the vigor explicit in individual differences.

In the immediate aftermath of Sarah's relocation, Big Mike faced the threat of impending insolvency. Sonora's economy had gone south, placing him on a financial tightrope between a dwindling consumer base and suppliers clamoring to be paid. Shortly after the birth of his fifth child Henry on July 27, 1858, he turned his business assets over to his creditors and joined his brother in Los Angeles.

Over the next few months, Big Mike engaged in a scramble that came to a dead end. He opened a combination billiard parlor and bar in the Belle Union Hotel, but the returns fell far short of the revenues he needed to support his growing family and relinquish the $3,260 debt he carried from the Sonora years. The first step in his cost cutting scheme was to relocate his family to a predominately Mexican American neighborhood in Los Angeles, where the aristocratic Sarah was forced to take in boarders. When even that drastic measure failed to stem the tide, Big Mike swallowed his pride and filed for bankruptcy. By the time the petition was finalized on March 19, 1860, his net worth was inventoried at one hundred dollars worth of household items and clothing valued at one dollar.

Joseph's situation was fortunately on the upswing. The tobacco shop he operated across the lobby from Big Mike's billiard hall and bar at the Belle Union Hotel was posting record profits. By the time of the 1860 census, he boasted a net worth of $3,000, a princely sum he willingly put at the disposal of his older brother, whose dire financial straits grew more so with the birth of his sixth child Lenora (known as Annie) on June 20, 1860.

A lesser spirit would have cracked under the weight of the pressures Big Mike faced, but as he had done in the past and would again do in the future, he reached down inside himself and found the will and ultimately the way to place himself back on the road toward the destiny that existed only in his dreams. He was no child of privilege, which meant he answered adversity with the anxious action known only to the hungry. Through his role as proprietor of the billiard hall and bar, he made the acquaintance of pioneer Los Angeles physician Wilson W. Jones, who had formed a merchandizing partnership with an entrepreneur named Alonzo Ridley near the recent gold strike known as Gila City, near the Colorado River. Jones alleged that the miners would welcome a peddler with a wagonload of 'Yankee notions.' Big Mike discussed the rumor with Joseph, who offered to underwrite the cost of a spring wagon, four mules and the necessary stock to enable his brother to don the cap of Jewish peddler.

During the late summer of 1860, Big Mike placed the billiard hall and bar under Joseph's care and set out on a journey that took him to Fort Yuma, where he crossed by ferry into Arizona. He traded at every stop along the way, ultimately pushing out to the furthermost outcroppings of miner's huts and houses. Currency was at a premium in mining camps, enabling him to exchange goods for gold and garner an even larger profit than he had initially expected.

When the newly minted peddler returned to Los Angeles and the returns were calculated, the Goldwater brothers immediately began to plot and plan. Big Mike had conducted a mental canvas along his journey with regards to the type of wares suited to the tastes of his customers. Joseph, in addition to overseeing their interests in Los Angeles, signed on as buyer for the goods his older brother delivered and sold on site. Over the next year, business boomed but so did the guns at Fort Sumner, which placed the brothers on the horns of a dilemma. Many of their friends were southern sympathizers, who abandoned their businesses to return home to fight for the confederacy. After minimal soul searching and debate, Joseph and Big Mike pledged their loyalty to the union by taking the oath as U. S. citizens respectively in June and July of 1861.

While the Civil War raged in the east, the Goldwater brothers turned their attention toward becoming successful capitalists by expanding their traveling wares, as well as opening stores at both the Belle Union Hotel and in the Mascarel Building located a half block away. Because Big Mike's bankruptcy had been widely publicized, both stores and the credit vouchers that enabled them to operate carried Joseph's name. A risk taker immune to the fear factor typically associated with poor odds, he pushed the envelope to the point of inspiring resentment on the part of his competitors and suppliers, who covertly plotted in unison to administer his comeuppance.

On September 12, 1862, Joseph signed an 'on demand' note with Leon Sylvester Wholesale House in San Francisco. Two weeks later, he signed a second note for $2,000 payable in gold coin. Two weeks after that, Sylvester called both notes due. When it became apparent that the brothers could not cover their obligations, he called in the sheriff, who placed all of their holdings on an auction block. Word soon spread to other Goldwater creditors, who likewise demanded repayment. The wagon and mule team were the last assets to fall under the hammer, leaving the brothers again penniless, but not totally without prospects.

The source of their potential salvation ironically stemmed from a philosophical approach to life that the elder Goldwater brother's famous grandson would later descriptively label "paying rent." Big Mike held the ethereal belief that ownership of anything was essentially a myth. Because human presence on the earth was both temporal and temporary, the individual essentially paid rent. He also held the Old Testament admonition that 'to those much is given, much is expected' as a self-evident truth, which made participation in community life less a matter of choice and more an issue of personal honor.

Widely known and respected as a man of great heart, Big Mike was typically the first to stand to the call in time of need, whether the problem was individual or community catastrophe based. He was a charter member of the Hebrew Benevolent Society of Tuolumne County and an energetic member of the Sonora Chapter of the Masons, an affiliation he cultivated further in Los Angeles. He also took an active part in various informal merchants' associations, which set the stage for his introduction to Bernard Cohn, a dry goods and pawnshop owner, who ultimately persuaded Big Mike to partner with him in a joint venture in the Arizona goldfields, specifically La Paz.

Rumors of the latest mother lode had been car-

ried on the wind for sometime, but the Goldwater Brothers initially discounted the gossip as little more than mineral trail embroidery. Their primary concern was establishing a niche for themselves in southern California, where competition within the mercantile trade was both fierce and unforgiving. The peddler's wagon was viewed as a temporary measure geared toward a more stable end that would enable Big Mike to be with his family. When the ax fell on that part of their operation, Joseph moved to San Francisco and worked for his older brother Abraham, who had relocated from Poland around 1860 and established a small store. During the final days of 1862 or the beginning days of 1863, Big Mike joined Cohn in La Paz, where he initially worked as a clerk, most likely on a percentage basis with an option to invest.

By the end of his first year in Arizona, the once penniless adventurer was an equal partner in the mercantile establishment of Cohn and Goldwater and boasted a personal purse valued at $15,000, a figure three times greater than the net worth of his business partner. By the end of his second year, he had expanded his interests further by backing Sol Barth and Aaron Barnett, two wilderness traders who initially marketed their wares in the new diggings springing up in central Arizona, before setting up a store in Prescott in 1864. Originally located on the southwest corner of the present day intersection of Goodwin and Montezuma Streets, the adobe housed venture was principally backed by Big Mike.

The old saw that 'the appetite comes with the eating,' seems to thereafter apply. Big Mike speculated and expanded into other partnerships, including a complicated and lucrative union with his old friend, Dr. W.W. Jones, who had retired from medicine to speculate in minerals, merchandising, freight hauling and road building. Through these ventures, Big Mike met Henry Wickenburg, a German prospector desperate to protect his Vulture Mine from the encroachments of poachers and claim jumpers. He needed to build a stamp mill and he approached Goldwater and Cohn for backing. With the aid of Joseph, Big Mike scouted out and purchased the necessary machinery and made arrangements for it to be shipped from San Francisco to La Paz by steamer, then freighted to the mine by wagon.

Over the next two years, Big Mike sold thousands

of dollars of supplies to the Vulture Mine. The debt soon exceeded the owners' ability to pay, a dilemma resolved by an arrangement between the parties whereby the Vulture Mine was 'delivered over' to Goldwater and Cohn for the time necessary to clear the $34,967 standing debt. The obligation was cleared within ninety days, marking the end of Big Mike's tenure as a mine owner. In 1866, Big Mike dissolved his partnership with Cohn and rejoined ranks with his brother Joseph to launch Goldwater Brothers Mercantile.

Events in his personal life were equally portentous. A few months before the Los Angeles auction that left him insolvent, Big Mike became a father for the seventh time with the birth of his son Ben on March 23, 1862. Four years later, he was called home to witness the birth of his eighth and youngest child Baron on May 8, 1866.

During a late summer visit that same year, Big Mike learned that his eldest son Morris wanted to work with his father in Arizona. Although only fourteen years of age, he had already completed all of the formal schooling available to him at the time. High school was still several years in Los Angeles' future and college educations were almost exclusively the domain of the upper classes. Sarah initially discounted the notion as ridiculous beyond all comprehension. Although she had never been to Arizona (nor would she ever go), she had heard enough stories and tales to make her nervous about her young son's safety. Father and son worked in unison to persuade her to the contrary by issuing assurances neither were in the position to deliver. She ultimately relented and Morris accompanied his father back to Arizona during the early fall of 1866.

Morris would later regale his famous nephew with tales of the eventful trip. He recalled that his father used the stagecoach trip to educate him about the people and places of Arizona. When the stage reached Dos Palmos, his father's words took on new meaning when they found a man lying in a pool of blood on the floor of the stage station. The victim was Herman Ehrenberg, a German mining engineer and Big Mike's closest friend and intellectual soul mate. Father and son stayed over and buried the body the next day, then solicited the aid of Indian friends in seeking justice for the fallen. A few weeks later, he told a reporter from the *Alta California* that:

The party of Chimahuevis Indians which made a raid on Saw Mill Canyon near San Bernardino last month were overtaken by a party of settlers and several killed. Among the party was the murderer of Herman Ehrenberg at Dos Palms—a man who also shot old Dr. Smith last Summer in San Gorgonio Pass. The murderer was followed by the friendly Cohuilas, who corralled him near Agua Caliente about the 28th of January and killed him. He was shot 20 times, but even after down he killed two of them.[3]

Big Mike's ability to mobilize his Indian friends on behalf of a personal need was a testament to the measure of the man. Mainstream relations with the Native populations were truculent at best. Tempers flared and arrows and bullets ricocheted often enough to keep both sides in a permanent state of discomfort. Big Mike's experience varied greatly from the norm. His La Paz store was a favorite hangout for members of the neighboring Mohave nation. When the Colorado River changed its course and Native crops were ruined, he opened his heart and purse to the victims. He was a friend who had firsthand knowledge of dislocation, prejudice, hard times and hunger. Rather than objects that other people did things to, he saw Indians as people who did things for themselves. He respected their humanity and they returned the favor by addressing him as 'Don Miguel' or 'Don Marcos.'

The same life experiences that kept Big Mike honorable also made him pragmatic. Sarah had been clamoring for sometime to leave Los Angeles and return to San Francisco. In 1867, he succumbed to her wishes and purchased a house at 722 Post Street. Although considerably larger than their crowded quarters in Los Angeles, the residence was far beneath the income level of the owner, who opted to close the deal with cash. Because most of the purchases for the retail end of his interests were made in San Francisco, he could save time and travel by consolidating family visits with business, which included opening a business office at 106 Battery Street to serve as a filtering agent for distributing goods to his growing Arizona mercantile empire.

With several minor and two major business busts painfully set in his memory, Big Mike systematically contrived a strategy that paved the way for the vast fortune his family would ultimately amass. He isolated the lack of merchandising and marketing knowledge on the part of himself and his brother as a major causative agent in the earlier ruins. In 1868, the decision was made to send Morris to San Francisco to serve an apprenticeship in the P. Berwin Company, a hat and cap concern owned by an old friend from the brothers early days in California. Morris began as an apprentice clerk and worked himself through the ranks, gathering valuable insights into business procedures and processes that later benefited the family business. The return from the experiment was such that Big Mike made working in a rival concern a rite of passage for each of his sons except Baron.

Big Mike was less successful in his efforts to curb the excesses of his younger brother. Unlike the approbation widely accorded to his tall, fair featured elder sibling, Joseph frequently fell victim to public suspicion and distrust. Short, dark and plagued with a lazy left eye that made him look guileful, he lacked his brother's diligence in seeing a task through to completion and honoring all deals. During his eventful life, Joseph was consecutively robbed, swindled, shot at, sued and falsely accused of crimes ranging from mayhem to murder. The one consistency in each crisis was Big Mike's steadfast support and protection.

By the time that the family business moved to the new town of Ehrenberg in 1869, Big Mike was clearly the brother in command. The impetus for the move came from the widespread devastation wreaked by the flood cycle during the winter of 1866-67. The Colorado River had radically shifted its course, necessitating the costly and time-consuming transshipment of heavy freight. Merchants began to scout out a new location, with the Goldwater brothers taking the lead. When a location was targeted seven miles to the south, Big Mike persuaded the founders to christen the new town in honor of his recently fallen friend. In the fall of 1869, he opened the largest, most modern store building in the town and affixed it with a new shingle: J. Goldwater and Bro.

On September 20, 1869, the U.S. Post Office Department named Joseph postmaster for Ehren-berg, an action Big Mike most likely engineered. The appointment gave the brothers inside information on such critical variables as the location of the next military installation and upcoming contracts required to provision the garrisons, along with the bids submitted by their competitors. By exploiting every avenue at their disposal, the brothers counted record profits in every arena from the Ehrenberg store to their ambitious pilgrimages as itinerant peddlers, but the real boon to their collective fortune came from military contracts wherein they inevitably ended in a favored position due to Joseph's propensity to pilfer the mail.

The hit and run tactics of Apache raiders made security for the caravans used to transport the goods fronting their newfound wealth an ongoing concern that carried a potentially life threatening penalty. Big Mike very quickly earned a reputation among Native ranks as a fierce and formidable fighter and expert marksman, who would willingly risk life and limb to protect his cargo. Wagons carrying the Goldwater logo were usually left alone, but such respect was not extended to the unmarked buggies he used during the summer of 1872 to attend a bidding convention for frontier freighters in Prescott.

After losing the widely coveted Fort Whipple concession to their principal rival, C. P. Head and Company of Prescott, the Goldwater brothers headed home, with Big Mike riding in the front carriage with then-freighting partner Dr. Jones and Joseph taking charge of the reigns in the rear buggy. Fourteen miles out of Prescott, the trio was attacked by a band of Mohave-Apache raiders. Dr. Jones suffered a minor scratch from a ricocheted bullet and Big Mike escaped unscathed except for two bullet holes in his new hat. Joseph suffered a direct hit to the lower back and another one to the shoulder. The men fled with the raiders in hot pursuit. A fortuitous encounter with a group of heavily armed ranchers ultimately routed the chase.

By the time the shooting stopped, Joseph had begun to lose consciousness. Dr. Jones bound up his wounds sufficient to enable him to be transported to the nearby ranch of E. F. Bowers in Skull Valley. Soldiers were dispatched to Fort Whipple for surgical instruments and medical supplies. The following day, Joseph was taken to Camp Date Creek for additional surgery. A week later, he was moved by army ambulance to Ehrenberg. After a brief respite to regain his strength to travel, he returned to San Francisco. His wife Ellen Blackman, whom he had married in 1862, nursed him back to health. For the next eight years, he managed the San Francisco end of the family operations. He did not return to Arizona except for brief visits to Ehrenberg and Parker, until the brothers dissolved their partnership in 1880.

During the years of Joseph's convalescence, Big Mike opted to expand the mercantile business. He purchased property in Phoenix, then journeyed to San Francisco to discuss his plans with his son, Morris, who had worked his way up from clerk to a key position in the P. Berwin and Co. sales force. On October 12, 1872 the editor of the *Arizona Miner* revealed that:

> *Morris Goldwater, son of M. Goldwater, is now a partner in the firm and may take charge of the business at Phoenix. He is said to be an exceedingly intelligent young man.*[4]

On December 11, 1872, J. Goldwater and Bro. opened their first store in Phoenix in a two-building complex located near the intersection of present day Jefferson and First Streets. Early newspaper advertisements tantalized readers with the promise that J. Goldwater and Bro.:

> *Have on hand a large & complete stock of general merchandise, comprising everything required in a farming country, and which they will sell at the lowest possible prices. Highest prices paid for grain.*[5]

The latter claim reflects Big Mike's desire to secure a contract to supply most of the area's barley to the army. Although he bid and lost the contract, Morris soothed his disappointment by arranging for him to receive a lucrative military contract to supply beans to three army posts. The deal was the first of many he engineered as a junior partner in the family business.

There is an element of *dejà vu* in the means Morris implemented to achieve this feat. Phoenix was less than two years old and without the transportation and communication networks necessary to sustain growth and development. In 1873, Congress appropriated funds for the construction of a military telegraph from San Diego to Prescott and Tucson, with supplementary lines to Yuma and Maricopa Wells. Through the rumor mill, Morris learned that upon the timely completion of the original project, a supplementary line had also been laid to Florence, with $5,000 left in the coffers for a new terminus. The messengers were Captains George M. Price and R. R. Rainey, two military officials assigned to the telegraph project, which he had quartered for a night. At the end of the evening, Morris had persuaded the two men to run the line through Phoenix. In exchange, he agreed to donate the first set of instruments, provide office space in the Goldwater store and serve gratis as the on-site operator. The deal struck, Morris was granted intimate knowledge of impending military contracts, the client lists of competitors and countless other bits of information that the enterprising Goldwater clan turned into gold.

The road to that fortune was filled with ruts and the Phoenix store proved one of them. With Big Mike divided between the Ehrenberg store, his high revenue freighting interests and his frequent trips home to be with his family, Morris was left to his own devices in determining the scope and span of available stock. The simple utilitarian offerings of yesteryear gave way to a splendid assortment of dry goods and hardware, as well as a fashionable line of ladies ready-made, all carrying premium prices early Phoenicians could or would not pay. In April of 1875, Big Mike journeyed to Phoenix to assist his son in closing operations.

Changes had already occurred that made the temporary loss of revenue insignificant. Big Mike had successfully dissolved his freighting partnership with Dr. W. W. Jones and placed Morris in his stead. In 1874, he scouted Prescott for a new location, but became distracted by difficulties in other parts of his growing empire, primarily Morris' ill-fated investment in The Arizona and New Mexico Express Company, which went belly up in less than a year.

Once the new financial encumbrance was quelled, Big Mike returned to Prescott with a more serious glint in his eye. He purchased a brick building under construction on the southeast corner of Cortez and Goodwin Streets. In October of 1876, J. Goldwater and Bro. opened for business, offering the largest and most diverse array of stock heretofore seen in the Arizona Territory. Big Mike took up residence in the town and was joined by his sons Morris and Sam in early December. Still smarting under the recent foiled investment in the stage line, Morris took responsibility for the store, Sam served as his apprentice and Big Mike scouted the town and surrounding areas for new opportunities to further enrich his growing coffers.

When Prescott recaptured the territorial capital from Tucson in 1877, he purchased lots on the corner of Union and Cortez Streets and contracted to construct a new building, which ended upon costing the unheard of sum of $15,000. He spared no expense in its layout, design and appointments, prompting a local newspaper editor to deem the structure "the most substantial, beautiful and convenient building in the Territory."[6] The handsome edifice was so solidly constructed that it remained in use for over a century, despite the fact that a July 29, 1880 fire exacted damages in excess of $3,000.

A few months prior to relocating the store to its new quarters, Morris decided to throw his hat in the ring for the mayor's seat. Politics was far from a novel venue for members of the Goldwater clan. In 1873, Morris had worked part time as a deputy clerk for the District Court of Maricopa County. The following year, all three Goldwaters ran for office. Twenty-two year old Morris made a foiled bid for a House of Representatives seat in the Eighth Territorial Assembly. Big Mike made an equally fruitless bid for a Council (Senate) seat, primarily because his pride and humility kept him from placing the usual announcement of candidacy in local newspapers. Despite his reluctance to play by the rules, the final tally was close, with Big Mike garnering 174 votes to his opponent Jose Maria Redondo's 212. Joseph won election as school trustee for District Two from Yuma County. In 1879, Morris won the mayor's seat in Prescott by a 208 to 114 majority.

While Morris was campaigning for the mayoral seat, Big Mike's efforts to "pay rent" brought him untold heartache. In the early part of 1879, a group of leading citizens formed the Arizona Development Company and elected Big Mike president. The ambitious collective's goal was to raise money for public improvements through the first public lottery. A $20,000 surety bond was placed with the Territorial Treasurer, with the Arizona Bank charged with handling income and approving necessary expenditures. In April, the scheme fell into disfavor when a local newspaper reporter discovered that the founders of the Arizona Development Corporation received kickbacks from the sale of lottery tickets.

While other incorporators denied and dodged, Big Mike admitted his part in the scheme in a newspaper ad wherein he promised to return the profits to the purchasers. No record exists as to the names or number of claimants, although Morris's log books cite a total of $690.00 was accrued through lottery ticket sales. By early July the issue was a moot point. The U.S. Postmaster declared the lottery illegal and forbade any further use of the mail toward that end. The Eleventh Territorial Assembly quietly repealed the lottery ordinance, but speculation continued for months over who benefited from the ill planned scheme and to what extent.

In the immediate aftermath of the crisis, Joseph journeyed to Prescott as a show of support for his brother. Recently widowed with three children of his own, he was accompanied by Big Mike's daughter Annie, making her the first of the Goldwater girls to actually visit Arizona. The brothers decided with so many children coming into the business it was time to disband their partnership. When the calculations were made and final line placed on the official documents in 1880, Joseph received a total of $60,000, a handsome sum rumored to be a fraction of the staggering net worth of his older brother. Big Mike ordered a new shingle for the store that read M. Goldwater and Son, while Joseph set out to parley his nest egg into a fortune of his own.

The first stop on his itinerary was the Castle Dome Mining District in southern Arizona, where he made a series of injudicious investments that left him penniless within a year. By 1881, he returned to his old tactics of buying goods on credit and wholesaling them to distributors across Arizona. When he failed to clear a $100,000 debt, California law officers cornered him at a dinner party in Yuma, placed him under arrest and returned him to San Francisco in handcuffs. Joseph ultimately talked his way out of the situation and returned to Arizona in July of 1881 in pursuit of P.W. Smith, a Tombstone merchant who owed him money. As fate would have it, Smith had lost most of his stock to a fire that had swept the business district a month before Joseph's arrival. He also owed a large sum of money to neighboring merchant H. K. Tweed, who had already commandeered the remaining stock as payment on the overdue loan. Joseph met with Tweed and ended up forming a partnership that included an obscure clerk named Paul B. Warnekos, mostly because the principals needed a clean name to establish credit.

After the shootout at the OK Corral and the subsequent departure of Joseph's old friends the Earp Brothers and Doc Holiday, he disbanded his union with Tweed and Warnekos and formed a new partnership with two other failed merchants, Joseph Guindani from Florence and Jose Miguel Castaneda from Yuma. Because all three men had bad track records for paying their debts, they billed the new enterprise as the A. A. Castaneda Company and listed Jose's wife as owner. The trio immediately launched a fast paced expansion in Cochise County, opening stores in Fairbank, Crittendon, Benson and Bisbee, where Joseph established himself as a banker by using an alias. During the summer of 1883, he brought his sixteen-year old son Lemuel into the business.

On December 8, 1883, Joseph unwittingly commanded a starring role in the legendary Bisbee Massacre. He was behind the counter when armed bandits appeared and demanded he open the safe and hand over the payroll for the mines. In a colorful interlude his famous great nephew would later research and write about, Joseph stalled for time under the guise that he neither knew how to open the safe nor had the stage carrying the payroll arrived. The sound of gunfire on the street soon convinced him that the robbers meant business. He relinquished the contents of the safe, as well as a bag of gold hidden under the pillow of his ailing partner Castaneda, who was lying on a cot in the back of the store. At the end of the tragedy, four people lay dead and Joseph was short $6,000 and a bag of gold. Evidently, the stage carrying the payroll had indeed been late.

Over the next few weeks, Joseph enjoyed community acclaim for his calm and collected demeanor during the crisis. He regaled all listeners with embroidered tales of the exploit and went on to earn himself a humorous page in the annals of territorial jurisprudence, through his colorful testimony at the trial. When the bailiff asked him to raise his hand to take the honesty oath, he raised both hands in the air. The judge pointed out that one hand was sufficient, but Joseph insisted that the very sight of the accused sitting at the defense table rallied his survival instincts to the extend that he felt it prudent to err on the side of safety.

While Joseph participated in the Territory's version of a media circus, Big Mike continued to have the Midas touch. Business was bullish across his growing empire and he was running out of excuses for Sarah, who insisted he retire and return to San Francisco. Old beyond his sixty four years, tired and forced to walk with a cane as a result of a busted kneecap acquired during a skirmish with marauding Indians intent upon purloining his wares, he continued to be troubled by the tarnish the lottery fiasco brought to his good name. Despite assurances from those close to him that no one remembered the folly, he was determined to set the record to right before he handed over the reigns to his children.

During the latter months of 1884, fate handed him an opportunity to recoup his standing in the public mind, when a citizen's committee petitioned him to run for mayor. Big Mike had never had more than a passing interest in politics, but he knew the people, the town and the needs. The race was a close one, primarily because the incumbent J. L. Hall was a seasoned campaign veteran with a host of influential friends. When the final returns were tabulated, Big Mike emerged the victor, garnering 289 votes to his opponent's 232.

From the onset of his administration, Big Mike provided vigorous leadership. He earned the approval of Bible thumpers and professional prostitutes alike when he championed a bill denying amateur 'B girls' access to the bars along Whiskey Row. He raised eyebrows among the ruling class, when he sponsored ordinances to build a fence around the courthouse square to keep stray cattle from destroying the lawn, as well as the construction of wooden crossings on downtown streets. Real estate owners rose in their collective ire, when he insisted that downtown property owners assume the cost of con-

structing wooden sidewalks in front of their holdings. Amidst the wave of protests from his business
associates and friends, he got a music stand built on
the square for public concerts, a lamppost installed
in front of city hall and a new bridge built along
Granite Creek.

More than any other measure, it was his private
war against stray dogs that led to a parting of the
ways between the mayor and the council. The situation was far from whimsical. Dogs, many of them
feral, drifted into town from the mining camps, ran-
domly attacking children and adults at will. On
more than one occasion, Big Mike was known to
make free use of his cane in an effort to protect himself or some other innocent bystander. Consequently,
the passage of stray dog ordinances were among his
first official acts as mayor and when Police Chief
James Dodson failed to enforce the new laws, Big
Mike called him to task him at a council meeting.
The wily official responded with insults and name
calling, prompting the determined mayor to fine
him $100.00 and suspend him from office until he
apologized.

When Dodson's friends on the council argued
that the fine was excessive for a public servant that
only made $150.00 a month and suggested it be
reduced by half, Big Mike submitted his resignation
and walked out. Consensus judgment held that he
would recant his decision once he had a chance to
cool down, but the mayor could not be placated.
Three weeks later, the council reconvened and
accepted his resignation *in absentia*, seven and a
half months into his term.

The following year, Big Mike retired from professional life. He sold his interest to Morris for the pal-
try sum of $11,858 and other considerations, which
neither father nor son chose to record or reveal. The
old warrior went home to Sarah in San Francisco
and the spacious mansion the couple had constructed at 716 O'Farrell Street, where he enjoyed his
children, grandchildren and the approbation of being
a beloved patriarch in the surrounding Jewish community. Even though he no longer had a direct hand
in the day-to-day operations of his empire, he
remained an advisor to his children both within and
outside the family business, whether he supported
or disapproved of their decisions and actions.

While Big Mike was enjoying the fruits of his
labor, his brother was still chasing rainbows and
finding mostly rain. In February of 1885, a massive
explosion in his Tombstone store wreaked $20,000
worth of damage after a fire in trashcans situated in
the alley ignited a barrel of gunpowder. Joseph stalwartly rebuilt the store, while son Lemuel assumed
command of the wholesale operation in Fairbank. In
1887, younger son Harry arrived to assist his
brother. Guindani ran the store in Contention and
Castaneda retired.

Around the time Harry arrived from San
Francisco, Joseph began to have a series of paralyzing headaches, most likely as a result of the bullet
wound he suffered to his spine during the Indian
attack in 1872. He moved from Fairbank to a hotel
in Tombstone to be near his doctor and the
Castanedas. Jose's mother-in-law, Manuela Arvizu, a
handsome woman a year his senior, soon took a
shine to him and he honored her attention by
requesting her hand in marriage.

When he confessed his intentions to his brother,
Big Mike suggested the couple should marry at his
home in San Francisco. The two boarded a train and
upon their arrival, Big Mike had a prenuptial agreement waiting for their signatures. Sarah stifled her
disapproval of her brother-in-law marrying outside
the faith and staged a grand reception for the newly-
weds, following their informal wedding on October
16, 1887.

Less than two years later, on August 31, 1889,
Joseph passed away in Tombstone at the age of fifty-
nine. At the insistence of his son Lemuel, he was
buried beside Ellen in the Hills of Eternity Cemetery in
San Francisco. Manuela received the $1,000 allocated
to her by the prenuptial agreement and relocated to
Nogales, where she lived an additional forty years.
Lemuel and Harry used their inheritance to buy out
Guindani, sold the Fairbanks location (the Bisbee store
had been sold and the Contention location closed
prior to their father's death) and continued to run the
Benson store for an additional three years. They ultimately sold their interest to Castaneda and relocated
to southern California, where Lemuel made a fortune
manufacturing "Boss" overalls. He also established the
Bank of Anaheim and served as one of the founders of
the Cedars of Lebanon Hospital.

The situation with Big Mike's children was a mixed bag of glory and grief. Daughter Carrie married Jewish businessman Peter Aronson during the fall of 1876. Extant records suggest that she neither worked in the family business nor did she visit Arizona until many years later.

Throughout his eventful life, Morris remained the golden boy and heir apparent. He drafted the company slogan "The Best Always" and remained adamant that it appear in the window of any establishment carrying the Goldwater logo, as well as all newspaper ads and handbills. Both before and after his father's retirement, he mentored each of his brothers in their quest to earn a niche for themselves in the family empire. He lived a humble bachelor existence in a boarding house owned by Sarah "Sallie" Shivers Fisher, until local gossip hounds began to disparage her character for continuing the arrangement after the death of her husband John L. Fisher, a Chino Valley rancher and former mayor of Prescott. More for Sallie's reputation than romantic impulse, Morris married her in Los Angeles on September 19, 1906. To the chagrin of his mother, who steadfastly insisted that her children marry within the Jewish faith, Sallie was a protestant and the wedding ceremony was a gentile affair.

Along with the key role he ultimately played in the life of his famous nephew, Morris' sterling contributions to political arenas earned him stature as one of the leading lights in both the Territory and state of Arizona. The evidence is in the resume: 1879: Mayor of Prescott; 1883: Council seat in the Twelfth Territorial Legislature; 1884: six year term on the Yavapai County Board of School Examiners; 1885: Clerk of the House of Representatives in the Thirteenth Territorial Legislature; 1888: Chairman of the Territorial Central Committee; 1890: two terms on the County Board of Supervisors; 1894: member of the Territorial Board of Equalization; 1894-97: Mayor of Prescott; 1898-01: City Councilman; 1899: President of the Council in the Twentieth Territorial Legislature; 1905-13: four consecutive terms as Mayor of Prescott; 1910: Vice President of the Arizona Constitutional Convention; 1914: President of the Senate in Second Arizona State Legislature; 1919-27: Mayor of Prescott; and, 1910-11: Tempe Normal School Board of Visitors.

In the interim between his business duties and electioneering, Morris served on the welcoming committees for such dignitaries as General William Tecumseh Sherman and General John Charles Fremont, whom President Rutherford B. Hayes appointed territorial governor. He also founded a volunteer fire company, a militia and remained a tireless railroad promoter, who led the foiled quest to bring a transcontinental line through Prescott in the early 1880s. He later invested in the narrow gauge Prescott and Central Arizona Railroad, which connected his home city to the mainline to the north, as well as played an instrumental role in the erection of the courthouse square statue of his archrival Buckey O'Neill.

Few details are known about daughter Elizabeth except that she evidently never married. Senator Goldwater once related his suspicions that she may have been mentally retarded, since little was said of her aside from passing references to her "sickness." She resided with her parents until the end of their lives. Thereafter, she was dependent upon her brothers for financial support, as witnessed by the $10,000 bequest Baron allocated for her maintenance in his will.

Son Samuel was born frail and lived his life in that manner. Rumored to be the quietest of the clan, he worked as an apprentice under Morris at the Prescott store for a brief time, then returned to San Francisco, where he operated a cigar store. He died in Arizona in 1888, after a prolonged and painful battle with tuberculosis.

Although son Henry was a dead ringer for his father in a physical sense, his nature was more attuned to that of his Uncle Joseph minus the elder's profound sense of loyalty to his kin. He came to Prescott in 1884, but found the town and family responsibilities too confining for a man of his particular genius. He journeyed to Mexico, where he secured employment as a clerk in a small railroad depot in Guanajuato for a time, but soon found the subsistence wages beneath his dignity.

Through Morris' intervention he was hired by Abe Frank in Yuma, only to abandon the position within a matter of weeks to explore the agricultural potential of the regions surrounding the juncture of the Sonora and Mohave Deserts. He joined ranks with a group of investors and formed the Mohawk Valley Canal Project, a joint stock company chartered to build dams and canals. Although the concept proved a solid scheme in subsequent decades, the group's irrigation plans collapsed due to a lack of adequate working capital and the requisite technical expertise to get the project off the ground.

Henry lost his shirt in the scheme, but he could not bring himself to lay the notion down. Over the next few months and years, he alternately worked as a postmaster in Ehrenberg, Parker and Howells, but lost most of his wages through ill-fated mineral investments. By 1888, Big Mike's patience was exhausted. He instructed Morris to bring his younger brother back to the fold, a dictate he honored by making his wayward sibling a full partner.

The following year, Henry fell in love with Julia Kellogg, a native of Keokuk, Iowa, who was teaching in Prescott at the time. Julia was a gentile which so displeased Sarah that she responded to Henry's announcement of his impending nuptials by sitting shivah, a Jewish rite typically reserved for a death in the family. Other family members found Julia delightful, particularly Morris and Big Mike, both of whom viewed her as a stabilizing influence on free spirited Henry.

After their wedding in Chicago on October 27, 1893, the couple purchased a handsome home at 217 East Union Street on Nob Hill in Prescott. Henry settled down for a time, while Julia earned community wide approbation for the stellar role she played in securing Carnegie Foundation funds to erect a public library. The bottom fell out of the dream in 1896, when the second Goldwater store opened in Phoenix and Morris put Baron in charge.

Henry was in a fury about being passed over for what he adamantly claimed was his idea. He broke with his brothers and entered an itinerant phase that reads like a testimonial of a soul lost to itself. From 1901 until his death in Los Angeles on September 22, 1931, he managed a furniture store for his brother-in-law Ralph Prager in San Francisco, built furniture in Richmond, California, worked as an accountant in Aberdeen, Washington, speculated in minerals in several areas around La Paz, installed a cost system for a film laboratory in Los Angeles, invested in beehives and strawberries in northern California and the list goes on. In 1916, he received U. S. patent no. 1045695 for a T-square he invented for draftsmen.

Several times during these years, both Morris and Baron tried to persuade Henry to return to the family fold, but pride kept him from accepting their largesse. He preferred to support himself by borrowing from friends and relatives, always convinced that the scheme at hand would enable him to repay his debts with interest. A true 'hale fellow well met,' his remains are interred in the Goldwater plot in the Hills of Eternity Cemetery in San Francisco.

Big Mike's sixth child Lenora [Annie] was the first of his daughters to visit Arizona, a journey that did nothing but confirm her mother's contention that the place was raw, rough and backward. She married Ralph Prager, heir to a Portland, Oregon clothing store chain. The couple had two daughters, Nita Winkler and Ruth Prager.

Son Ben was a gentle spirit, who never married. He earned his spurs in the business world as a traveling salesman for B. Blumenthal and Company, a California-based glove manufacturer, before moving to Prescott in 1895 in a fruitless effort to combat the ravages of tuberculosis. He was living with his brother Henry at the time of his premature death at the age of 33, on July 13, 1897.

As the youngest of Big Mike's large brood, Baron was both the most coddled and arguably the most creative. He attended schools in Los Angeles and San Francisco, possessing both the marks and the money to attend the college of his choice, but he would have none of it. He wanted to enter the family business and, after years of relentless petitioning, Big Mike reluctantly succumbed to his request. At the age of 16 in 1882, he arrived in Prescott, where he immediately exhibited a genius for marketing that rendered both his father and older brother speechless with awe.

During the early days of his residency, Baron was an obedient and observant pupil of all phases of the mercantile industry. Self-directed and motivated beyond his years, he quickly perfected the basic skills of retailing, including the uncanny ability to calculate lengthy columns of figures in his head without the aid of an adding machine. Unlike his father and older brother, neither of whom suffered fools gladly, he possessed a sublime gentleness that enabled him to dispatch even the most irate customer with a smile that proved contagious.

Baron was an ambitious perfectionist, who knew what he knew without knowing how he knew it. When his older brother vetoed his suggestion that existing stock be expanded to include fine pianos and other musical instruments, he established an independent outlet for such wares. After his relatives viewed his balance sheet, Baron's comments and concepts were accorded greater respect and attention. It soon became apparent that he had an almost supernatural knack for accurately predicting the public palette, which translated into more patrons and higher profits.

Because Baron was a self-possessed man who did not see fit to keep a journal, it is impossible to ascertain the exact epistemology of his thinking with regards to making a second attempt to conquer the Phoenix market. Morris later recalled that he initially pitched the idea to the family partners as early as 1890. With the earlier disappointment fresh in his memory, the elder brother's gut level reaction was to reject the notion without discussion, but Baron proved relentless. Family folklore holds that the issue was finally settled, when the younger brother emerged the victor in a game of casino.

Whatever the course of the decision, the Goldwater brothers drew up a partnership agreement between themselves and their Phoenix based banker, E. J. Bennitt, marking the first time since the days with Cohn that Big Mike or his descendants formally forged a mercantile association outside bloodline ranks. Baron was charged with conducting the preliminary information gathering canvas, which took a year to complete. When the brothers convened to discuss the younger Goldwater's findings, he exhibited the scrupulous and fair-handed attention to detail that would soon become his calling card as a businessman.

Baron reported that Phoenix already boasted seven stores catering to the mercantile needs of an increasing population, primarily as a result of the political wrangle that swept the capital away from Prescott in 1890. From surface to substance, the town was a study in contradictions. Unpaved streets connected an urban core that barely spanned a three-block radius out from the midpoint at Center and Washington Streets. Situated within the power nucleus of government and business were blacksmith shops, livery stables, saloons and houses of questionable repute. Tree lined opened canals provided both aesthetics and recreation, while the surrounding agricultural community expanded the resident customer base of approximately 3,000 to an estimated 10,000 exclusive of winter visitors and other tourists. Transportation networks were improving by the day and the town was rife with talk about erecting a dam to grant the settlement a steady supply of water.

The Goldwater brothers sensed potential, which they resolved to exploit to the full extent of their collective wisdom and energy. A reasonably priced building was rented at 18 and 20 North First Avenue on the Fleming Block. Baron was dispatched on a series of buying trips to Los Angeles, New York and other points east. A massive publicity campaign coincided with his homecoming, touting the illustrious return to the Valley of the Sun of M. Goldwater and Son, purveyors of "The Best Always."

Several shipments of goods failed to arrive by the official opening date on March 21, 1896, but the Goldwater brothers covered their flanks with daily newspaper advertisements advising potential customers of new merchandize as it arrived. Early press reports promised an expansion of basic frontier mercantile stock to a broad slate of items of the finest quality. Six weeks later, a Goldwater ad confessed that, "The meaner sorts of merchandise we have no time to bother with," complete with the tantalizing promise to potential customers to "give your money back if you are not pleased with the purchase."[7]

Because Baron was already a veteran of several well publicized buying trips prior to the opening of the Phoenix store, he had already determined to test the reaches of practical merchandizing by offering an essentially frontier populace fineries foreign to its prior experience. Local reporters waxed poetic about the quality and compass of his appeal to the discerning palate to the point that he soon became the unwitting arbiter of both women's and men's fashion in Arizona, through both merchandise and method. Along with establishing exclusive rights with prestigious cosmetic lines like Elizabeth Arden, Helena Rubenstein, Dorothy Grey and others, he was the first Phoenician to abandon the male precedent of a business suit for short sleeved, white cotton shirts and a simple tie during the sweltering summer months.

The new location prospered to the extent that it soon outgrew its space. Baron reviewed the available options and chose a building located at 134 Washington Street, which boasted a large sales floor and full basement for storage. He added skylights and a balcony to serve as a mezzanine and waited until the end of the Christmas rush in 1899 to orchestrate the relocation. A few days into the New Year, a *Gazette* reporter again dubbed both the store and the stock "the Finest in the Territory."[8]

Subsequent years brought both gain and pain. At the same time Baron was expanding his wares, he was also extending his reach. Leaving politics to his older brother in Prescott, he focused on other aspects of community life. In 1897, he was appointed to the board of the Phoenix Chamber of Commerce, joined the Elks and Arizona Clubs, donated countless dollars to local charitable campaigns and served as a founding director of the Iron Springs Outing Club, which built a popular resort near Prescott in 1900. He also lost his brother Ben to tuberculosis in 1897, his brother Samuel to the same malady in 1888 and witnessed the dissolution of the old family partnership, when Henry left for California on February 15, 1902.

More devastating still was the loss of his father on April 19, 1903. Since his retirement, Big Mike had lived the life of a gentleman aristocrat attentive to both his family and adopted community of San Francisco. Following a final visit to the Phoenix store in 1896, he is not known to have returned to Arizona, but absence did not lessen the communal memory of the battle-tested pioneer whose life read like a western epic. Newspapers throughout the territory mourned the passing of the courageous and committed immigrant, whose ambition, marksmanship, vigorous fists and unsullied honor laid the basis for a fortune his talented sons would quadruple over the next few decades.

The next generation of Goldwaters accomplished the monumental task through a combination of hard work, Yankee ingenuity and the willingness to check their egos and play off of their collective strengths. Because Baron possessed both the eye and taste for fine things, he made countless excursions to New York and abroad to acquire the fineries that set M. Goldwater and Son apart from their competitors. These trips often lasted months in duration, which

necessitated that Morris serve as overseer for both locations, including lengthy stays in Phoenix during the stultifying summer months. By the time Big Mike passed away, the frontier establishment he had launched had transcended into Phoenix's first modern department store, headed by a sharp, ambitious son well attuned to the needs and tastes of a boisterous community caught on the treadmill of constant redefinition.

Aside from his respected savvy as a businessman, Baron was widely touted as both the best dressed man in Phoenix and the city's most eligible bachelor. Straight backed and slight of frame, he had the look of a dandy about him and a well-guarded shyness that made him seem aloof. A victim of more than one parlor scheme hatched by coy maidens and their mothers, he kept his own counsel, until fate brought him face to face with a petite redhead with a glint in her eye and a noticeable purpose to her step. Cupid's arrow had hits its mark, but the prize quickly proved a rose with petals perpetually unfolding.

Hattie Josephine Williams was an enigma wrapped in a mystery, because she chose to be. She shared few details about her early life, beyond citing Nebraska as her place of birth and Chicago's Cook County Training School for Nursing as the issuing institution for her registered nursing certificate. Inquiries from her children were pushed aside with colorful tales of her adventures en route to Arizona and memorable escapades experienced during her early residency. They respected her privacy, until her eldest son turned detective during the years immediately succeeding her death.

These investigations revealed that she was born in Bowen, Nebraska on March 19, 1875. She was less than two years old when her parents relocated to the sod house frontier in the rural reaches of York County, outside a small farming settlement named Waco. She received her education at the neighboring one room schoolhouse, before relocating to Chicago to study nursing. The evidence suggests that her early life was both mean and meager, which hints that she most likely exchanged domestic work for room, board and tuition, a commonplace practice within turn of the century training schools for girls.

Cruel fate intervened shortly after Josephine

received her nursing certificate. A visit to her physician netted the grim prognosis of tuberculosis, which if left untreated constituted a death sentence. In keeping with the medical temper of the day, her doctor prescribed a warm, dry climate as the only available cure. She gathered what money she could and bought a one-way ticket to Ashfork, Arizona, where she disembarked and began walking southward along the railroad tracks. After a few miles, a considerate conductor took pity on her and allowed her to hitch a ride in the caboose to Phoenix.

During her early tenure, Josephine lived in a tent city near present day Sunnyslope, where she traded professional skills for room, board and treatment. A trained nurse was a rarity in the Arizona Territory at the time, which made her services greatly in demand. In addition to privately ministering to the needs of patients in their homes, she was frequently called upon to assist local physicians like Dr. E. Payne Palmer, who engaged her to assist him in the first surgery performed at St. Joseph's Hospital.

By the time she met her future husband, she was living in Phoenix at 305 East Monroe Street. Josephine spent her spare time exploring her new setting, including window shopping at stores with prices she could ill afford. It was on one of her frequent visits to the new Goldwater store that she was introduced to Baron, who was immediately smitten by her stark beauty and plucky demeanor.

A spirited two year courtship followed wherein Jo-Jo, as she was eventually known to family and friends, revealed herself to be a woman of many layers. She knew as much about guns and fishing rods as she did about the traditional womanly arts of domesticity. She was also a practicing Episcopalian, a staunch conservative and a shrewd businesswoman, who elected to purchase the goods for her trousseau at Korrick's, under the guise that Goldwater's prices were too high.

The couple married on January 1, 1907 at St. Luke's Episcopal Church in Prescott, with Reverend Fredrick Trotman Bennett officiating and brother Morris standing as best man. Following a combination honeymoon and buying excursion to New York, they set up housekeeping in a humble adobe at 818 North Central Avenue. The following year, Jo-Jo discovered she was pregnant and plans were immediately enacted that led to the purchase and remodel of a spacious two story house at 710 North Central, which boasted an attic, basement, large yard and a barn in the back. Three children followed in short order: Barry Morris (January 1, 1909), Robert Williams (July 4, 1910) and Carolyn (August 13, 1912).

Although her husband's wealth kept her from returning to the work place for economic reasons, Jo-Jo remained steadfastly loyal to the profession of nursing and the health needs of the community in general. Along with the private assistance she gave to needy patients in the community, she served as the hands-on director of the American Red Cross during the influenza epidemic that coincided with World War I. In the 1940s, she donated $25,000 to the residents of Show Low for the construction of a hospital, which was named in her honor.

During these same years, Josephine became enamored with the then all-male pastime of golf. She shocked local residents when she appeared on a Phoenix golf course in pants prior to the liberality associated with the Jazz Age. She ignored her critics into social silence by becoming Arizona's first female golf champion, with numerous city, state and regional titles to her credit.

A profound passion for the game was but one of many attributes Jo-Jo passed down to her children, who steadfastly remained her top priority. She was a freethinking child of the western frontier who believed that person and place were inextricably entwined in a partnership that necessitated both exposure and personal investment. She led by example, practiced more than she preached and punished only for the cardinal sin of lying. No stranger to the local party scene, she drank her fill, danced holes in her stockings and smoked in public. She kept herself exclusive to her husband, loved her children with a passion and never found cause to apologize for being rich. If she taught her children one lesson above all others it was that life was about living down to the very moment at hand.

Several years older and considerably more reserved in demeanor, Baron's parental guise was more in line with the teachings and value system imparted by his immigrant parents. He held fast to the traditional values of family, heritage, hard work, individual initiative and productive self-sacrifice. Never a hands-on caregiver, he was nonetheless a force in his children's lives who earned the respect he demanded by practicing the same set of rules he established for their behavior, including his father's dictum of "paying rent." Although his lofty standards were meted out to each of his children in turn, the greater onus fell on his eldest son Barry, whom he fully expected to both shoulder the Goldwater family mantle and extend its reach through the sheer force of honest achievement.

Talking the Talk, Walking the Walk

As a child of affluence and heir apparent to a birthright much larger than mere financial fortune, Barry Morris Goldwater's childhood was both privileged and purposeful. He entered the world with a full tool chest—strapping good looks, a quick and cutting wit, a hunter's instinct for new experience and a puzzling genius for all things mechanical. Like his grandfather before him, he possessed an impatient temper, a searing tongue that could clip a hedge and a soul-level sense of fair play that kept him honorable, often to his own detriment. Plagued by a restless curiosity that alternately proved a bane and a blessing, he became adept at transforming idle talk into direct actions that changed minds, lives, and ultimately the course of a nation.

Goldwater was born with an innate sense of adventure and a mother with the good sense to recognize that the human child's needs extended beyond the physical. She gave him rope, which he stretched to maximum length, usually in collusion with his brother Bob and best friend Harry Rosenzweig. Sister Carolyn and Harry's older sibling Newton were running buddies as well, but social dictates surrounding gender and the indelible civility of the elder Rosenzweig brother kept them from engaging in many of the street urchin activities that caused conservative eyebrows to raise and gossipy tongues to wag.

'Mun' or 'Munjie' (as she was known to her children) remained nonplussed by the criticism, confident that her sons possessed the gumption and grit to survive the rigors of their desert setting. The evidence was as clear as the lessons she administered in the open-air classrooms stationed at every stop along the trail during the family's frequent wilderness outings. Firearms, fishing rods and the facts of life as she saw them were taught by direct experience and reinforced by personal example. Problem solving and principles went hand in hand, with pride in self and place natural outgrowths of repeated, face-to-face encounters with situations frequently fraught with danger.

These colorful excursions set the stage for Goldwater's initial introduction to photography, which in turn intensified his growing passion for all things Arizona. The process began when his mother purchased a box camera to create images for the family album. Although her children were expressly forbidden to touch the sensitive device, her eldest son violated the parental edict at every opportunity at his disposal, unmindful of the fact that visible evidence of his perfidy would appear on each processed roll of film. He began with safe shots of the landscape and an occasional scene from Indian life, surreptitiously shot from beneath a blanket in the back of the family's touring car as it was parked outside one of the trading posts his mother was fond of frequenting. Within a short amount of time, he expanded his repertoire to portraiture of family and friends, including those enrolled at the Phoenix Indian School, many of whom stood center stage in the sterling array of Indian portraiture he later executed as a seasoned professional.

Rather than mete out fruitless punishments for his disobedience, Goldwater's mother pragmatically encouraged his fledgling attempts at photography under the belief that his interest would wane once the novelty wore off. When the reverse proved the case, she did what came naturally and supported her son's efforts down to exhibiting his amateur imagery to her friends, including her genteel husband, who preferred to limit his communion with nature to an occasional camping trip that extended no more than a day or two in duration.

The brief interludes favored by the father were little more than appetizers to his eldest son, whose taste for wild and woolly places grew with each exposure. He particularly relished treks off the beaten path, where Mother Nature flourished unsullied by human hands and unchecked by technology. From his early youth forward, his ideal of paradise was a bedroll by a campfire in the midst of a virgin setting limited only by a star-studded sky that hinted eternity lay somewhere over the horizon. If some sharp-toothed creature carrying a poison pack or painful stinger entered the scene, the situation was deemed all the more hospitable.

The spare accoutrements and tin canned suppers experienced on the wilderness excursions were so far contrary to the opulent comforts explicit in daily life in Phoenix as to constitute a separate zip code. The Goldwaters lived in a spacious, well-appointed home, ate the best food, wore the finest clothes and enjoyed regular seaside escapes from the summer heat. Along with the full retinue of bicycles, trains and sporting equipment favored by youth across time, Baron's profession and purse enabled his children to enjoy a full spectrum of expensive toys outside the fiscal reach of most of their contemporaries, including the premium priced, crystal radio set, which the future statesman built, perfected and ultimately transformed into a tool to shatter distance, save lives and prop up the flagging patriotism of his constituents during the Vietnam War.

Goldwater's interest in ham radios inadvertently benefited his growing attraction to photography, if for no other reason than it helped to fine-tune his mechanical skills. He first became intrigued with the technology, after learning about it in the scientific journals he was fond of reading throughout his life. In his early teens, he talked his parents into buying him his first crystal set, which he systematically modernized and perfected over time. The minute attention required to assemble, operate and repair the touchy apparatus helped keep his eye sharp and his hand steady, skills that became critical building blocks in his ongoing quest to create the perfect photograph.

Goldwater's privileged caste and mechanical eccentricities did not keep him from participating in all of the youthful rites common to his time and place. He swam in the canals that ran through town, played baseball on sandlots and operated a soft drink stand with his brother Bob, who had to maintain a stern vigilance less his elder brother spend profits either before or immediately upon their acquisition. Along with the Rosenzweig brothers, Bob and several others, he formed the Center Street Gang, which met in the open space above the family garage to plan track meets, bicycle races, boxing matches, mud ball fights and various other competitions with rival groups from other parts of town.

When he was not conspiring with his gang brothers, Goldwater typically did those things he had been told not to do such as hiking to the top of South Mountain before it was a park or terrorizing locals caught in delicate situations with his mother's camera. Pranks netted him more than one parental lecture, particularly his propensity for wreaking disharmony upon a neighborhood church by using a toy cannon to launch rag bags filled with garbage into the midst of the faithful as they gathered for Sunday morning services. He was a scrappy little boy known to hold his own in a fistfight or wrestling match, as well as a western style Artful Dodger, who had the temerity to pawn his brother's saxophone to cover the cost of his courting rituals, which began early and continued unabated until his introduction to his future wife in 1932.

Regardless of the penalty enacted or the consequence suffered, young Barry early and often challenged rules as little more than someone else's opinion. He was blessed with enough natural cunning and wit to conceal most of his trespasses. On those occasions when exposure loomed certain, he typically charmed his way out of the situation. Barring that eventuality, he suffered the punishment and learned the lesson in virtually every childhood arena except the one his parents viewed as sacrosanct—formal education.

School was a place where Goldwater excelled in everything except academics. During the early years at the Kenilworth School, he was never the star pupil, but he managed to hold his own with the aid of an occasional tutor. With the onset of adolescence came an interest in girls and a growing litany of hobbies such as cameras, ham radios and lettered sports. Parental patience finally ran out when he ended his first year at Phoenix Union High School with few credits beyond his role as freshman class president. Baron decreed that more discipline was needed, with the prestigious Staunton Military Academy in Virginia selected as the administering institution.

Although his mother initially objected to the notion of exiling her eldest son to military school, Baron stood firm for reasons relating to both bloodline and class. As a first generation U.S. citizen, he was weaned on the immigrant notions of ambition, hard work and diligence to task. He knew firsthand the price his father had paid for the family's privileged caste and he expected his oldest son to behave in accordance with his entitlement as a Goldwater, which meant running every race to win. By his way of thinking, formal education was a critical component in garnering the edge necessary to do more than merely go the distance.

Goldwater's lack of scholarly focus was a variable he openly acknowledged later in life, always with a tongue and cheek awareness that through whatever means necessary he acquired his own style of education at his own speed. The student whose test scores found him lacking in basic learning skills could master virtually any mechanism, spew scientific facts like a gentleman scientist and create on-the-spot lines and limericks others found quotable. What he could not manage to do was show up on time, lock down on any exercise extant to his own immediate interests or forfeit the moment at hand for some rumored future reward. He needed to learn the fine art of focus and, as he later confessed, the Staunton years proved a critical watershed in that process, for reasons far beyond the rigors implicit in a military setting.

The first lesson came from the unspoken motivations of a father determined to turn a boy into a man. Baron was less than two years older than his slacker son when he entered the competitive world of retailing, which meant he had no concept of an extended childhood. He hailed from a time and place when a man's worth was largely measured by his ability to be a good provider. By his way of reasoning, learning and earning went hand in hand. The fact that his youngest son Bob was a solid straight A student added more weight to his firm resolve that the time was right to corral and channel his oldest son's talents in a direction more conducive to a future compliant with established family standards.

Once the Staunton decision was handed down, Baron made it clear that he would entertain no further arguments to the contrary. Plans were put in place for the recalcitrant pupil's academic transfer, the requisite clothing and supplies purchased and a departure date selected that coincided with one of Baron's slated buying trips to New York. He accompanied his son on the train, using the intervening miles to reinforce the full spectrum of his expectations. When they pulled into the station, he pointed

his son in the direction of Staunton Military Academy, bid him a fatherly adieu and boarded a connecting train to New York.

A stunned, fourteen-year-old Barry traversed the two miles to Staunton Military Academy on foot carrying both his bags and a chip on his shoulder over what he perceived as an unfair sentence. For the first time in his life, he was alone, far away from home and surrounded by strangers, many of whom were callous-tongued easterners that held views about the American West and its inhabitants that were far from egalitarian. These unfortunate prejudices led to more than a few arguments, fistfights and disciplinary demerits during the difficult adjustment phase, but they also served as the catalyst for a level of introspection that life up to this point had given him little cause to practice. He thought about himself, his heritage and his homeland, systematically laying the preliminary groundwork for the renegade regionalism that would later serve as his calling card in international political arenas.

The adolescent ethnocentrism born out of Goldwater's first trek as an outsider made him curious about sides of Arizona he had heretofore taken for granted, specifically the history that existed outside of the realm of family folklore. He had been raised on stories about the fearless grandfather who came, saw and conquered; enjoyed a close personal bond with the popular uncle who was widely revered as one of the infant state's leading political lights; and, stood direct witness as his trendsetting father transformed what was essentially a frontier supply depot into a modern department store. He remembered his mother sewing the forty-eighth star on Old Glory when the Territory of Arizona became a state in 1912, but he wanted to know more about the force of circumstances leading to that eventuality and all the other unknown happenings that were part of his regional birthright.

When Goldwater returned home after his first year at Staunton, he resolved to fill the gaps in his knowledge with factual information. The first stop was the local library, a venture that left him sadly empty-handed and intellectually dissatisfied, particularly when further inquiry revealed that the only institution centered upon the study of Arizona was the Arizona Pioneer Historical Society in Tucson. Through a combination of municipal rivalry and natural inclination, the collection's principal focus was on southern Arizona, when Goldwater's primary interest was on the history of the central part of the state. Unable to solve the dilemma on his own, he took his case to his Uncle Morris, who served as guide and benefactor in his nephew's beginning steps as an Arizona bibliophile and rare document connoisseur.

Goldwater acquired and diligently devoured all of the published accounts on Arizona at his disposal. From these narratives, he learned that human habitation of his homeland dated back more than twelve thousand years to the ancient Anasazi Indians of the plateau country and the Gila Valley Hohokam, who engineered the extensive irrigation network that led Phoenix founder Jack Swilling to raise the 'city out of the ashes.' He also learned that modern Arizona was essentially the product of an endless cycle of invasions, beginning with the dual Athapaskan (Navajos and Apaches) and Spanish *entrada* during the 16th Century, followed by the northward march out of Mexico City during the 17th and 18th Centuries. The next wave came from the mainstream traders, trappers and prospectors that drifted into the area during the years intervening between the Mexican Revolution of 1810 and the 1848 Treaty of Guadalupe Hidalgo, which ceded all lands (except the 29,142,400 acres acquired through the 1853 Gadsden Purchase) to the United States. The floodgates were then opened to the frenzied invasion of speculators, investors, health seekers and tourists destined to increase with each passing decade.

The more Barry learned about the human side of Arizona, the greater his appreciation for her natural landscape. Wilderness excursions transformed into fact-finding missions wherein his ever-present camera served as an invaluable ally. He continued to turn his lens in the direction of a beautiful face or place for aesthetic reasons, but more often than not these were serendipitous sights encountered en route to a specific place because a specific event happened there. When he shared the results of his findings with friends and neighbors, he discovered an audience of residents hungry for the same information he craved. An idea began to germinate in his fifteen-year-old brain that took shape in adulthood as a lifetime quest: saving Arizona through the

ground glass-eye of his camera, as it existed during his lifetime, for the benefit of posterity.

Goldwater later recalled that his newfound interest in Arizona's history made him a better student in other arenas. When he returned to Staunton to begin his second year, the once defensive shirker systematically gave way to a serious scholar who could not get enough of the difficult curriculum he had previously shunned. Classes in American history proved especially interesting, particularly the lives, achievements and philosophies of men like Alexander Hamilton and Thomas Jefferson, whom he quickly adopted as personal heroes. Knowledge about the United States' historic evolution into an emerging super power made him realize the profound importance of a strong national defense, which led him to master military science to the extent that he earned prestigious honors as Outstanding Cadet during his senior year. He immediately set his sights on the Military Academy at West Point, fully intent upon pursuing soldiering as a profession.

Shortly after his acceptance letter from the United States' oldest and most renown center of military study arrived, Baron's health began to fail and his mother called her oldest son home. Goldwater spent the summer renewing old acquaintances, adding materials to his growing collection on Arizona and visiting the wilderness with his camera in tow. Retracing the path of his pioneer ancestors was a passing fancy that inadvertently transformed Goldwater into a scholarly detective adept at separating fact from fiction and rumor from reality, invaluable skills he would later fine-tune as an elected official.

During one memorable foray, he accompanied his Uncle Morris to Ehrenberg to witness the demolition of the old post office. The deed had already been accomplished by the time they arrived, but the trip was far from futile. After some minor shifting of planks and other debris, they unearthed passels of mail from Joseph Goldwater's tenure as postmaster that he evidently neglected to deliver. Barry recovered the readable samples for his library, then spent the next few years researching and writing about his colorful uncle, whose wanderlust ways and fast dealings suggested that fortune and failure were relative concepts in a setting where purpose routinely shape-changed at the whim of promise.

Goldwater enrolled in the University of Arizona during the fall of 1928, with no immediate plans beyond acquiring a college education. He pledged to Sigma Chi Fraternity, joined the swimming team and was elected president of his freshman class, before fate dealt him another cruel hand. Halfway through his second semester, his father passed away and he was forced to drop out of school to take his place in the family business.

Baron had been battling angina pectoris for over a decade prior to his death on March 6, 1929. After consulting with local physicians, he sought treatment from medical professionals in both California and New York, always with the same grim prognosis. Consensus medical opinion held that he should abstain from alcohol and over exertion, but the prescription was incompatible with his personality. In 1927, he expanded the store's operations by opening a shop in the San Marcos Hotel in Chandler. The night before his death, he donned a tuxedo and journeyed to the new Arizona Biltmore to greet guests at the opening of an even grander location off the hotel lobby. He drank too much, partied too hard, woke up the next morning feeling out of sorts and died mid-day at the age of sixty-two, with his stunned wife by his side and his daughter Carolyn innocently engaged in teenage acrobatics on the lawn.

News of Baron's death fell hard on his son Barry, who was just in the beginning stages of getting to know the father whose emotional distance and reserved demeanor paled next to Jo-Jo's high drama style of parenting. Although he later came to honor each of his parents within their own context, he essentially spent his youth tied to his mother's apron strings. She was an affectionate teacher, protector and wilderness guide, who could don the executioner's hood at a moment's notice if he dared offer up a falsehood. She taught him the meaning of patriotism, raised him as an Episcopalian and introduced him to the political tenets of the Republican Party that he would later help reshape and refine. More than all else, his mother instilled him with the self-confidence, courage and conviction to live each day of life as though Armageddon was upon him. She encouraged his interests, celebrated his feats and looked past virtually all of his youthful foibles,

including his adolescent and forward fondness for the ladies.

Baron's style of parenting stemmed from his own peculiar situation as the youngest child of parents who essentially occupied separate universes. The prolonged absences of his father placed Sarah in the role of primary caregiver, a responsibility she had shouldered with enough élan to convince her son that children were a responsibility best left to the female sphere. Like his father before him, he only stepped in when heavy-handed discipline was necessary as in the case of his eldest son's cavalier attitude toward his studies. For the most part, he remained the calm, collected benefactor that used his purse to impart lessons more at point with the mental mold crafted by the teachings of his immigrant parents.

A favorite tale of his oldest son provides a descriptive example of Baron's style of parenting. During their mid-teens, the Goldwater boys petitioned their father for an automobile and he suggested they earn the money to buy their own. When the Rosenzweig brothers underwent a similar proceeding with their father Isaac to the same end, the foursome put their heads together and decided to hire themselves out as cotton pickers to earn the necessary sum to purchase the new Ford they had targeted as goal. It took the better part of two years filled with cuts, scrapes, bleeding fingers and painful sunburns to accrue the $480 listed on the sticker price. When the final tally was taken, it soon became obvious that Newton had contributed the lion's share of the money, which gave him command of the keys.

As an elder statesman, Senator Goldwater often reflected upon the experience as one of those rites of learning that carried multiple lessons. On the most primordial level, he came to appreciate the dynamics of hard work from pain to gain. He also received an object lesson in the value of friendship as a special partnership that can join at many points and emerge stronger from each contact, as witnessed by his pleasantly productive and highly protective brotherhood with best friend Harry Rosenzweig. The experience renewed his respect for the pragmatic business savvy of his friend Newton, whose opinions on all things large and small remained an influential force up to the end of his life. Although he would have to have children of his own before he realized the magnitude of the lesson surrounding the purchase of his first car, he ultimately credited Baron as the catalyst for his early awareness that hard work and high reward are ancillary sides of the same coin.

When cast against the colorful hands-on attention accorded by Jo-Jo, Baron's reserve cast him in the role of disinterested witness in the minds of his sons, if for no other reason than his failure to prepare either of them for the rigors of pedaling pricey wares in a setting more accustomed to broadcloth and beans than caviar and silk. The younger Goldwaters had certainly grown up in and around the store, but Baron had not seen fit to offer either of them the type of mentoring he had received at the hands of his father and older brother. His eldest son was never certain whether his reticence related to his desire that his sons pursue careers in different fields or simply the human propensity to deny one's own mortality. Whatever his reasoning or lack thereof, his sons were left to their own devices in proving their mettle in the world of business.

As he had done so many times in the past and would do repeatedly in the future, Morris stepped up to direct the action. He suggested his eldest nephew begin his apprenticeship as a clerk and work his way up through the ranks, garnering in the process a first person view of retailing from the basics to the bottom line. Barry began his journey in the piece goods department, followed by a stint in ready-to-wear, where he set a store record during Christmas season with over two hundred separate sales. He ultimately worked the sales floor in every department, gathering sufficient knowledge to enable him to quickly advance to the more prestigious role of store buyer, a position he perfected during several lengthy trips to New York.

Merchandizing and mechanism came easy to Barry, whose long list of credits in each arena suggest he inherited more than a little of his father's penchant for modernization. Along with the famous "Antsy Pants" brand of men's briefs and the Desert Style Shows that featured the latest fashions against a southwestern backdrop, he created a number of regional signatures like Pedro, the advertising symbol, and the highly popular, brandishing iron patterns printed on piece goods. He also equipped the store with the first electric-eye door in Phoenix and arranged for the installation of a vacuum tube system to transport fiscal transactions from the floor to the office. The latter innovation triggered his always keen wit, which led him to place a live mouse in the cylinder and send it to the assembly office to the delight of all except the accountant.

Barry's principal weakness as a businessman was finance, but he was blessed with a younger brother whose natural acumen for figures more than compensated for his own lack of aptitude. Bob graduated from Stanford University a year after Baron's death and entered the family business just as his older brother took the reigns as store manager. The brothers quickly agreed upon a division of labor that allowed them to play off their individual strengths. Both excelled at merchandising, but Barry was better at buying and Bob better at bookkeeping. Through trial, error, trauma and travail, the brothers formed a working relationship that enabled them to both maintain a competitive edge and survive the ravages of the Great Depression without once missing a payroll, a feat that required each of them to forfeit their own salaries on more than one occasion. Through hard work and cautionary spending, the brothers managed to shepherd the store through the hard times on a break-even margin.

During these difficult years, Barry found solace from his business woes in his growing fascination with his home state. He journeyed near and far gathering materials pertaining to Arizona's past, present and future, some by donation but most by purchase. After meticulously organizing his growing collection, he sent the word through the community for all would-be Arizona Argonauts to come, see and savor. A steady train of residents accepted the invitation, then spread news of the boon to their peers. Within a short time, researchers at his door became as predictable as the Arizona sunshine.

A new camaraderie was born that simultaneously brought Goldwater great intellectual pleasure and intensified his desire to master the finer points of photography. During his many visits to the library, he had grown enamored with the stark and seamless images of California Master Edward Weston, whose "New Objectivity" theories and practices had given birth to a nascent school of thought that emphasized precision lighting, high definition and succinct patterning. The so-called "straight tradition" abandoned the artifice explicit in the soft-focused pictoralism of earlier years in favor of sharp, in-your-face photographs that captured "the very substance and quintessence of the thing itself,"[9] a realistic posture that proved a balm to the senses of a self-ascribed historian who was increasingly growing more convinced that the past was indeed prologue.

Bob's presence in the family business also freed his older brother to pursue his growing interest in aviation. His earliest exposure to planes and pilots came from the scientific journals he read as a child. When the Irving Kravitz School of Flying opened in Phoenix in the aftermath of World War I, he enrolled as a pupil without informing either of his parents of the decision out of fear they would squash his ambition as dangerous. When his mother caught him sneaking back through his window after one early morning lesson, she suspected he was returning from an all night tryst with some local maiden. Upon discovering the real reason for his covert behavior, she applauded his cunning and agreed to subsidize the cost of instruction. He accepted her generous offer, but soon devised a more ingenious scheme for banking enough cockpit hours to qualify for a license. During his frequent trips to Luke Field, he adroitly transformed his ever-present camera into an instrument of barter by trading photographs for flight time with Air Force cadets interested in portraits of themselves in military uniform.

By 1931, Goldwater had acquired sufficient skill to make his first cross-country flight. The following year, he tried to enlist in the Army Air Corps aviation program, but failed the eye exam. He purchased his first plane during these years, but did not officially obtain his commercial license until 1940, primarily because real life got in the way and he had less time to engage in the pursuit that he later likened to "the ultimate expression of individual freedom."[10]

The responsibilities associated with his leadership of the Goldwater store was an ongoing concern, particularly after Bob signed on as a one dollar a week trainee at Bullock's in Los Angeles and Morris closed the Prescott store to pursue his interests in politics. By the time Bob returned to the family business in 1937, Barry had been promoted to president of Goldwater's Inc., a position he held until 1953, when he assumed the title of Chairman of the Board. He continued in that capacity until the family sold the department stores to The Associated Dry Goods Company in 1962. At the time of his brother's return from his self-imposed apprenticeship, Barry's principal concern was reopening the Prescott store, a feat the brothers ultimately accomplished during the spring of 1938 to great fanfare.

Events in his personal life had taken a pleasantly portentous turn when he met Margaret "Peggy" Johnson at the Goldwater store during the winter of 1932. The chemistry between them was intense, but the woman he immediately targeted as his intended initially proved far from an easy sell. Pre-World War II Phoenix was essentially a small town with a vigorous rumor mill that kept few secrets. She knew about his pioneer heritage, unquenchable thirst for desolate places and widely celebrated reputation as a ladies man. He likewise knew that she was a wealthy winter visitor, who was fast cutting a swath in social circles as a cultured debutante maiden of great charm, beauty and breeding, with a bevy of potential suitors at her beck and call.

Never one to step down from a challenge, Barry spared no effort or expense in his efforts to win Peggy's hand. The days immediately following their official introduction found him dispatching notes, sending flowers, making phone calls and in general haunting her every waking hour. A short time into the mating ritual, she left on a worldwide cruise with her mother. He slyly scored a copy of her itinerary prior to her departure and made the necessary arrangements for a bouquet of roses and a love letter to be waiting for her at every port. Upon her return, he turned up the heat further, ultimately persuading her to officially take his name by holding her hostage in a phone booth during a grueling midwestern snowstorm.

During the two years leading up to their nuptials on September 22, 1934, they each learned that the other was more than just a pretty face. Barry was a charismatic, wilderness adventurer turned reluctant businessman, who ran the gauntlet between his duties at the Goldwater store and a full litany of spine chilling adventures that left timid jaws agape. Peggy was a somewhat shy, modern woman more attuned to the comforts of the parlor, with an impressive resume that included fashion and creative design at the Grand Central Art School and the David Crystal Company in New York City. He was a western diamond in the rough; she was an eastern charm school demoiselle urbane enough to recognize his potential.

Despite their surface differences, the popular couple possessed an essential sameness that led to a fairy-tale romance that ended in a lifetime union, which produced four children. Daughter Joanne arrived in 1936 and was named in honor of her grandmothers. Barry, Jr. made his worldly appearance two years later in 1938, followed by brother Michael Prescott (named for his great-grandfather and the town where the Goldwater's first gained a stable foothold) in 1940 and Peggy, Jr. in 1944. In accordance with the custom of their time and all the variables explicit in the juncture of two private fortunes, the couple practiced a loose division of labor whereby Barry remained the primary breadwinner and Peggy served as overseer to their comfortable home in Phoenix Country Club Manor, as well as principal caregiver for their spirited children.

Through force of personality and circumstance, the handsome couple fast became a social force in the community. They frequented local A-list parties, as well as hosting a number of memorable soirées on their own, including the frequent weekend getaways with a tight cadre of friends that Barry whimsically dubbed the Hiking, Singing and Loving Club. These colorful gatherings typically ended at the Grand Canyon, the majestic natural wonder known in inner circles as "Barry's mistress." Within a very short amount of time, they acquired a reputation as a fun loving, high energy couple that worked, played and contributed to the quality of community life with the same passion they felt for each other.

Having been raised on Big Mike's dictum of paying rent, Barry already had a reputation as a philanthropist and civic activist at the time of his marriage and the list kept growing right up to the end of his life. There were countless acts of private generosity in conjunction with his brother Bob such as clothing entire families after a fire, feeding woebegone strangers trying to get a foothold in Phoenix, and bailing out various Goldwater employees who had fallen on hard times. The more public side of his largesse entailed a combination of time and money

pledged to causes such as the Young Men's Christian Association, the Boys Club of Phoenix and the Community Chest (which later became the United Way), where he served a successful stint as president, as well as general chairman for the 1937 fundraising drive. He also served on the advisory boards of St. Lukes and St. Josephs hospitals and a long list of fraternal organizations that pledged funds toward disease and disaster relief.

As a businessman and local booster, Barry was active in a broad slate of activities earmarked toward making Phoenix, in particular, and Arizona in general, a hospitable setting for free enterprise. He served as president of the Phoenix Chamber of Commerce, as well as a charter member of its Royal Order of Thunderbirds. He also taught a class on tourism to local merchants and joined Prescott's Smoki Clan, a fraternal organization of mainstream professionals who dressed in Native American regalia and performed traditional dances to publicize Arizona's cultural diversity.

Along with standing shoulder-to-shoulder with her husband in his community efforts, Peggy had social concerns of her own. The cause closest to her heart was unplanned pregnancy and all of the health and human costs therein implied. In 1937 she joined with other local women and founded the Mother's Health Clinic, which targeted Mexican-American women for assistance. Working hand-in-hand with Margaret Sanger, she helped direct the successful collective into Arizona's first chapter of the Birth Control Federation of America, which later changed its name to Planned Parenthood. Then as now, birth control was an issue that raised hostile debate, but she persevered and her husband stood solidly in her corner down to openly soliciting funds for the cause.

During these busy years, wilderness jaunts were both frequent and laden with consequence, particularly with regard to Barry's aspirations as a photographer. Peggy's talents as an artist proved a pivotal ally in her husband's concerted quest to translate an extraordinary scene into an extraordinary photograph. Under her direction, the noisy compositions and amateur arrangements of the earlier years soon gave way to balanced images that paid liege to New Objectivity standards for high aesthetics. The only remaining shackle on Barry's imagination was technical reach, a shortcoming Peggy set to rights on the occasion of their first wedding anniversary in 1935, when she gave her husband his first professional camera outfit, a 4 x 5, twin lens Graflex, with a rapid lever film winder, eye-level focusing through a pentaprism and a built-in exposure meter.

The acquisition of a state-of-the-art light-tight box next to a built-in aesthetic mentor closed the gap between the dream and the deed. Modern equipment gave the master photographer in-the-making a decided edge in terms of focus, format and reach, specifically the critical elements of lighting controls and the untold options offered by the varied lens system he purchased in short order. Curiosity got the best of him, his mechanical genius came into play and Goldwater was suddenly in transit toward a future that unfolded into a wider social canvas with each passing decade. It was a life drama wherein his camera creations would hereafter enjoy a perpetual starring role.

Goldwater's immediate goal came from his twofold quest to add to his expanding library on Arizona and answer the research needs of its growing army of users. An impromptu request from a student about Peach Springs became the precipice for transforming a youthful inkling into a private pledge to record Arizona as it existed during his lifetime, a difficult but worthy challenge that found ready succor in the vast array of changes going on around him. The small town atmosphere of his youth was showing signs of the nascent beginnings of urbanization as more and more visitors heeded the call of boosterism and traded the mantle of tourist for that of permanent resident. Economic opportunities abounded and eastern investors took notice, particularly during the post-Depression years when the federal government launched an unprecedented era of large scale spending in the region.

The latter phenomenon raised an ambivalence that would haunt Goldwater until the end of his days. As a businessman and civic leader, he welcomed the flush of ready cash as a necessary stimulus for perpetuating the economic promise and potential that kept his family in comfortable stead. As a conservative, he feared the underside of sudden wealth, particularly the propensity for free flowing dollars to stick to fast hands. The wilderness addict lamented the restructuring of the landscape and the irreparable costs of lost traditions, especially among

the ranks of Arizona's First Nations. He ultimately assuaged his fears by accepting change as inevitable and the past as a place filled with critical lessons, seemingly opposite concepts that spurred him to marshal his instincts and go see, study and save telling slices of his beloved homeland for the benefit of posterity.

A high stakes gambler and natural risk taker, Goldwater craved action, adventure and the thrill of fresh experience. Arizona, with her vast unspoiled reaches and low-density settlement patterns, was balm to his senses. Although fully cognizant that she was too big to ever be completely known and too cagey to ever lay up all of her secrets, he pursued her with a diligence known only to the smitten, crisscrossing her nethermost reaches in every form of transport from foot power to state-of-the-art aircraft. He climbed her towering cliffs, hunted her forests, fished her streams and challenged her major waterways in wooden boats and rubber rafts, systematically attaining a full resume of cuts, bruises, broken bones and cancer inducing sunburns, which he proudly viewed as battle scars garnered in the age old struggle between man and nature.

A place fraught with the potential for high adventure was only part of the impetus behind Goldwater's passion. Arizona's First Nations proved a powerful lure to a native son who chose to attain the finer points of his education through direct experience. Never one to adhere to a theory that could not withstand the test of practical experience, he looked past the prejudices characteristic of his time and simply made friends, initially with the students at the Phoenix Indian School and later with citizens of First Nations from across the country.

Many of these acquaintances ended up in his photographs. As often, an Indian face or custom was captured for its aesthetic or historic intrigue. The collective result is a broad stretch of imagery that ranges from character studies to spectral frames featuring traditional indigenous practices and pursuits. Their collective power comes from more than their obvious technical savvy. These images bespeak a special understanding held by a mainstream aristocrat, who beheld Indians through a highly personal lens shaped largely by intimate exposure.

Rather than impoverished wards of the federal government, Goldwater viewed Arizona's Indian nations as independent cultures with a rhyme and rhythm discreet to each tribal unit. He opened his mind to their own unique brand of wisdom and caught an intimate glimpse of the varied and complicated relationships existing between humans and gods and goddesses and conversely, gods and goddesses to humans. He drew fresh analogies between belief, practice and historic experience and added a new dimension to his views toward the human role in nature's vast spectrum. He ate Indian food, hunted by their methods, slept in their homes, honored their traditions and showed them the respect of learning words from their languages. Arizona's First Nations each in turn eventually answered his civility with prestigious appointments as honorary chief.

Perhaps the most important aspect of Goldwater's Indian photography is that which is seldom conceded by his critics. The knowledge behind their evident magic took a lifetime to acquire. It took root in childhood with his first trip to the Hopi village of Oraibi at the age of seven. It matured as he made friends, established contacts and commenced to acquire the massive Kachina collection that he ultimately donated to the Heard Museum. More than pretty photographs, he created intimate portraits of people, practices and rituals, many of which were fast falling through the hourglass of history.

Goldwater's photographic race against time netted a stunning visual diary that spanned the spectrum from close-up portraiture to wide-angle views of the landscape. Appreciative friends took note of his growing talents and pressed him to seek a wider audience for his wares. Through their insistence, he began to submit photographs to local newspapers to illustrate stories on the Grand Canyon and other scenic settings around Arizona. Word soon reached then *Arizona Highways* editor Raymond Carlson, which led to a professional relationship that began in 1934 and continued with respectable frequency until the photographer's death in 1998.

Around the same time Goldwater forged an alliance with the *Arizona Highways,* he also learned the vocabulary of formal exhibition. He began by submitting images to juried exhibitions advertised in the backs of photography and art journals. The response was immediate and overwhelmingly positive from all points of the globe, earning the stunned cameraman ribbons, prizes and cash awards.

Recognition from his peers came in short order, winning him tomes of favorable reviews, consistent critical applause and ultimately inductions into summit organizations that officially mantled him with the title of Master Photographer. By the time war broke out in Europe in 1936, he was one of the widest exhibited photographers in the world, with an excess of three hundred exhibitions to his credit.

During a time when the Colorado River constituted 265 miles of some of the roughest water in the North American continent, Goldwater added further to his laurels by becoming the seventy-third person to retrace John Wesley Powell's second river voyage. The year was 1940 and the trip was more an expedition than a vacation. Along with still film cameras, he carried a movie camera, which he used to make what is believed to be the first color, feature length film shot in Arizona, a 29-minute, expertly captioned, highly learned documentary about the Colorado River, complete with original musical score. At the behest of his friends, he showed the film to sell out audiences around the state. He later credited the experience and subsequent fanfare with granting him the necessary notoriety to make a successful bid for public office, an as yet unforeseen fate that in essence took root when the Japanese bombed Pearl Harbor during the early morning hours of December 7, 1941.

When news of the attack reached stateside, Goldwater was on fire to do his patriotic duty. He discussed the situation with his brother Bob, who agreed to cover his duties at the Goldwater store. Garnering Peggy's approval was a different matter. Along with the obvious threat such action posed to his personal safety, she would be placed in the role of single parent to three rambunctious children, ranging in age from one to five. Through his powers of persuasion and his wife's considerate understanding of his profound need to do his part, Goldwater finally won the support he sought, only to have his patriotic ambitions temporarily derailed by rules and regulations surrounding enlistment standards.

Military officials initially rebuffed Goldwater's efforts to enter military service under the guise that he was too old and too blind, but he fought to fight and won. He had already begun the preliminary steps a few months prior to the United States declaring war on Germany and Japan by using his position as chairman of the Phoenix Chamber of Commerce committee (charged with seeing to the off base needs of troops and airman stationed at Luke Field) to persuade the base commander to admit him as a reservist assigned to the Air Corp. A few months preceding U.S. entry into the war, his division suffered a shortage of pilots to ferry planes and haul critical supplies such as the mail to U.S. military bases situated on foreign soil. A new service pilot division was formed, which was open to aviators with a minimum of 400 hours in aircraft with over 400 horsepower, provided they could pass a flight test on the AT-6.

Goldwater qualified on all fronts and was accorded his first set of Army Air Corp wings in October of 1941. A few months after the U.S. officially entered the war, he assumed the duties of flight instructor at the Yuma Air Base, a position that gave him experience on a broad slate of aircraft, including the AT-9, PT-40, A-20, B-26 and a twin-engine Cessna, which he whimsically labeled 'the bamboo bomber.' By fall, he had been promoted to captain and reassigned to the Second Ferrying Command in Wilmington, Delaware, where he served as operations officer for the 27th Ferrying Squadron, an experience that enabled him to extend his aviator skills to even more aircraft: B-17s, A-36s, P-39s, B-26s and P-47 Thunderbolts, one of which he christened the *Peggy G* and flew in the first and only attempt to ferry fighter planes across the Atlantic in 1943, a 3,750-mile journey that marked Goldwater's first solo flight over an ocean.

By the end of the war, he had flown cargo missions in both theaters and commanded the first, all-female squadron of service pilots. The failure to actually take part in combat remained one of his biggest disappointments, but he took great pride in the contribution he had been able to make to the war effort. Near the end of the fighting, the aviation cadets of class 43-E of the Army Air Force Advanced Flying School at Yuma Army Air Field dedicated the yearbook to him, complete with a flattering inscription that deemed him "the type of Officer and Gentleman after which we would like to pattern ourselves."[11]

When Goldwater left active service, he took a reduction in rank from Lieutenant Colonel to Captain in order to found the Arizona National Guard, where he served as Chief of Staff until 1952. He remained active in the Air Force Reserve for thirty-seven years, retiring in 1967 with the rank of Major General, USAFR. By that time, he had 15,000 flying hours and over 255 different types of aircraft to his credit, as well as the distinction of being the first non-rated test pilot to fly the U-2, the SR-71, the B-1 Bomber and the F-16.

Goldwater's immediate concern at the end of the war was renewing his acquaintance with his family, which now numbered four children. He arrived home laden with the bounty of gifts characteristic of the returning soldier-father of his era, only to discover a larger present awaiting him. While he was flying cargo missions over The Hump, Peggy secretly arranged for him to become a partner in the Rainbow Lodge and Trading Post, which had been built around the turn-of-the-century by S. I. Richardson, the descendant of a pioneer family who boasted both long roots and a long reach in trading operations across Navajo country. At the time of the purchase, former Goldwater store manager Sam Wilson's brother William and his wife Katherine served as the live-in managers and caretakers of the lodge.

Although Goldwater was never able to spend more than a week or two in residence at Rainbow Lodge, he went to great lengths to make it amenable to his needs. He borrowed equipment from the Babbitt Brothers in Flagstaff and constructed a two thousand foot runway near the lodge, which enabled him to close the distance from Phoenix in less than two hours. After installing a five-watt generator and a walk-in icebox, he contracted developer Del Webb to construct a half dozen one room cabins to house the bevy of friends and eastern tourists, whom he lured to the area with promises of personally conducted adventures like climbing Navajo Mountain, mule train trips down to Rainbow Bridge and various hiking and camping excursions in virtually every direction imaginable. Cameras were commonplace equipment on these excursions, which translated into a wide array of new photographs of people and places to add to his award winning visual oeuvre.

After the war, Goldwater became acquainted with an English pilot with connections in East Germany that enabled him to secure camera equipment at wholesale rates, which he graciously extended to

American friend for a period that stretched across several years. Premium priced German optics were highly coveted by professional photographers, because they offered mirror-like clarity through precision ground lens systems that were interchangeable between different camera models built by the same manufacturer. Through this ad hoc arrangement, Goldwater expanded his equipment arsenal to include new Rolliflex and Leica cameras, compatible lens systems, tripods and other devices that gave him a wide range of technical choices previously outside his reach.

Piecemeal equipment updates kept him abreast of the latest through the lens options, but Goldwater wanted full range control of his photography, which meant mastering the language of the darkroom. Prior to World War II, his efforts toward this end had essentially been self-directed with the aid of various mail order manuals in a makeshift facility he installed in his basement next to the air-conditioning equipment and all the other hardware, toys and discards characteristic of a home occupied by four energetic children. During the post war years, he took his case to his friend Claude Bate, a local portrait photographer who earned his spurs at his brother's Prescott studio, before hanging his own shingle off the lobby of the Biltmore Hotel. Weeks and months of sporadic lessons grounded Goldwater in the basics, but his natural curiosity led him to continually push the envelope, which in turn fed his insatiable desire to claim mastery of the technical end of photography down to the most mundane detail.

The next formal wave of darkroom instruction came from gratis advice rendered by the legendary Ansel Adams, whom Goldwater met during a haphazard wilderness encounter, a few months after he became a partner in Rainbow Lodge. Both men were scouting camera scenes near the head of the Rainbow Bridge Trail on the southwest side of Navajo Mountain at the time of their introduction. Their discussions soon revealed that they had much in common, not the least of which was a twin allegiance to the western landscape and the philosophies of Edward Weston. A lifelong, mutually beneficial friendship took root whereby Goldwater taught Adams how to behave on an Indian reservation and Adams taught Goldwater how to transform the dark-

room into an aesthetic partner in his quest to master the finer points of film development and print production.

Full scope knowledge of photography from composition to chemistry lit a fire in Goldwater for a state-of-the-art darkroom of his own, a hunger ultimately satiated with the construction of *Be-nun-i-kin* (Navajo for house on the hill) in 1957. Situated on acreage he had bought from Frank Brophy in the late 1940s, the 6300 square foot estate caused a stir in local circles both for its post-modernist design and then remote location. Goldwater's darkroom sat in the center of the main structure, enabling him to generate prints at will, many of which ended up as wallpaper for the guest bathroom. The stench left behind by the chemicals offended Peggy's sensibilities, but she tolerated the smelly encumbrance as part of the downside of sharing quarters with a Renaissance Man far too humble to ever lay claim to the title.

Although Goldwater began to experiment with color film shortly after he acquired his first professional camera in 1935, he seriously set his sights on mastering the specifics of the medium during the post war years. The Arizona landscape and Native American portraiture remained his favorite subjects, but his expertise with color opened up new markets for his photographic wares, particularly after regional publications began to abandon black and white formats for new printing technologies based on four color separations. When the *Arizona Highways* made the transition in December of 1946, editor Raymond Carlson selected a Goldwater photograph of two Navajo girls herding sheep in the snow for the cover image, granting the magazine and the photographer a mutual historic first.

Goldwater continued to submit photographs to international exhibitions and fine arts publications during this time, but the lion's share of his attention was focused on reclaiming his place in a community caught in the throes of a frantic costume change. The years surrounding World War II and the subsequent Cold War era, with its overt emphasis on national defense, proved a pivotal force in the unprecedented growth and development Arizona in general and Phoenix in particular were destined to wrestle with across upcoming decades. Military installations and related support industries such as electronics and aviation, which Goldwater personally championed, spurred a population shift that raised Phoenix's population from 65,414 in 1940 to 106,818 in 1950 to an astounding 439,270 in 1960. The situation in Maricopa County was even more dramatic, with the 186,193 residents posted in the 1940 census jutting to 331,770 in 1950, only to double to 663,510 in 1960.

The sum of these changes caused an internal war within Goldwater that placed his perspective as a businessman at odds with his own unique brand of patriotism, which from start to finish decried federal interference in the lives of its citizens. On the surface, he viewed growth as a necessary precursor to wider social and economic opportunities, a view assisted by both the proliferation of new industries and the remarkable rebound of the traditional sectors of copper, cattle, cotton, citrus and tourism. Although the new "clean industries" would ultimately emerge as the dominant horse in the regional economy, Goldwater feared the underside of federal involvement and he said so early and often, as the following excerpt from a 1940 newspaper interview reveals:

> *Of extreme importance to retailing in all its branches has been huge expenditures of public money in this area. Arizona ranks near the top in per capita money received from the New Deal. It is sheer folly for any of our numerous branches of business to consider this money as a permanent source of income to business…If it continues, it will be at the expense of business and is, so to speak, robbing Peter to pay Paul.[12]*

Goldwater continued to voice his concerns to an audience that was initially of no mind to listen. Between the years 1940 to 1960, Phoenix eclipsed El Paso as the premier metropolitan complex in the Southwest, a feat aided and abetted by the city's stature as the 'Air Conditioning Capitol of the World.' City leaders practiced an open arms approach to new industries, while turning a blind eye to the growing list of urban ills and environmental concerns left in the wake of uncharted and unchecked growth.

Although a composite of these forces ultimately prompted Goldwater to cast his hat in the political ring, the immediate outgrowth of his observations and concerns brought new urgency to his quest to record Arizona as it existed in his lifetime. Wilderness escapes were commonplace and most often carried double duty as vacations and fact-finding missions wherein his camera proved an invaluable ally. He traveled to all points of the state in every form of transport at his disposal, systematically amassing a vast opus of new views of people, places and indigenous practices, which he feared circumstance had earmarked for history's graveyard. The more artistic of these images were fed to formal exhibitions, where he continued to earn awards and critical acclaim, including back to back twin inductions as an associate into The Royal Photographic Society of Great Britain and as an honorary member of the Photographic Society of America.

Goldwater later revealed that these honors prompted him to consider pursuing photography as a profession, but events were fast unfolding in Phoenix that mantled him with a different destiny. At the end of World War II, thousands of defense workers and military personnel settled in Phoenix, which taxed existing housing, transportation networks and social services beyond their capacity. Vice was rampant, but citizen complaints toward that end essentially went unnoticed, until a combination of rioting and venereal disease cases among servicemen prompted local commanders to declare Phoenix out of bounds to military personnel. The edict tarnished both the city's reputation and curbed its profit making potential, since servicemen constituted one of the largest sources of consumer spending.

When a new sheaf of complaints went unheeded by city officials, forty concerned citizens formed into the first Charter Government Committee. Regular meetings were held from January to August of 1948, which entailed members reviewing literature provided by the National Municipal League, particularly its Model City Charter. They collectively drafted a sheaf of recommendations, which the voters approved by a three-to-one margin, only to have the newly elected officials emulate the same corrupt tactics of the predecessors.

In July of 1949, a second citizens group met and formed the new Charter Government Committee (CGC), a bipartisan collective intent upon drafting a slate of candidates committed to the implementation of the revised charter. Through the combined influence of newspaper publisher Eugene Pulliam and friend Harry Rosenzweig, a reluctant Goldwater threw his hat into the ring and claimed a decisive victory by carrying every precinct in the city, garnering 16,405 of the 22,353 votes cast. Fully convinced that his trek into local politics was a timed engagement limited to a single term, he pledged himself to the task at hand with single-minded devotion and the local press took notice. Rumors began to circulate about his political future and the Republican Party approached him to run for governor, an offer he refused under the guise that he had barely commenced his term.

By the time of his election to the Phoenix City Council, Goldwater had already made a name for himself as a popular local author and public speaker. His maiden trek in the former arena began in 1940, when he self-published *Arizona Portraits*, a humble collection of his photographs, which he sold through the Goldwater store for the benefit of local charities. The following year, he published two separate volumes featuring excerpts from his 1940 river diaries: *A Journey Down the Green and Colorado Rivers: From the Diary of Barry M. Goldwater* and *An Odyssey of the Green and Colorado Rivers: The Intimate Journal of Three Boats and Nine People on a Trip Down Two Rivers*. The film he shot during that portentous voyage and unveiled to sell out audiences around the state proved but a stepping stone to a whole slew of speaking engagements that earned him followers statewide, including the famed Lincoln Day dinner speeches he gave at Republican fundraisers. With his straight shooting style and fine-tuned sense of humor, he cajoled audiences to stop wasting their energies apologizing for being Americans, Republicans (Arizona was a Democratic stronghold at the time) and capitalists. Instead of "planning for socialism," he argued that their time would be better spent, "planning for the continuation and the improvement of our free enterprise system."[13]

When Republican candidate Howard Pyle selected Goldwater to manage his second gubernatorial campaign in 1950, the reluctant politician was exposed to even a wider audience. He flew Pyle from one whistle stop to the other, often on opposite sides of the state in a single day, marking the first political campaign in the state's history to use aviation as a primary means of transportation. The handsome aviator's unique ability to find words in common with people from all walks of life next to his off-the-cuff wit made him a star attraction on the campaign trail, leading more than one observer to conclude that the wrong man was running for office. Rather than resent the usurper, Pyle joined in the chorus. Along with crediting Goldwater's charisma as a major component in his gubernatorial victory, he made a concerted attempt to convince his one-time manager that the time had come to write his own chapter in the political history of his time.

Through a combination of Pyle's victory and influence, Goldwater abandoned his earlier hesitation and accepted his party's nomination for a U.S. Senate seat in 1952, a race he won by a nervously close margin. With the exception of a single term hiatus to run for the presidency in 1964 (the only election he ever lost), Goldwater was elected continuously until his retirement on January 2, 1987. From junior senator to senior statesman, he held steadfast to the principals of free speech, free people and free enterprise. He favored no-holds-barred, public debate of the issues, a strong national defense, a foreign policy that granted overt preference to other democracies, minimal taxes and a hands-off policy toward commerce. His enemies were big government, tax and spend liberals, liars and traitors of every stamp.

From start to finish, Goldwater's straight to the heart of it style and eclectic interests caused a firestorm in Washington. He was an aristocrat who claimed no special privilege for the caste; a technology addict that revered the past as the blueprint for the future; and, a political renegade who gave old line Republicans and spin doctors alike more than a few Maalox moments. He was also a high profile Republican who openly claimed Harry Truman as a personal hero, a Vietnam War hawk who lent a scholarly ear to the arguments posited by the doves and a staunch Nixon supporter who told the beleaguered president that it was time to hit the trail, once his mendacity and complicity in the Watergate scandal became apparent. Although media critics frequently made sound bite glory by misquoting Goldwater's humorous quips as serious statements, few questioned that his my-country-right-or-wrong patriotism and with-no-apologies-style championship of the free enterprise system laid the bedrock for the modern conservative movement that essentially came of age as he was leaving office.

The consistency of his views, the soundness of his supporting arguments and ready willingness to stand against the popular tide for principle earned Goldwater respect from audiences worldwide, including those who took exception to his political views. More than the issues he addressed, challenged and championed, it was the way he conducted himself and his homespun style that got right to the heart of the matter with minimum elocution. His uncanny popularity with people on both sides of the aisle prompted erstwhile political rival and life-long friend Roy Elson to whimsically label him "a real life Marlboro Man."[14]

Goldwater's own views toward his uniquely universal appeal inevitably pointed back to the Arizona wilderness and all those life-threatening encounters that kept him both humble and honest. More than colorful rhetoric, his frequently quoted mantra that the state was nothing less than "114,000 square miles of heaven" was a soul level belief born out of exposure to and experience with an unforgiving landscape equally laden with peril and potential. Later in life, he confessed that anytime he felt his ego swell or his confidence sag all he needed to do was visit canyon country and the corrective comeuppance was forthwith delivered.

Trips back to Arizona were commonplace occurrences, particularly after Peggy deemed Washington, D. C. an inhospitable environment to raise four young children. In a fashion dangerously reminiscent of the arrangement existing between his grandparents, Goldwater's life became a steeplechase between his duties within the beltway and his responsibilities to his Arizona-based family. Even though he never ceased to lament all that he had missed during his prolonged absences, he went to great lengths to make every trip home count, including frequent family outings into wild lands, where he taught his children (and later his grandchildren) his own version of the survivalist tactics imparted to him by his mother, as well as introduced them to a unique cuisine that boasted such novel entrees as peanut butter gravy.

Annual sojourns to the Grand Canyon were a popular mainstay on the family's wilderness itinerary. Through the years, Goldwater had become a walking repository of information on the Grand Canyon's natural history, down to the evolution of specific rock formations, crevices, monuments, spires, flora and fauna. Equally versed in the human side of the drama, he collected stories and tales, which he used to regale his children and their friends over campfires, on river odysseys and more hiking trips than they can collectively recall.

Cameras, tripods and film were standard equipment on these adventures, enabling Goldwater to instill each of his sons with more than a passing fancy in the discipline. Although neither Barry, Jr. nor Michael ever pursued photography with the intensity of their father, several of their compositions conveyed a similar level of skill, talent and artistic merit. Michael ultimately passed his interest to his daughter Anna, who received a degree in fine art photography from the University of Arizona in 1994.

The demands of the U.S. Senate limited the time Goldwater had to pursue his own photographic ambitions, but he never ceased to generate new images at every opportunity at his disposal, including his many sojourns to other countries both as an elected official and a private citizen. Photographs captured during these trips mirrored the subjects he favored at home, namely indigenous faces and the natural landscape. In Old Country settings, he frequently turned his lens toward ancient architecture or slice of life scenes that served as visual metaphors of some larger event or circumstance he wished to share with family and friends back home.

As much as Goldwater enjoyed his photographic forays in foreign lands, Arizona-related themes remained his subject field of choice. Many of his landscape scenes and Native portraits graced the walls of his senatorial offices, where they steadfastly elicited favorable commentary from peers and constituents alike. An even larger number of Arizona images were handed out as gifts to appreciative family members, friends and colleagues.

Along with commanding a starring role in most of his political literature, his photographs also graced the pages of a large scale, limited edition book entitled *The Face of Arizona*, which was used as a fundraiser for his 1964 presidential campaign.

Three years later, Random House issued his *People and Places: Text and Photographs*, a coffee table collection of new photographs of his trademark Arizona themes.

By the 1970s, Goldwater had become such a powerhouse in political arenas that his achievements in other fields were eclipsed by his manifold contributions as a statesman. The temper of the times was toward specialization, compartmentalization and pigeonholing personality types into neat little boxes amenable to surface interpretation. An odd sort of labeling occurred that limited public recognition of Goldwater's talents to those directly relating to issues and causes he championed as a politician. Critics were quick to acknowledge his skills as an aviator because of his staunch support of military matters. His stellar arguments on behalf of cyber age communication, along with his generous decision to patch radio transmissions between families throughout the United States and their relatives on the battlefields of Vietnam, called public attention to his contributions as a ham radio operator.

Since photography could not be tied to any existing political issue, it was reduced in rank to a hobby, an inaccuracy that unfortunately took false support from the time constraints that kept Goldwater from showcasing his photographs through the time honored rites of juried exhibitions. The level of media interest he steadily generated typically netted references that cast his photography in the shallow role of an aristocrat's passing fancy, rather than an influential force that facilitated the rise of a gifted statesman who fathered a new brand of conservatism that reshaped American politics during the last half of the 20th Century and beyond.

When Goldwater's arguments to the contrary fell on deaf ears, he discounted the misrepresentations as little more than another example of shallow reporting in the sound bite age. Those close to him knew the importance he placed upon his self-ascribed mission to record Arizona as it existed in his lifetime and it was to that end that he never lost focus. As a sitting United States Senator, he was often privy to changes before they occurred, which enabled him to capture scenes and settings growth threatened with obsolescence. There was also a constant stream of letters, phone calls and requests from other Arizona history buffs, which he went to great lengths to answer both as a brother in arms and as the founder of the Arizona Historical Foundation, central Arizona's oldest regionally specific historical repository and publishing arm.

The latter feat was an unplanned venue that fell on Goldwater's head when public access to his private library became a problem after he was elected to the Senate. Peggy was logically uncomfortable with having strangers appear regularly at her door, which netted numerous complaints to her husband, who ultimately solved the dilemma in 1959, when he joined with his friends and took his collection public. Rather than christen it with his own name, he opted for the broad title of The Arizona Historical Foundation (AHF) as a means of keeping its reach fluid and its purpose on track with the original impetus behind its evolution. Using his private library as its seed collection, he drafted and chartered AHF with the clear and simple mission "to collect, preserve and disseminate the history of Arizona and the Southwest," then spent the remaining years of his life and much of his private fortune ushering it toward that end, initially as Founding President and later as its first Chairman of the Board.

On the eve of Goldwater's 1964 campaign for the presidency, officials from Arizona State University approached him with an offer to move AHF from its original location on North Central Avenue to the Tempe campus. He initially refused the offer under the guise that its mission could best be served if it remained a private sector concern. Early in 1965, ASU President Homer Durham contacted Goldwater with a new offer more suited to his temperament. In exchange for relocating AHF to the proposed Hayden Library and making the collection available to researchers, the university would provide space, salary and material support, as well as maintain a firm hands-off policy with regard to its autonomy. Goldwater turned the matter over to Harry Rosenzweig, who engineered a three-part deal that included the Sun Angel Foundation, the newly founded Goldwater Chair for American Institutions and AHF under the terms set forth in the Durham offer, which had been extended to include the promise of a future senatorial library wherein his political papers would share the stage with those of his friend Senator Carl Hayden and other present and future elected officials.

When Hayden Library opened in 1966, AHF moved to its current location on the fourth floor. Goldwater administered it from a distance, but he was far from an absentee proprietor. In addition to acquiring a steady slew of new collections from other pioneer families, he solicited funds from business leaders and donated stipends from his speaking engagements to offset the cost of daily operations. In 1970, he published another diary from the 1940 river trip under the title *Delightful Journey* and reserved all proceeds for the exclusive benefit of AHF. He kept his ear to the wind for historic materials to round out its holdings and his checkbook open to answer its needs, which included everything from equipment updates to outright purchases of rare and relevant research materials and artifacts.

Along with the documents, maps, books and historic images he regularly purchased for AHF, Goldwater created an endless array of new photographs for the joint benefit of its patrons and his loyal audience of international fans, many of whom knew him from his days as a frequent contributor to fine art exhibitions. With his growing fame as a political leader came media interest in his life and pursuits, which led to an endless array of pictorial spreads in newspapers and magazines that typically featured a selected image or images from his growing visual catalog. In 1976, a fourth collection of his photographs was published under the descriptive title, *Barry Goldwater and the Southwest*. Rounding out the showcase was a prohibitive list of local and national charities, which either used his photographs to illustrate their literature or as auction items to generate funds for a full spectrum of causes, ranging from health care to historic preservation.

The glory and applause Goldwater enjoyed throughout his life in virtually every arena he entered was always tempered by the inevitable loss of loved ones to the ravages of age and disease. On April 11 1939, he bid farewell to his beloved Uncle Morris, who passed quietly to his reward at his Prescott home at the age of 87. The next blow came with the death of his mother on December 27, 1966. Goldwater grieved her passing with all of the passion characteristic of a self-professed Mama's Boy, but ultimately reconciled himself to the loss on the basis that she had lived a long, productive and happy life.

Goldwater was without such consolations after Peggy fell into a coma and died two weeks later on December 11, 1985. Although her health had been declining for a number of years, he was beside himself with grief over the loss of the gentle spirit who had stood at the center of his life for over fifty-one years. He held himself together through the funeral, but struggled privately with all of the hellish feelings of denial, anger and fear associated with the loss of a cherished soulmate. A few weeks into his grief, Goldwater sought relief from his anguish by returning to the site of Rainbow Lodge, which lay in ruins. The buildings had been lost to a fire in 1951, but memories are seldom fettered by creature comfort constraints. As he later revealed in his autobiography, the loss of Peggy punched a hole in his heart that no amount of rationalization or reasoning would ever fully heal:

> *The trip took me back to our honeymoon. For an instant, the face of my beautiful young bride appeared in the emptiness of the lodge and my heart. Then she was gone. We flew home. But Peg was there—in the face of the desert and the brown hills. My tears clouded the clear blue sky.*[15]

Depressed and dispirited, Goldwater returned to Washington to finish out what remained of his final term. On December 10, 1986, three weeks prior to his official retirement on January 2 1987, he was honored with a Department of Defense Distinguished Service Medal, an Army Distinguished Civilian Service Award, a Navy Distinguished Public Service Award and an Air Force Exceptional Service Award. Subsequent months and years brought additional honors, including the Thayer Award from the United States Military Academy in 1987 and the James H. Doolittle Award from the Hudson Institute in 1995.

Retirement for Goldwater was more a case of stepping out of one spotlight into another. Public interest was piqued by everything he did, leaving him minimal private time to grieve the death of his wife or celebrate events in private with his children, grandchildren and friends. Each public appearance sparked a new round of requests for his time; each social or political issue sent a herd of reporters to his door seeking his opinions and commentary. He remained sanguine in the madness, fully convinced that the attention would wane with time.

Goldwater did not sit idle while he waited for the peace that never came. He kept his official finger in national affairs as Chairman of the United States Air Force Academy Board of Visitors and his distinguished service as a presidential appointee to the board of the COMSAT Corporation. Unofficially, he rendered tomes of learned advice to upcoming and seated leaders on issues ranging from campaign reform to foreign affairs.

One of the most rewarding venues during his final years was Goldwater's ad hoc role as educator both in his official capacity as Goldwater Chair Professor at Arizona State University and the countless elementary and high school classrooms he regularly visited as a guest speaker. He delighted in sharing details of his life, heritage and homeland with young Arizonans, whom he steadfastly encouraged to study, experience and explore the boundless beauty and potential of their birthright.

The same passion that enabled Goldwater to excite young minds to appreciate Arizona added new fire to his determination to transform the Arizona Historical Foundation into the premier research facility he envisioned as a youth. During the years intervening between its relocation to Arizona State University and his retirement, several disputes arose with regard to encroachments upon AHF's autonomy, which he stalwartly resisted on the basis of both personality and principle. As a western man with western opinions, he was completely wedded to the dual concept of honoring all deals and a man's word being equal to his bond. The promised senatorial library had not been forthcoming and the proffered support dispensed in a piecemeal fashion that fell far beneath documented need. Since the conservative standards he championed as a statesman were as much a personal creed as they were a political position, he was adamant that AHF function as an independent, non-profit corporation, which adhered to the rules and standards operative within the private sector.

During the final years of his life, Goldwater reaffirmed his conviction by direct action and the results were dramatic. AHF's less than 2,000 linear feet research library increased tenfold, its membership a hundredfold, its patron base turned international

and its outreach activities expanded to include several fruitful partnerships, not the least of which is seven satellite galleries featuring alternating exhibitions of historic photographs and rare artifacts. Its once idle publishing arm was revamped and revitalized, leading to the publication of four new book titles exclusive of the present volume, which holds the distinction of being the last authorized account of his life.

Goldwater's concerted efforts to turn the Arizona Historical Foundation into a one-stop reference on all things Arizona were interspersed with other activities and events that kept him center stage in the public mind. Along with publishing two separate autobiographies, he authored tomes of political commentary, delivered countless speeches and lent his support to charitable activities across the spectrum.

In February of 1992, Goldwater raised a storm in media circles when he married Susan McMurray Wechsler, a registered nurse turned health care administrator, thirty years his junior. The newly minted couple accepted the intrusive scrutiny with good-natured equanimity, using their collective energies to contribute to the quality of community life in a broad slate of charitable arenas. Private time was rare and almost exclusively reserved for activities with their blended family, which included eight children and over a dozen grandchildren and great grandchildren.

Scholarly interest in Goldwater followed him into retirement and continues unabated in the present. Along with innumerable newspaper and magazine articles about his life and pursuits, he served as subject for over half a dozen books centered upon his political philosophies and contributions as a statesman. Film crews came calling early and often, but a combination of time limitations and personal interest compelled him to limit on-camera interviews to local television stations and two historical documentaries produced in conjunction with AHF: KAET's *Photographs and Memories* (1995) and A & E's *Biography This Week* (1996).

The combined force of these sterling productions refocused public attention on Goldwater's photography, an unexpected boon that brought him great personal satisfaction. Throughout the years, he had steadfastly told reporters and researchers that his camera was not a toy, but a tool that played a pivotal role in virtually every aspect of his life from aviation to politics. The sheer volume of his skills and interests muddied the water to the extent that critics inevitably reduced photography to an avocation, when it was in reality a lifetime habit that enabled him to parley his intense passion for Arizona into a high profile position that allowed him to seriously 'pay rent.'

Goldwater took immeasurable delight in the new wave of curiosity seekers sparked by the in tandem airings of the PBS and A & E films, for reasons beyond the obvious ego stroke. Enough time had elapsed between his foot race against time and the present to make him appear a sage in the minds of a new generation of fans, many of whom had come of age in the wake of the changes he had so diligently sought to chronicle. The fact that each photograph carried its own story added to the enticement, granting him the late life privilege of acting out on his personal passion for Arizona in his imitable tell-it-like-it-is-style. With rare exception, he left his listeners astounded, particularly those sentient enough to calculate the gap between his lack of formal instruction in photography and the fanciful talent that earned him the distinction of being the first Arizona photographer to be inducted into the Royal Photographic Society of Great Britain, a highly covetous caste that remains the brass ring for camera carriers across the spectrum.

The widespread popularity of Goldwater's photography stemmed in large part from his unique ability to capture a timeless story within the confines of a single frame, a masterful feat that required what he possessed in great abundance—knowledge of his subject and the technical savvy to render it amenable to a two dimensional format. Along with the precision inherent in regular practice, he remained a loyal student of the discipline from technique to philosophical theory. He was particularly enamored with French Master Henri Cartier Bresson's concept of the "decisive moment," or that rare and fleeting instant when all of the necessary elements for the perfect photograph appear in unison. The photographer becomes one with the photograph, a state Goldwater sought with deliberation and maintained by design.

Because he held the "The Street-sweeper" image featured on the cover as his most definitive success in capturing the "decisive moment," we thought it more than befitting that it provide the visual introduction to the present collection of photographs. The setting and circumstances surrounding its capture were a 1966 vacation with his wife to Spain, specifically a leisurely afternoon drive along the road from Madrid to Escorial. The sightseers decided to stop for a late cocktail in a historic hamlet before embarking on the final leg of their journey, when they happened upon two men sweeping the cobblestone streets with old brush brooms. Let the Master-turned-artistic-mentor resume the tale:

> *I asked the street sweeper to stand near the center of the street so that the trees in the back would frame him and at the same time break up the long rays of the setting sun as they filtered through the smoke. The fire itself was off to one side but the smoke drifted across and up through the trees and gave just the effect that I hoped I would find. The negative that came as a result of this composition was a pleasing one, and particularly so to the young members of my family for whom I have made seemingly countless prints of this picture to be given to their friends for presents. The printing of the negative requires a bit of control because as one can imagine, the brightness of the sun's rays dominates the negative, requiring the holding back, as we put it, of the darker areas during printing to allow the full development of the effect of the sun coming through the smoke. This control, by the way, is one of the most rewarding experiences in photography because it gives one the chance for additional creativity; and it presents a constant challenge to the darkroom worker who wants to get better prints out of his negatives.*[16]

Aside from various experiments in adherence with theories advocated by other photographers, Goldwater generally left his thematic tableaux unplanned, choosing instead to simply follow the lead of his senses and fire his shutter on instinct. Time and place remained self-imposed constraints, but he was an inveterate picture taker and picture maker who could not resist the urge to savor novel experiences encountered outside Arizona through the lens of his camera. Even though his aesthetic decisions kept him in good stead across time, his individualistic tendency to push the envelope raised eyebrows within the profession on whether he should be classed as a professional or merely a gifted amateur.

While traditional critics puzzled over such minutia as titles and status, cutting edge connoisseurs treasured Goldwater's diligence and direction, particularly his penchant for rendering an ordinary scene extraordinary by conveying it from a different vantage point. Practice sharpened his perspective to the point that he systematically adopted a full litany of aesthetic motifs that gave him a signature style. Paramount on the list was his preference for contrast and trademark addiction to sharp lines and angles, particularly those sculpted by Mother Nature. Trees became framing devices and clouds unfettered beacons across desert vistas only the most intrepid souls were ever likely to directly witness.

Throughout his productive career as a photographer, Goldwater favored slow films shot at the lowest aperture setting possible. He seldom used a light meter, preferring to rely solely on natural light. Although he experimented widely with the full range of film types produced by different manufacturers, he favored Kodak black and white film printed on fiber-based papers. The actual size of his images ranged from the traditional 8 x 10 and 11 x 14 formats to large-scale prints suitable for formal exhibition. Until his acquisition of a Nikkon 35-mm camera during the final decades of his life, he had an express allegiance for German optics, specifically a 4 x 5 Graflex and 2 1/4" Rolliflex and Leica units, which he used with equal frequency.

Each of the photographs featured in the upcoming Portfolio section were chosen as representative samplings of Goldwater's artistic skill, perspective and practices across time. The captions are a combination of his own words as they appeared in print and extracts from stories he related both on tape and in informal conversations during the preliminary planning stages of the project. Because he passed to a higher reward before the task reached fruition, we felt honor bound to present the images in a fashion complementary to his personal priorities.

More than pretty pictures of a bygone time, Goldwater's photographs should be viewed as visual love letters crafted by a gifted artist with a facile mind wedded to a cause larger than his own axis. What began as a hobby turned into a lifetime pursuit that enabled him to 'pay rent' in ways and arenas as boundless as the landscape he routinely celebrated as home. Beauty stirred his senses, but conscience controlled his hand. The evidence rests richly in his photographs, which are best viewed as two-dimensional windows into the soul of a human dynamo far too intrigued with the fine art of doing to ever pause long enough to admire the sophistication that kept him forever uncommon.

Evelyn S. Cooper
Tempe, Arizona

Endnotes

1   Barry M. Goldwater, interview with author, 19 June 1998, Phoenix, Arizona, Private Collection.

2   Troy and Marilyn Murray, eds., *Barry Goldwater and the Southwest* (Scottsdale, Arizona: Troy Publications, 1976), 3.

3   Michel Goldwater quoted in *Alta California* newspaper, 9 November 1866. Press clipping. Goldwater Family Collection, Arizona Historical Foundation.

4   *Arizona Miner*, 12 October 1872, 1.

5   J. Goldwater and Bros. Advertisement, *Arizona Miner*, 11 December 1872.

6   *Arizona Miner*, 4 December 1879.

7   M. Goldwater and Bros. Advertisement, *Gazette*, 23 May 1896.

8   Press clipping, *Gazette*, 7 January 1900, Goldwater Family Collection, Arizona Historical Foundation.

9   Edward Weston, "Photography—Not Pictorial," *Camera Craft*, 37, 7, 1930; reprinted in Nathan Lyons, ed., *Photographers on Photography*, Englewood Cliffs, N.J., and Rochester, N.Y. 1966, 155.

10   Barry M. Goldwater quoted in Peter Iverson, *Barry Goldwater Native Arizonan* (Norman and London: University of Oklahoma Press, 1997), 48.

11   Barry M. Goldwater quoted in Peter Iverson, *Barry Goldwater Native Arizonan*, 54.

12 Barry M. Goldwater quoted in Bradford Luckingham, *Phoenix, The History of a Southwestern Metropolis* (Tucson, Arizona: The University of Arizona Press, 1989), 105–6.

13 Barry M. Goldwater quoted in Peter Iverson, *Barry Goldwater Native Arizonan*, 72.

14 Roy Elson Lecture, Barry M. Goldwater Lecture Series Collection, Arizona Historical Foundation.

15 Barry M. Goldwater with Jack Casserly, *Goldwater* (New York: Doubleday, 1988), 71.

16 Barry M. Goldwater, *People and Places* (New York: Random House, 1967), 69.

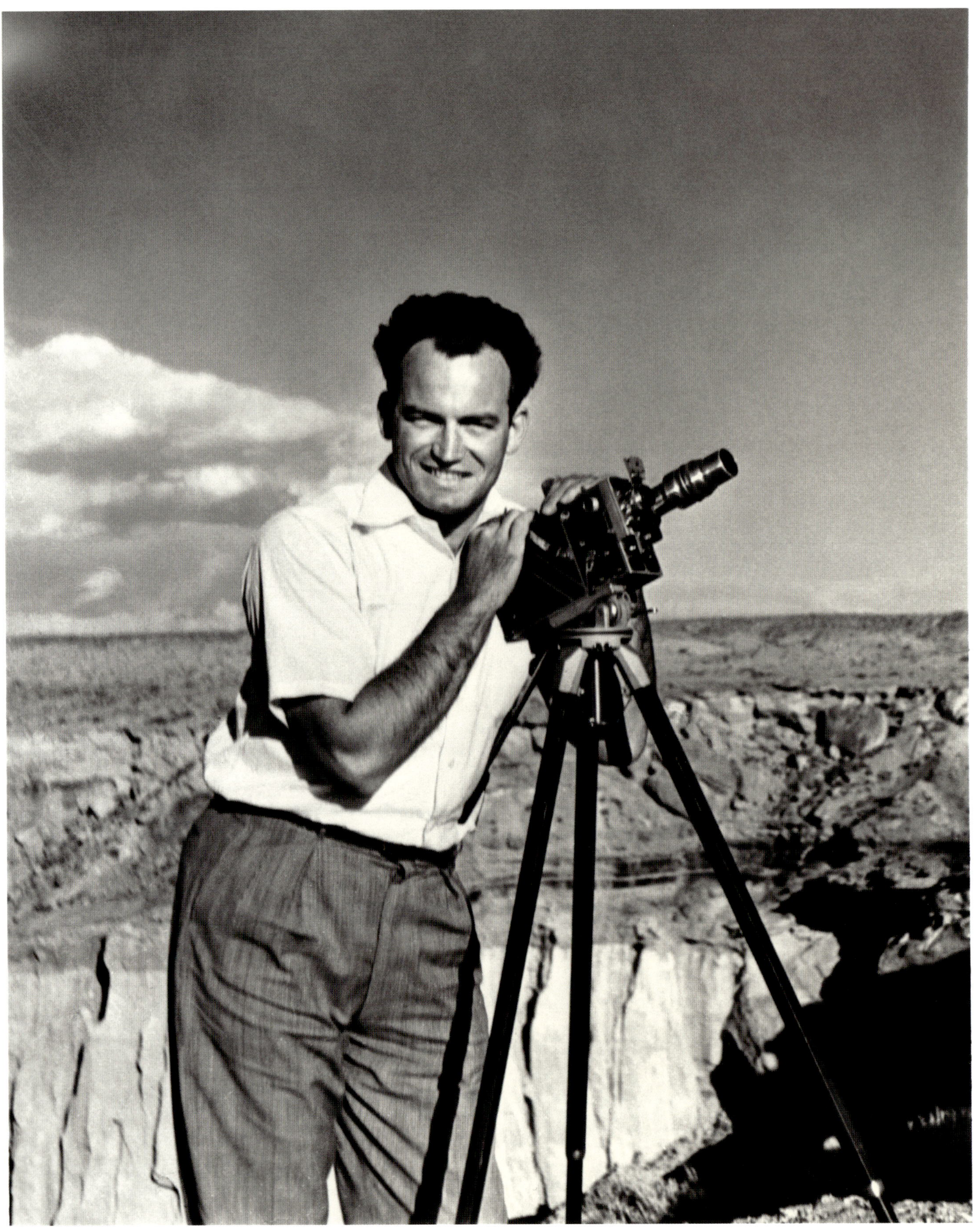

Portrait of the Artist as a Married Man, Coal Mine Canyon between Tuba City and Third Mesa, c. 1935.
Photo by Peggy Goldwater

ABOUT THE PHOTOGRAPHS

I grew up in the darkroom. My brother Barry, Jr. and I would earn a nickel a print enlarging Dad's negatives into 8 x 10 formats when we needed spending money. Having such a close familiarity with the negatives quickly transformed the exacting task of choosing a representative sampling of photographs from a collection built over the course of several decades into a pleasant walk down memory lane.

Dad's cameras were as much a part of our daily lives as our frequent camping trips into the wilderness, where we amassed a full slate of colorful adventures that have now become part of Goldwater family lore, always backed with photographs he captured on-site. He also carried his camera with him to Washington, D.C., and during his many trips abroad, thus lending the present portfolio a natural thematic division based upon frequency of occurrence: Family, Homeland and Statesman Abroad.

Within those headings, featured photographs are presented as capsule studies of Dad's favored subjects, aesthetic motifs and technical skill across time and various equipment updates. The breadth and scope of his interests made the selection process no mean task, as did his penchant for sometimes failing to accurately record dates, locations and other pertinent information about a given photograph. Rather than second guess the master, we chose to admit the confusion and just let the photographs stand on their own merit.

Most of his negatives and the equipment he used are now safely stored alongside Edward Weston's Archive at the University of Arizona's Center for Creative Photography in Tucson. Examples of his color photography join his massive Kachina collection at the Heard Museum in Phoenix. The images featured here were selected from the Barry M. Goldwater Fine Arts Photograph Collection at the Arizona Historical Foundation at Arizona State University in Tempe, or from the private collections of his children and grandchildren.

Although Dad was stylistically within the Weston school of New Objectivity, he was a wise and wily cameraman, whose tendency to push the artistic envelope gave him a signature style as stark and direct as his own unique brand of plain speaking. Famed photographer Yousuf Karsh, on assignment for *Life* Magazine, arrived at our home in Phoenix during the 1964 presidential campaign and spent three days surveying sites and checking the light without clicking the shutter once until the last day. The photographs were beautiful. Dad told me later that I had just learned an important life lesson from a Master Photographer that he greatly admired.

The magic Dad made through the lens was often enhanced by manipulations in the darkroom that smoothed out the rough edges without forfeiting the historical value of the image. He often said that half of the work in creating a memorable photograph occurred within the darkroom.

The captions are a combination of Dad's own words, stories he told, personal memories and facts extrapolated from the written record. Because he believed that every picture told its own story, viewers should read each of the featured images as an autobiographical sketch from the life of a gifted artist, who pledged his own peculiar brand of genius toward enlightening others to the dynamic majesty of Mother Nature and the broad diversity of her human children.

Michael P. Goldwater
Scottsdale, Arizona

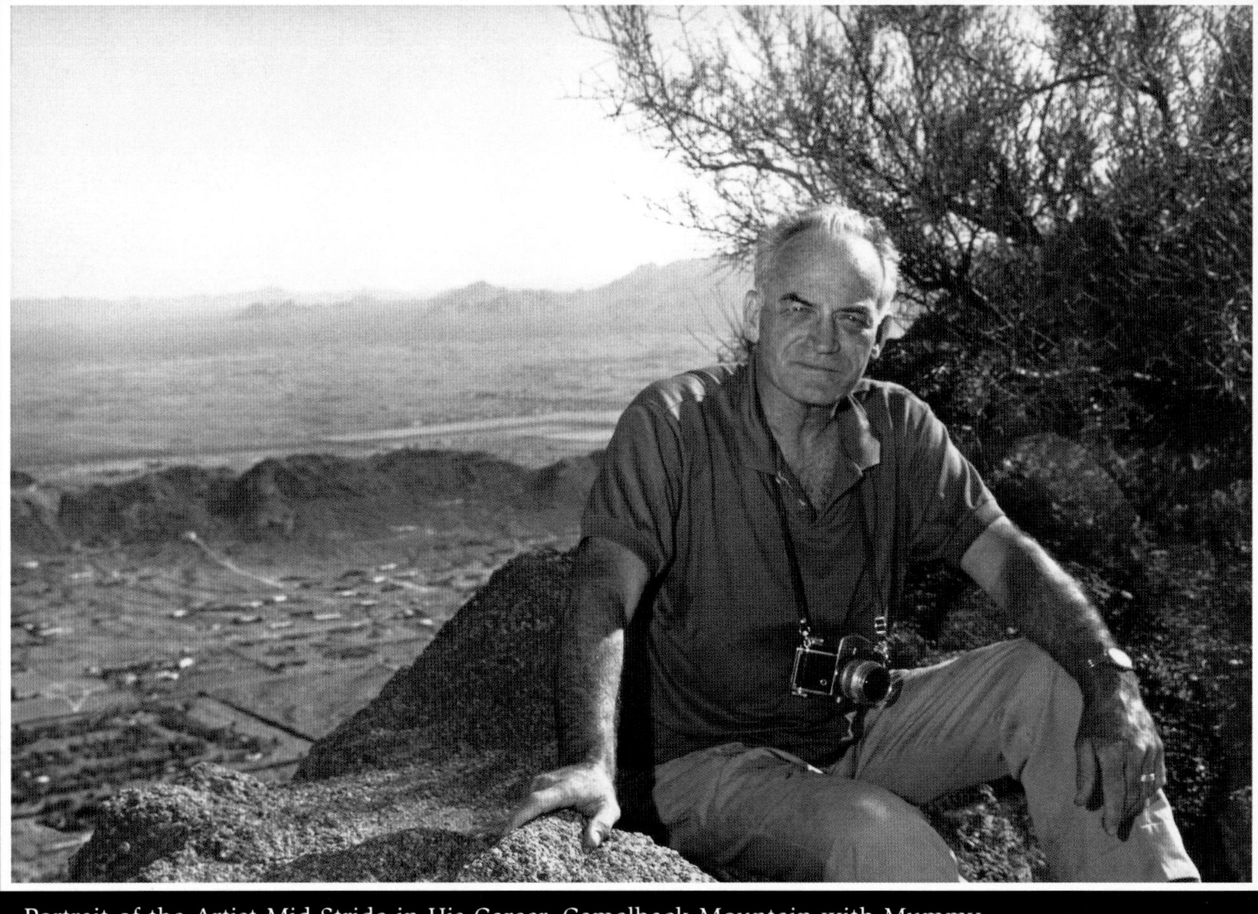

Portrait of the Artist Mid-Stride in His Career, Camelback Mountain with Mummy
Mountain and Paradise Valley in the Background, c. 1970

PORTFOLIO

My photo books on Arizona are my last will and testament to my love for my native state. So are the miles of amateur film and thousands of negatives that are being left to history.

Barry M. Goldwater
in *Goldwater,* 1988

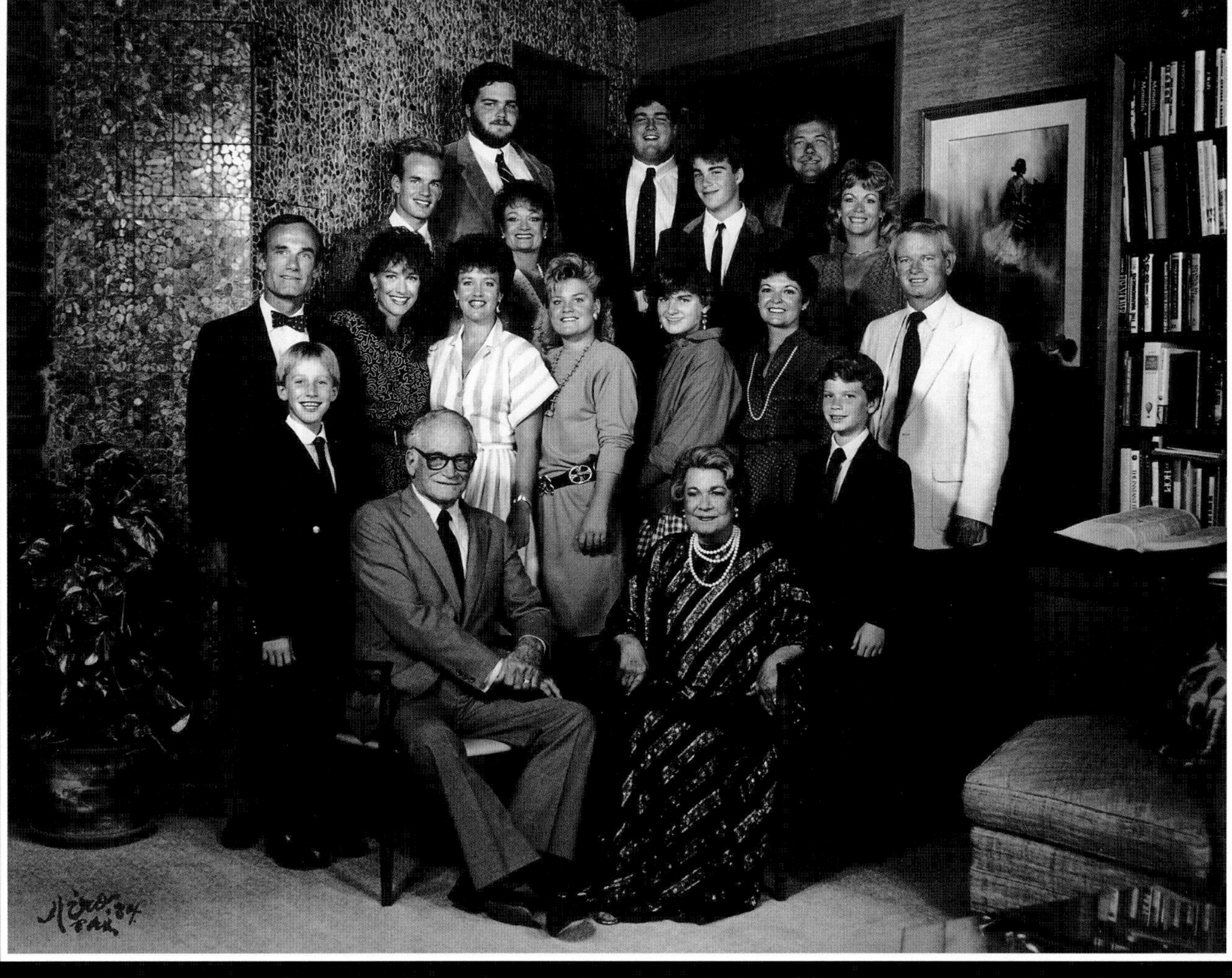

Portrait of the Artist With His Family, on the occasion of his 50th Wedding Anniversary, September, 1984

FAMILY

My conscience has sometimes suffered because I took time and energy away from my family....Later, I'd try to make it up. We'd take photos on a camping trip or fly somewhere for a few days of vacation. A man with one or several hobbies often walks a fine line between family and job.

Barry M. Goldwater
in *Goldwater,* 1988

PEGGY, 1941

Christmas is The Season in the dry goods business. Holiday sales can make the difference between profit and loss for a full year. I went to Muncie the day after Christmas 1933 to spend the rest of the holidays. New Year's Eve Peggy and I were at a dance. She wanted to call and wish her mother a Happy New Year. When we were in the telephone booth, I told her I was running out of money and out of patience. For the umpteenth time I asked her to marry me. She said yes.

We were married in Muncie almost ten months later on September 22, 1934....

There are many moments of triumph in a man's lifetime, which he remembers. I have been to the mountaintop of victory—my first election to the Senate, and my reelection; that night in Chicago, in 1960, when the governor of Arizona put my name in nomination for office of President of the United States; and another night in San Francisco when the delegates to the Republican Convention made me their nominee. But above all these I rate that night in Muncie, Indiana.

Peggy and I have had four children. We have known joy and sorrow together. We have encountered pain and illness. We have suffered separation for long periods of time. Through it all she has been my strength, my companion, a part of my private world where no other human beings, not even our children, have been allowed to enter. Peggy doesn't like flying or camping, but she has done a lot of both with me.

Barry M. Goldwater
in *With No Apologies,* 1979

Negative 2228

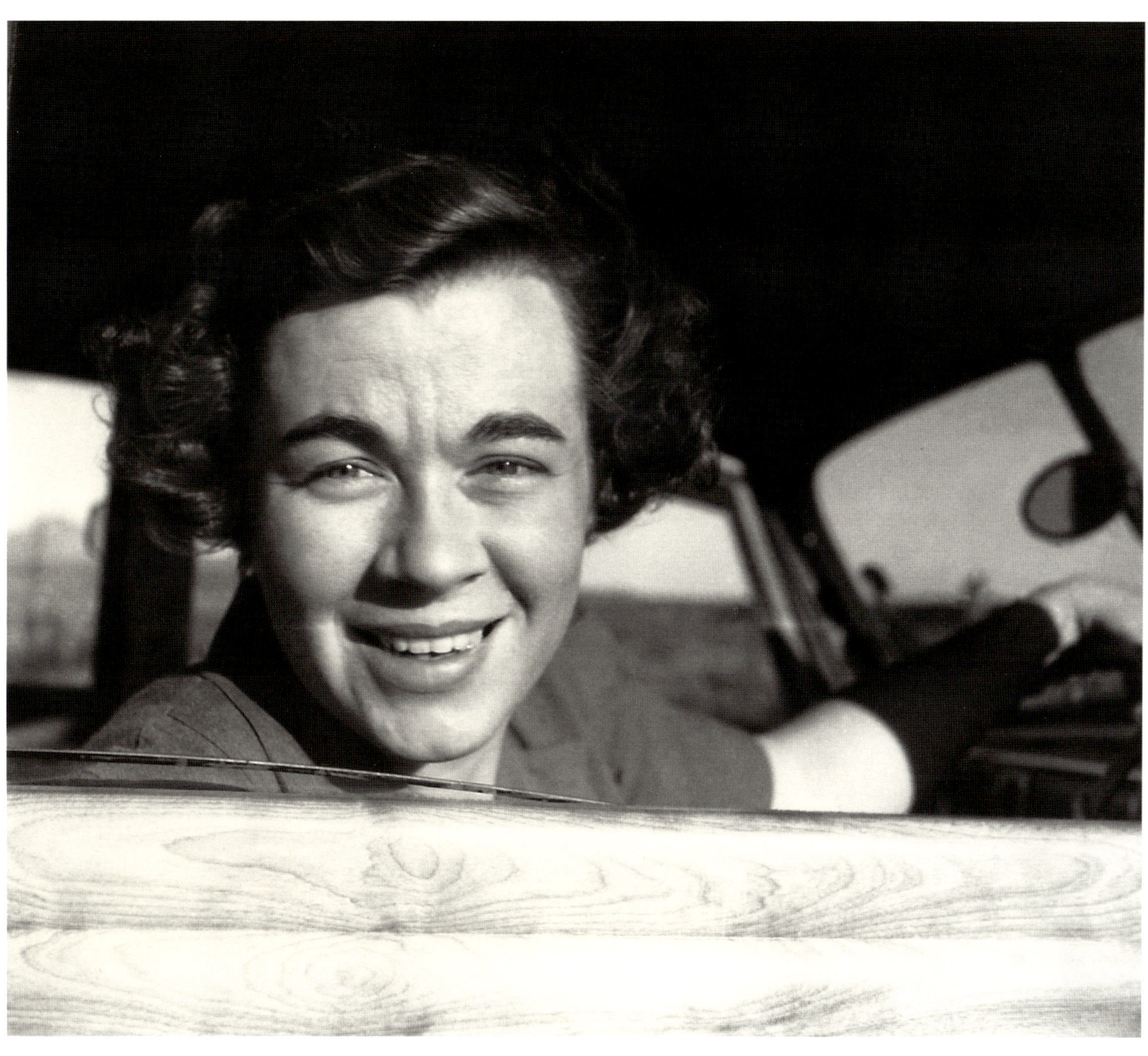

JOANNE GOLDWATER, 1939

As the oldest child, my sister Joanne was one of Dad's favorite and most frequent photographic subjects. Shown here frolicking on the beach at La Jolla, California as a toddler, she was fortunately extremely gregarious and highly photogenic.

Joanne entered the world in January of 1936 and was named in honor of both of our grandmothers. From start to finish, she enjoyed the special relationship that exists between oldest daughters and fathers down to a similarity in disposition and temperament.

Negative 2071

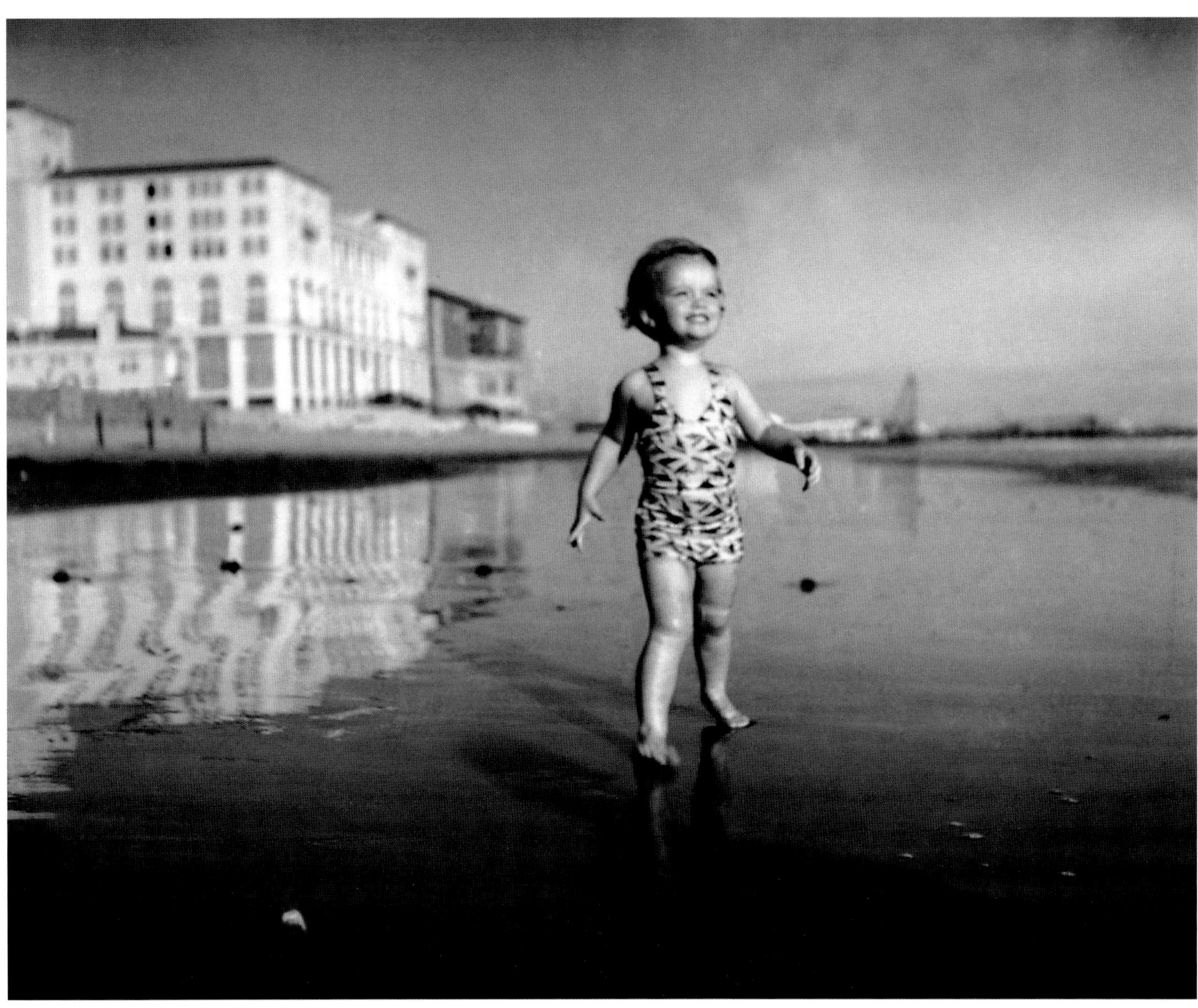

THE GOLDWATER GIRLS, 1948

(l-r): Joanne, Peggy, Jr. and Peggy, Sr.

When Joanne, Barry and I were really small, Mom frequently dressed the three of us in matching outfits. She abandoned the practice after Peggy was born except for the ensembles featured here.

Known in family parlance as the "Joan Crawford Image," the photograph captures the first and final time Mom participated in the mother-daughter fashion trend popular in the post-World War II years.

Negative 2245

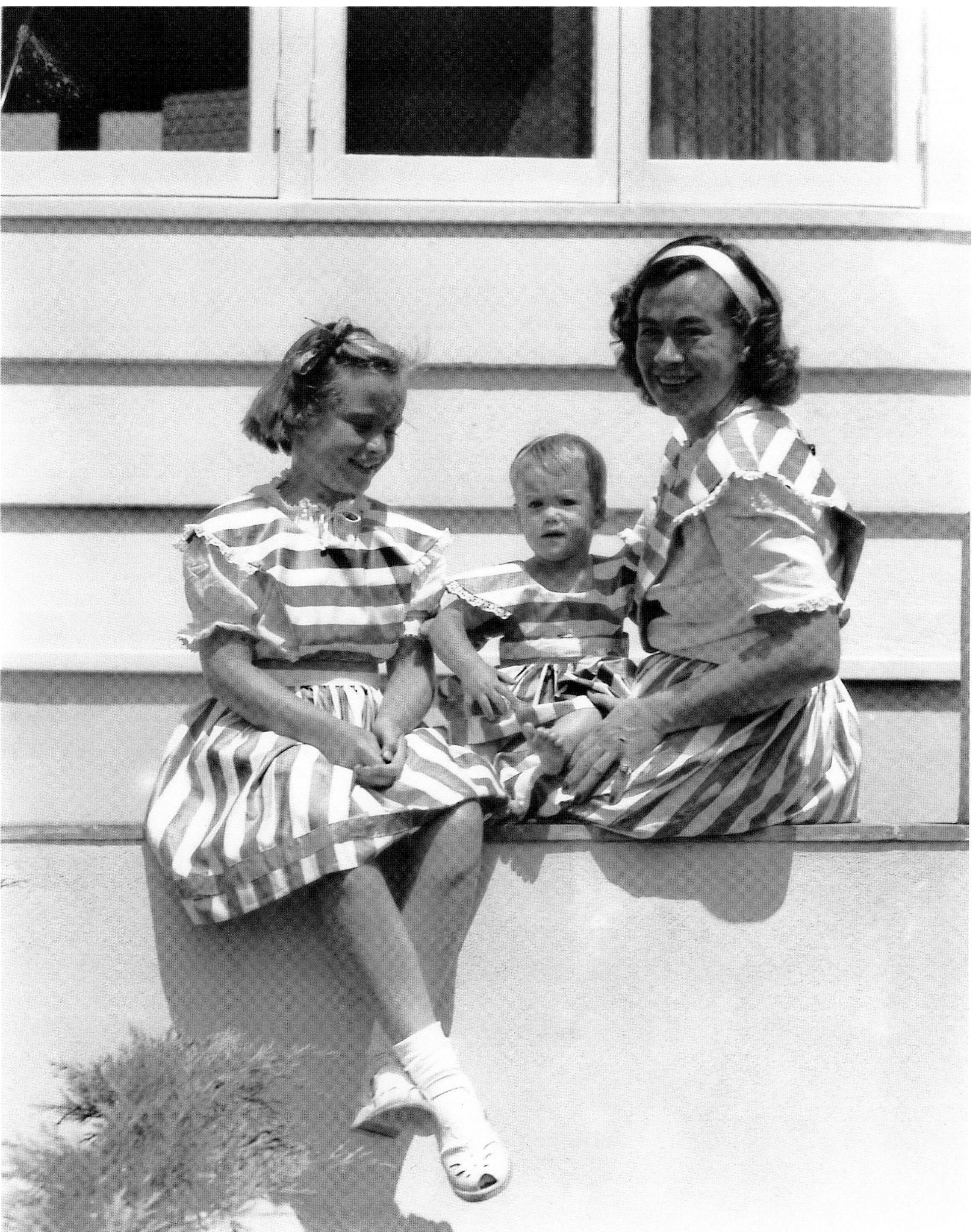

BARRY, JR. GIVING MICHAEL A HAIRCUT MIDDLE FORK OF THE SALMON RIVER, 1960

The practice of giving each other haircuts began during our years at Staunton Military Academy, when cadets in need of a barber had to walk to town. To circumvent what was essentially an eight-mile journey, Barry and I put our heads together and reasoned that since we both wore flat tops, we could cut our own hair.

As the featured scene reveals, our confidence in our ability as barbers was such that we required only the most basic tools.

Negative 977

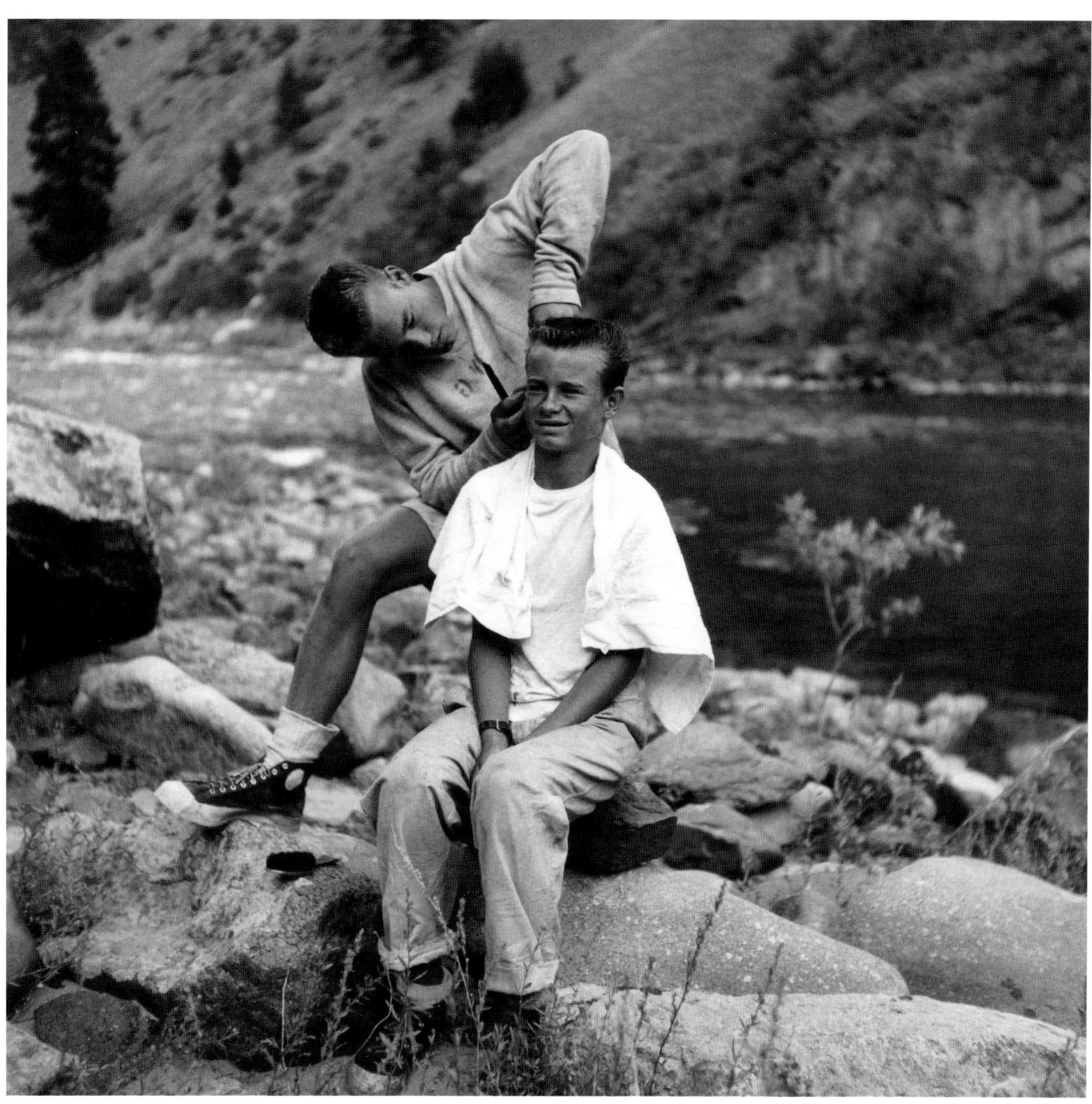

FAMILY OUTING, 1950

Camping and wilderness jaunts to the northern part of the state were such commonplace occurrences for our family that the present image could rightfully be captioned the 'Goldwaters at Play.'

Dad's belief in the value of direct experience was such that he oftentimes pulled us out of school for these trips, under the guise that we were off to study Arizona. And study Arizona we did to the extent that all four of us came to share his passion for off the beaten path Arizona.

It is an addiction we have subsequently passed to our children.

Negative 2375

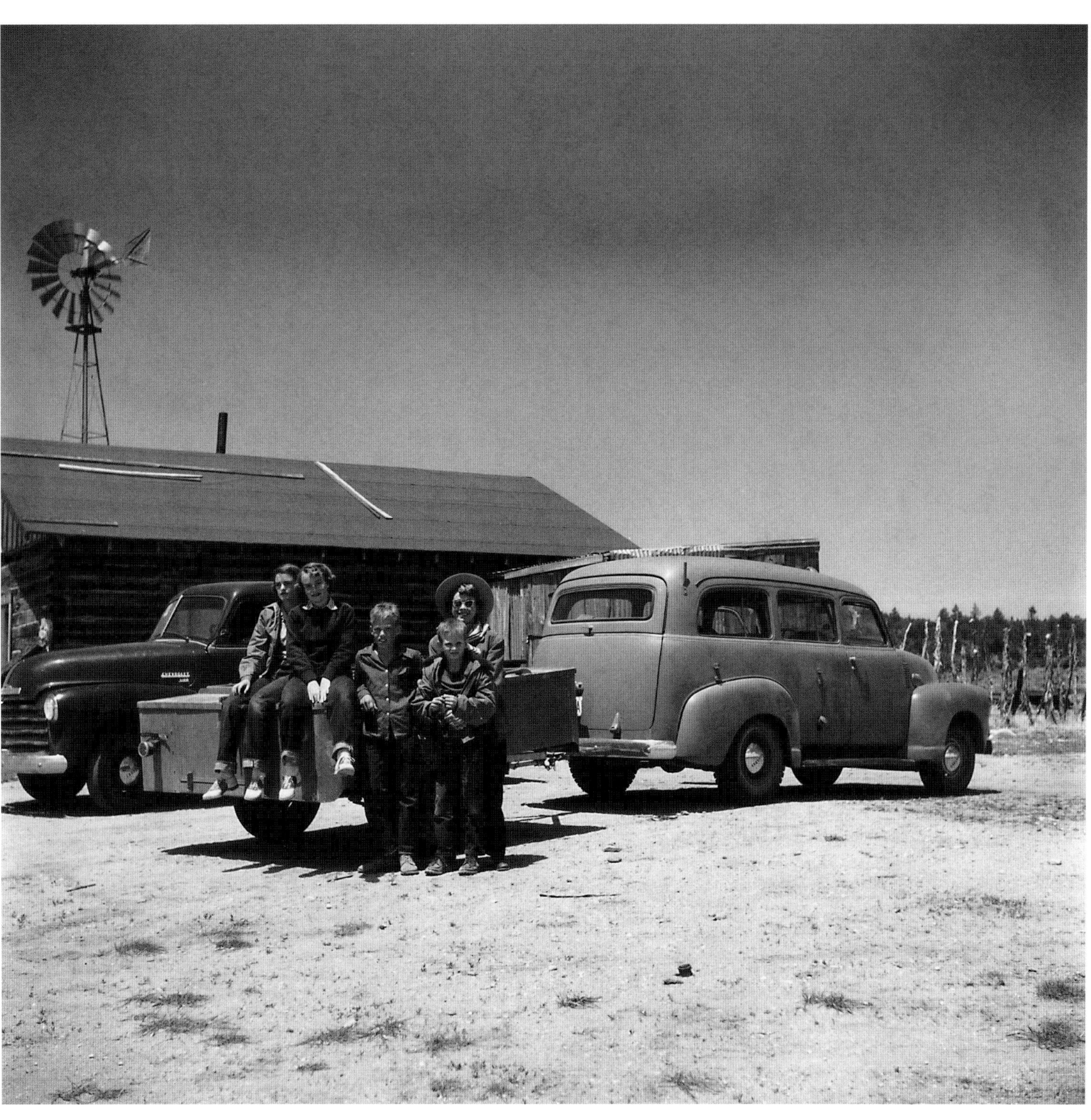

IMPROMPTU FAMILY PORTRAIT, 1948
(l-r) Joanne, Peggy, Jr., Barry, Jr. and Mike

As both a long distance father and a skilled photographer, Dad went to great lengths to capture our childhood at every stage. He was particularly fond of group portraits, which served as visual enhancements during times when he exercised his bragging rights as a parent.

The featured image was taken outside our home on West Manor Drive in front of the family car.

Negative 2271

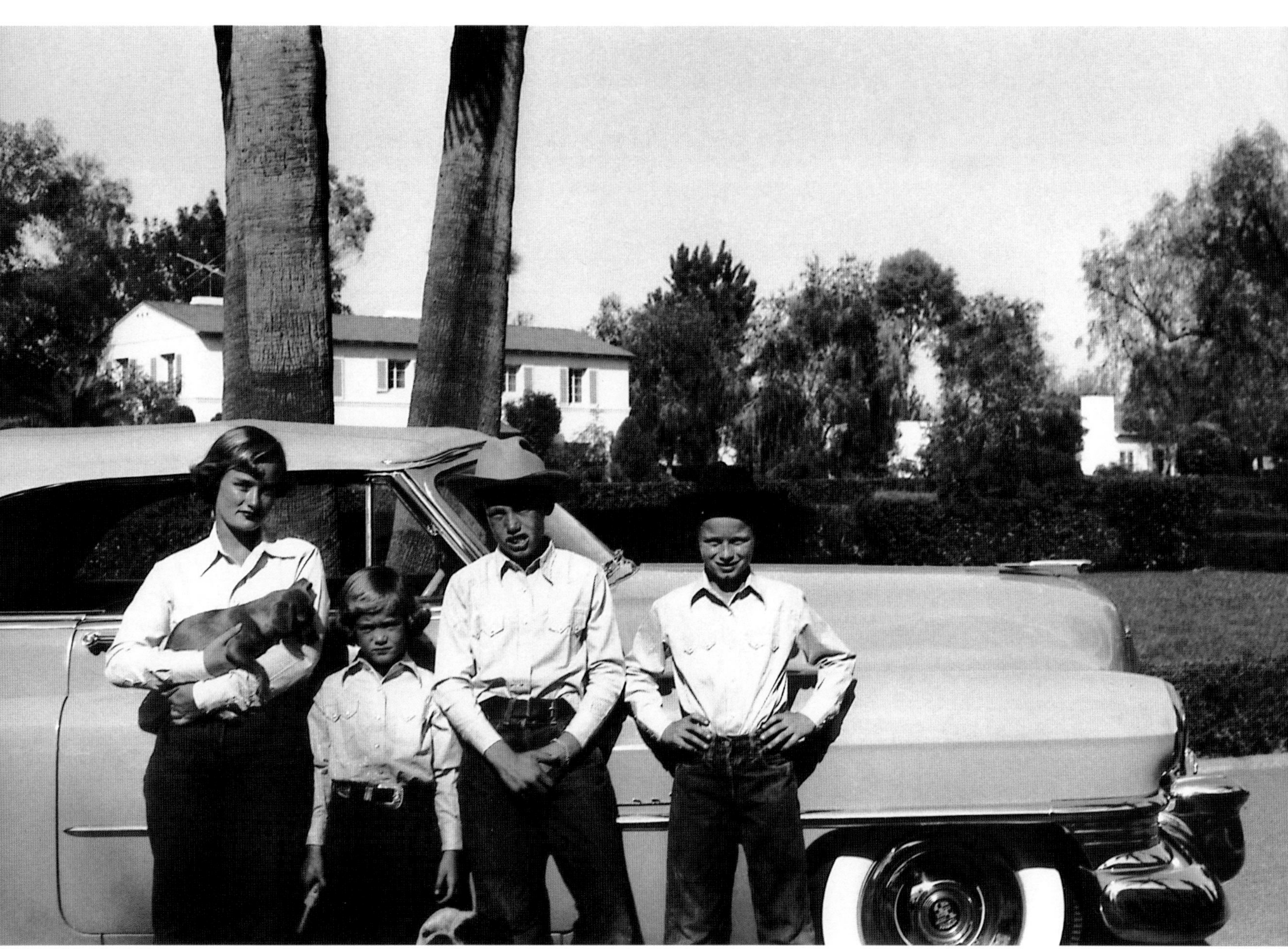

PEGGY THE FISHERWOMAN,
MIDDLE FORK OF THE SALMON RIVER, 1950

I rose this morning while you still slept to see the sun come up. It's a symbol not only of warmth and light for the world, but as full as your love and constant companionship have been for me. Through times of deepest darkness, your love has lighted the path for me. In nights of cold lonesomeness, the warmth of your affection has been my blanket....

The gratefulness I feel in my heart can never be shown by material things. The happiness that has been mine for these years cannot be expressed by words or even by a caress, kiss, or hand that feels hopefully for yours.

The thrill and pride that is mine, given me by you in our children, cannot be sufficiently shown by any action or thought on my part. The only one in the universe who fully knows the things that dwell in my heart is God. I have thanked him from a thousand canyon bottoms, from beneath a million trees, from the heights of His heavens in the cathedral of His clouds.

As I grow older in the warmth of your love, I will pray that, one day, I will meet Him face to face so that I might shake His hand and thank Him for giving me you.

Excerpt from a letter from Barry M. Goldwater to his wife Peggy, on the occasion of their seventeenth wedding anniversary on September 22, 1941.

Negative 1057

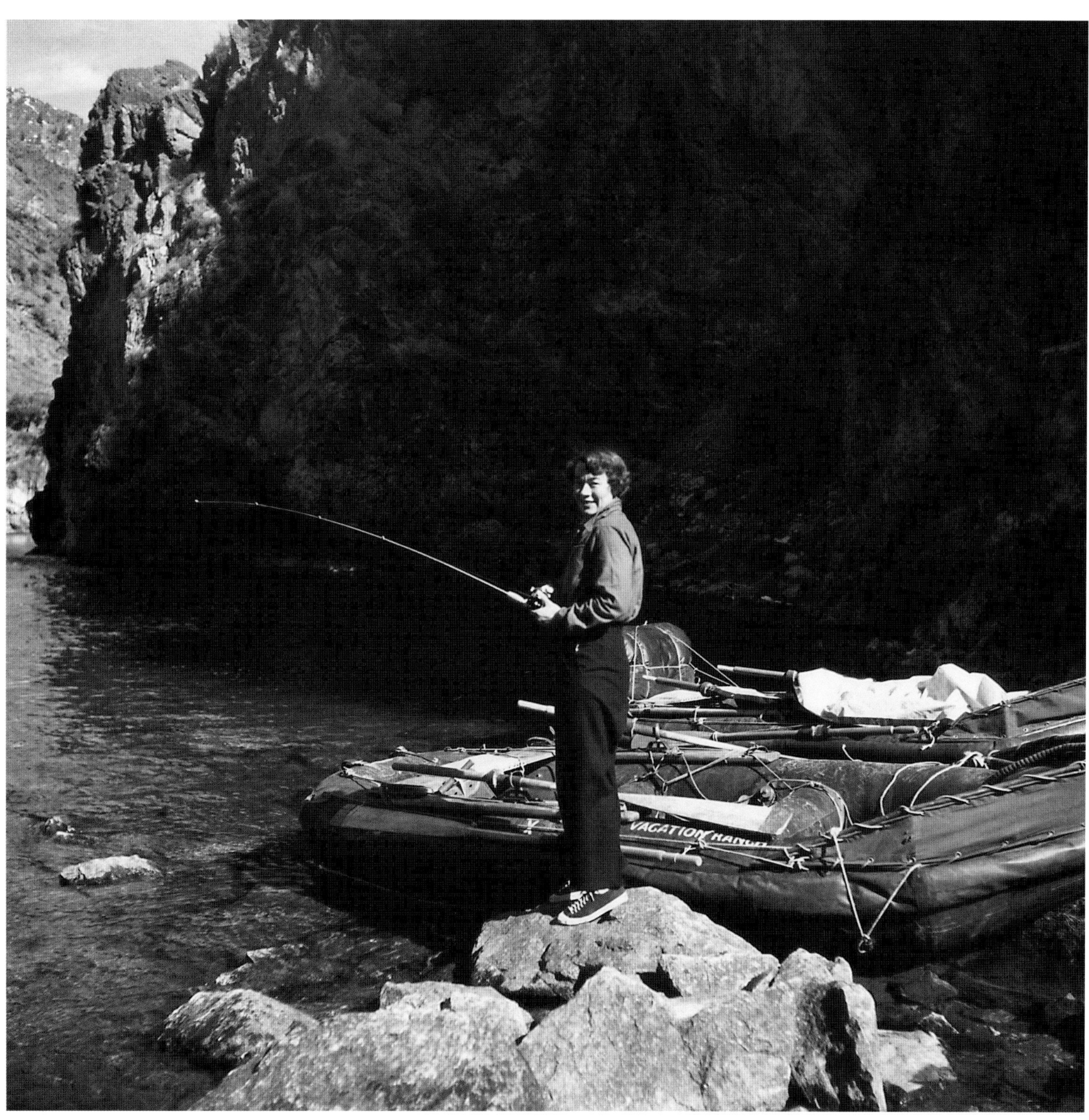

SELF-PORTRAIT, 1948

Mom and Dad shared a common view that every citizen should give back to the community. They practiced what they preached and found a way to have a good time in the process.

The featured image shows them working on a charitable event. It is an example of the wacky sort of whimsy that served as a ground wire for their lifetime commitment to each other.

Negative 2383

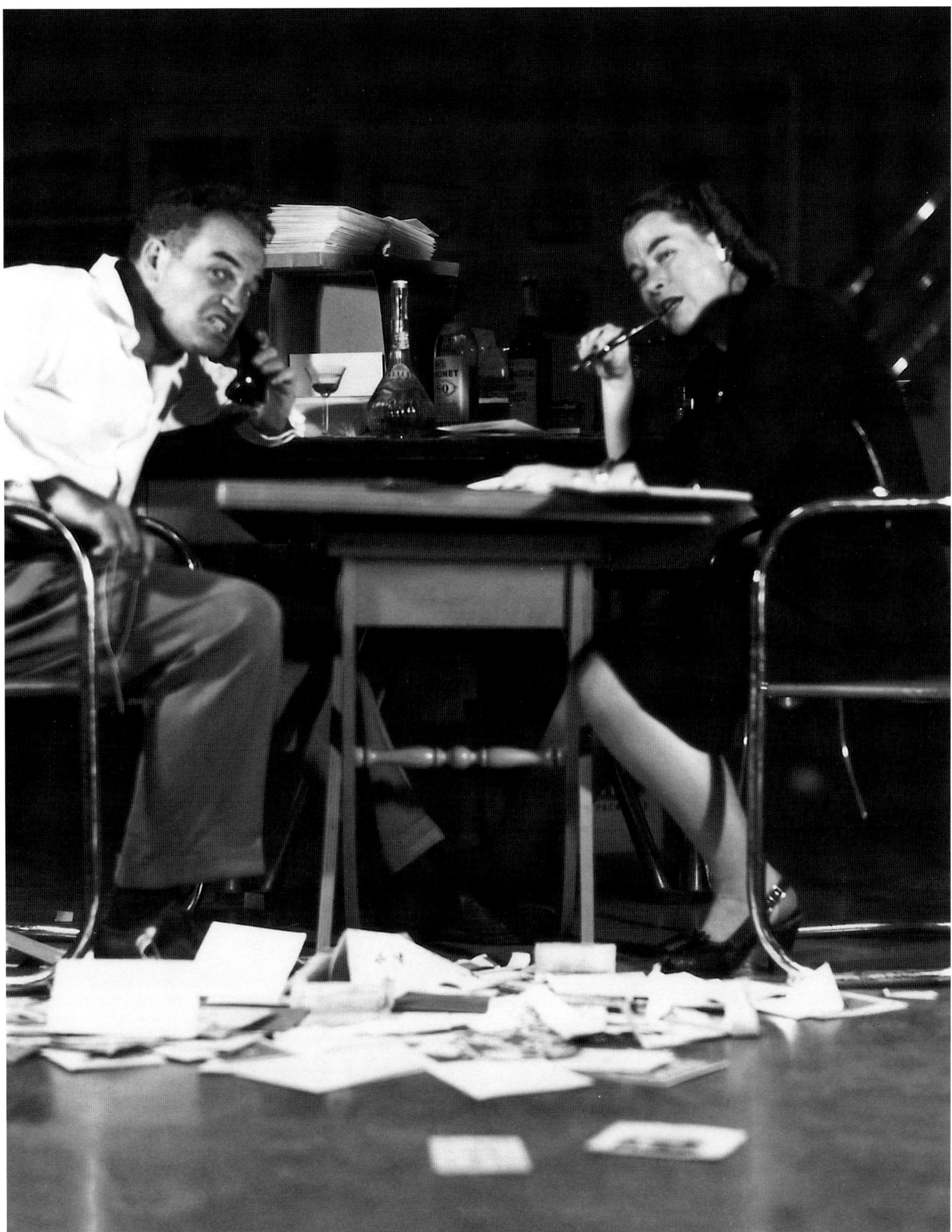

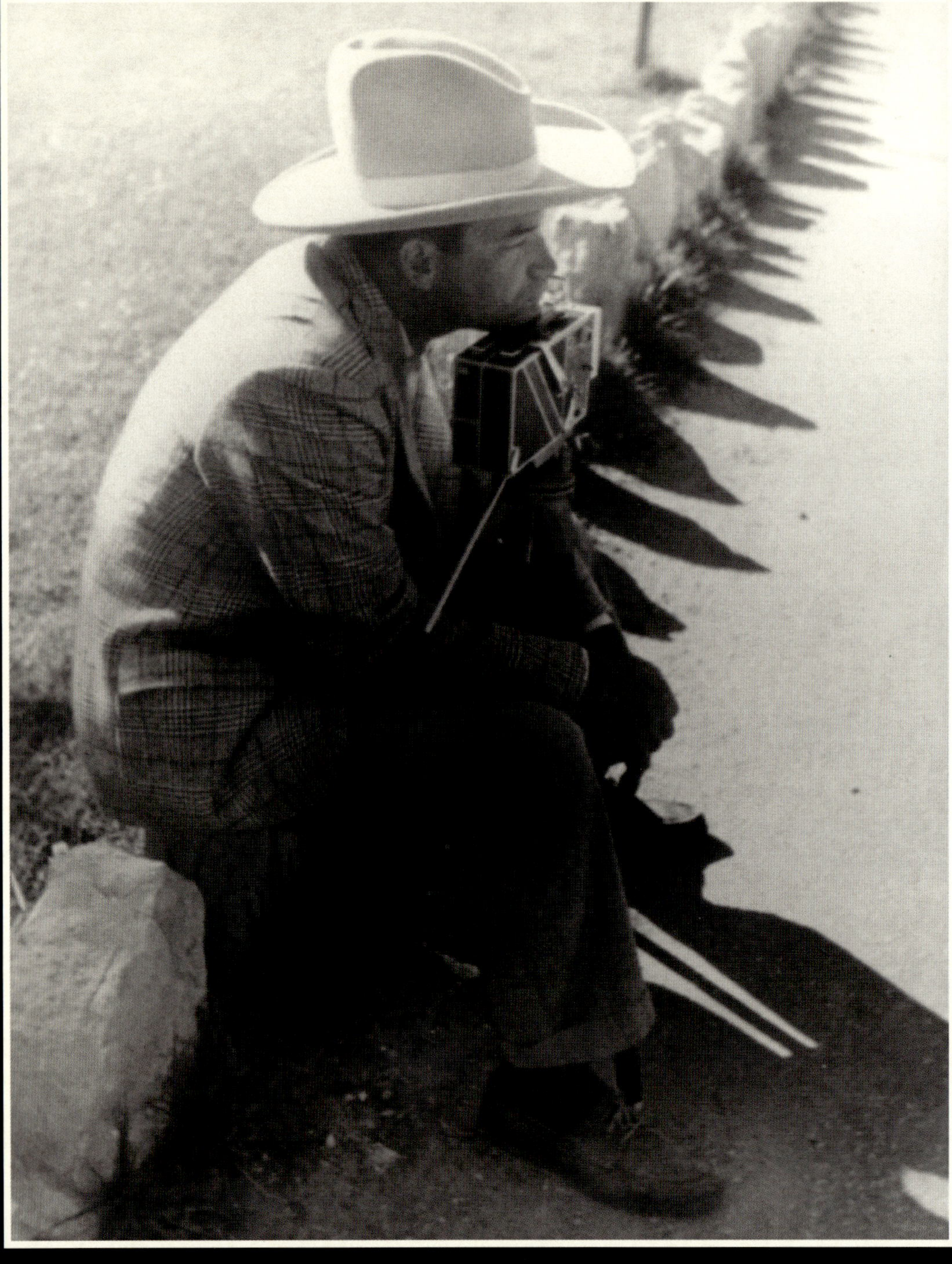

Portrait of the Artist on His Mission, Grand Canyon, c. 1945

HOMELAND

For more than fifty years, I've been studying (Arizona) history, visiting all parts of the state and sometimes other states for more information on our people and places. I've gone to libraries, talked with thousands of natives, studied all types of documents—from city and county to state and federal files as well as personal diaries and other sources—and rummaged through whatever family papers were available. I've taken thousands of photographs of people and places. Maybe I've been looking for myself much of the time.

Barry M. Goldwater
in *Goldwater,* 1988

CANYON SNOW, 1951

Dad's attraction to the Grand Canyon was such that he ultimately dubbed the Great Natural Wonder his "mistress." He was a walking repository of its lore and legends, as well as one of its most passionate suitors, who discovered fresh cause for its timeless allure upon each new visit.

"Canyon Snow" epitomizes his quest for contrast and serves as a visual testament to an attraction that forever left him awestruck and spiritually renewed. He applied the present caption, although he was known to ascribe a different title to an image with each new usage.

This photograph appeared in one of his early books and a number of exhibitions, including salons in Tokyo and Milan.

Negative 767

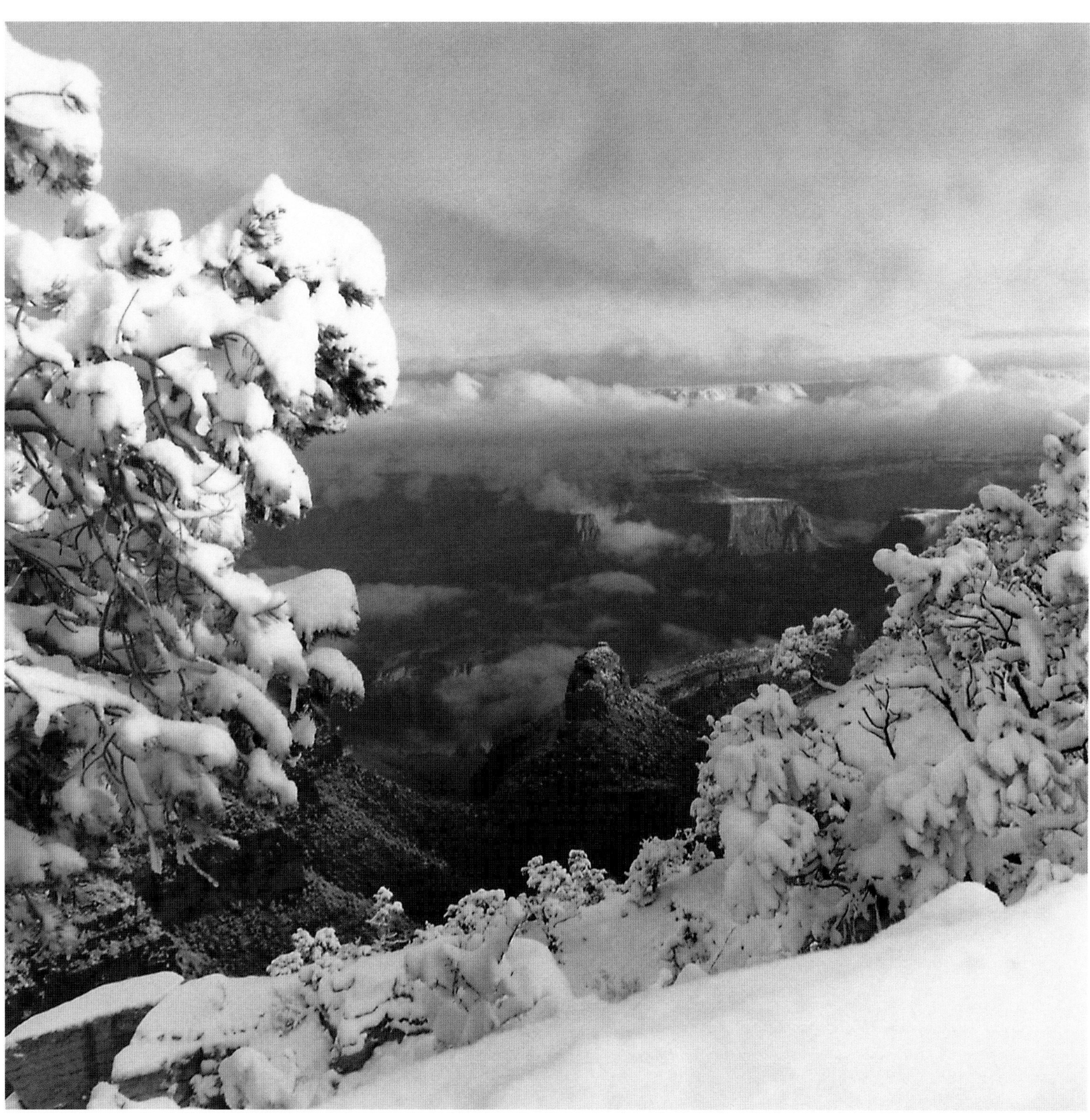

THE VALLEY, 1967

Situated not far from Goulding's Museum & Trading Post, which was owned by his friends Harry and his wife "Mike" Goulding, Monument Valley was another favorite target for Dad's lens.

Its Navajo name is *Tse bii ndisgaii*, or "valley in the rocks." Although the valley is part of the old Paiute Strip, the western and northern sections were annexed to the Navajo Reservation by Executive Order in 1884. Parts were later restored to the public domain, only to be returned to the Navajo Nation by Congress in 1934.

Over the years, Dad shot a vast series of frames of the mesas, spires and buttes that rise as much as a mile high out of the majestic valley. This image conveys both his love of place and his technical precision at maximizing depth of field.

The present photograph is one of a series of images he made during two trips to Monument Valley. A selection of those captured from the valley floor appeared in *Venture* magazine in 1967. He returned to the area the following year and took a new series of images from the top of the mesas, which he used to promote his 1968 re-election campaign.

Since the present photograph emanated from the earlier trip, he opted for "The Valley" as an appropriate title.

Negative 733

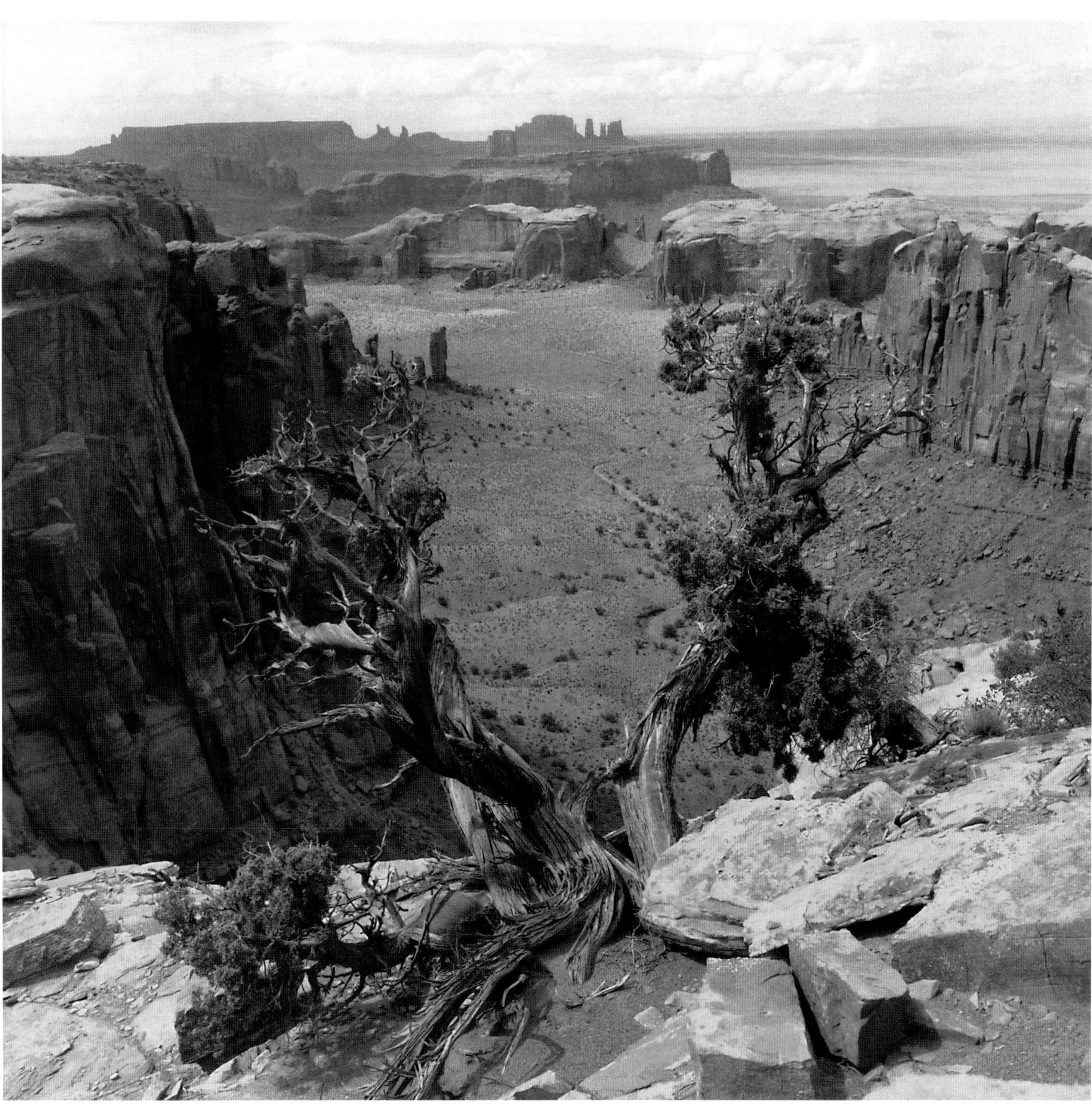

BIG COUNTRY, 1953

A good friend of mine described Arizona as the "Big Country." As I sit here and write these short captions, I think of that description and come more and more to accept it as the best one yet.

Arizona is 114,000 square miles in area. It rises from a hundred and fifty feet above sea level to twelve thousand feet; the land goes from sandy desert to verdant desert to a vast stand of ponderosa pine to another desert. On some days the temperature within a couple of hundred miles ranges from one hundred degrees down to zero. We are peopled from all states, as well as from Mexico, Spain, China, Japan and many other countries. Since ancient times Indians have lived on our lands, or maybe I should say we have lived on theirs, but the important thing is that we share the land.

This piece of the "Big Country" is between the lumber town of McNary and the sportsman's center, Springerville. It is high here, above seven thousand feet, and in the winter it is covered with snow. Spring and summer, though, bring the grass and the flowers and a new greenness to the pines as well as the aspens, whose leaves become golden before they drop off in the fall. The hill in the distance is an extinct volcanic cone, one of many that dot this White Mountain area, reminding us that out of the violence of evolution has come the quiet beauty which is ours.

Barry M. Goldwater
in *People and Places*

Negative 765

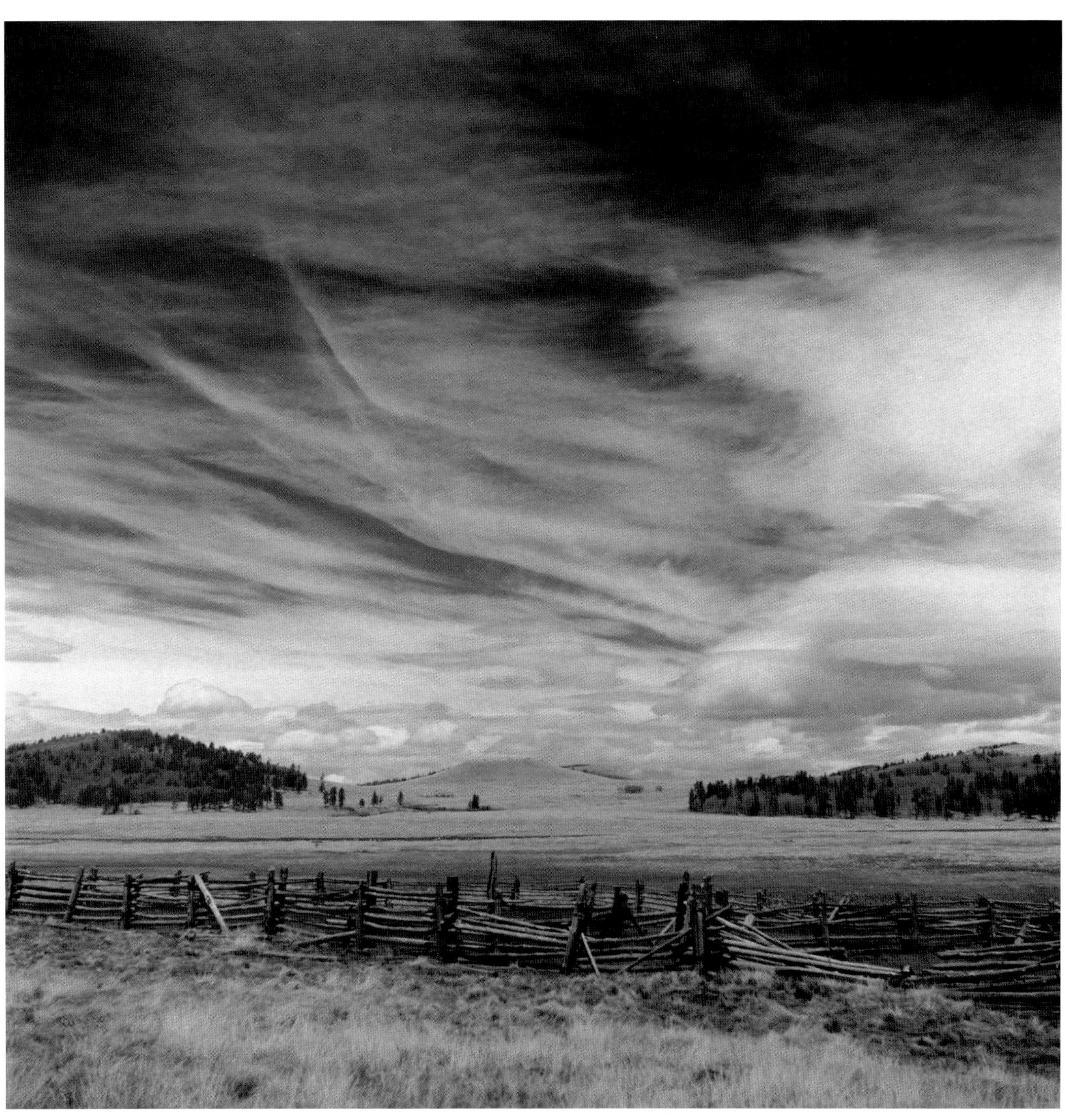

BASALTIC SCHIST, 1965

"Basaltic Schist" is another of Dad's visual love letters to his "mistress." Situated at the bottom of the Grand Canyon, the unique site is a dark basaltic formation left by volcanic activities, which occurred several millenniums ago. This violent action created a dam and a lake many times larger than present-day Lake Powell. Over the years, the river cut through the lava dam, leaving in its wake the areas we now know as the Basalt Cliffs and Lava Falls.

Although there are other basaltic outcroppings in the Grand Canyon, Dad's vantage point for this image is probably near Lava Falls at milepost 179.

Negative 942-B

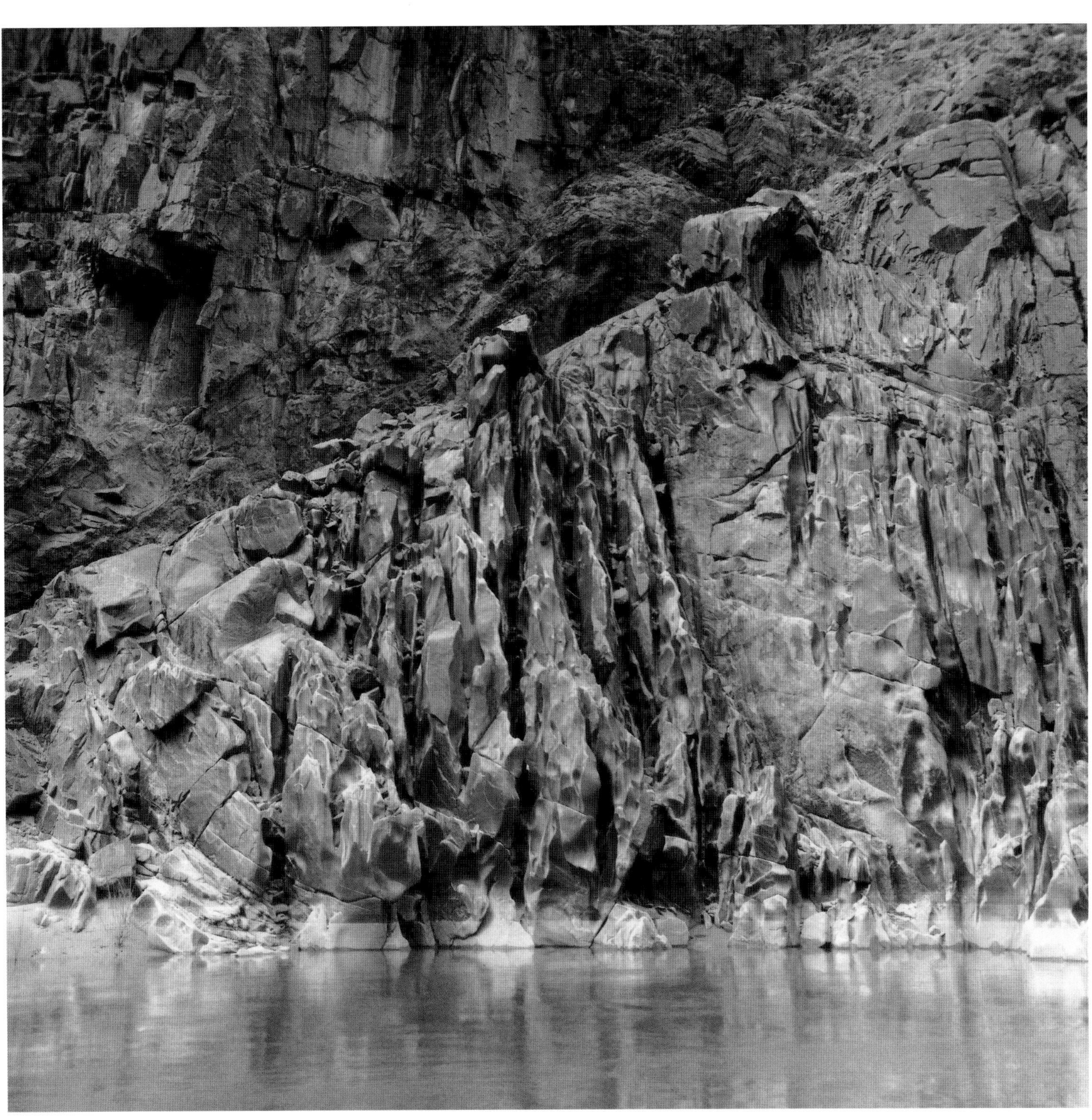

HOLE IN THE ROCK, 1938

The great difficulties my grandfather and great uncle had in gaining a foothold in the spare reaches of Arizona during the middle decades of the 19th Century made Dad hyper-sensitive to similar sufferings experienced of other early pioneers. As the following description reveals, "Hole in the Rock" should be viewed more as a historical document than an artistic photograph, particularly since most of this site is now covered by Lake Powell:

The canyon is short, not over three quarters of a mile or, at most, a mile to where it tops out. It is most difficult of ascent and descent, even on foot. I spent nearly three hours walking up and down because of my knee and my cameras. On the way down, I slipped and fell about ten feet, landing on my belly on the camera case. Cursing appropriately, I went on, none the worst for my clumsiness.

This narrow slit in the wall of the canyon was the site of one of the most heroic and determined efforts at colonization by pioneers of the West. Mormons, having ever been farmers, soon occupied most of the good land in northern Utah. The one place left for large companies of these industrious people to migrate was the little known country of the San Juan. This was confirmed in 1878 when scouts sent south for the purpose reported back to the successor of Brigham Young, John Taylor, that arable land could be had for the settling along the San Juan River.

Consequently, late in the winter of 1879 a company of Mormons departed, bound for this new land to the south. They were to follow a trail (roughly traced on a map by Taylor) that would lead them through Parowan, Bear Valley, Panguitch to Escalante, then across the Escalante Desert, the Colorado, and on to the vicinity of what is now Bluff, Utah. This brave company was composed of nearly two hundred-fifty men, women, and children, traveling in eighty-two covered wagons, and accompanied by nearly one thousand head of cattle. Though little was known of the country that lay between Escalante and the river, the party started with every expectation of arriving at its destination in good time.

They reckoned without knowledge of the miles of deep canyons that had to be crossed or of the labor that traversing this eroded land would entail. The early miles sped by, if miles in a covered wagon can be said to speed by, and the party's spirits remained high. A tremor of concern went through the group, however, when the train had to cross the Sevier. Climbing out of the deep valley of that river taxed man and beast to the utmost.

This concern must have increased when the scouting party that had been sent ahead on November 28 returned with a description of rugged country before them. This news must have particularly disheartened men who had labored hard to construct a passable road between Forty-mile Spring and Fifty-mile Spring. A meeting of the company revealed that everyone was determined to go on. They felt that to retrace their route would have been nearly impossible owing to the scarcity of grass for feed. At this time they had been on the road more than the total number of days they had planned to use for the entire trip, and they had scarcely started on their journey.

Barry M. Goldwater
in *Delightful Journey*

Negative 1113

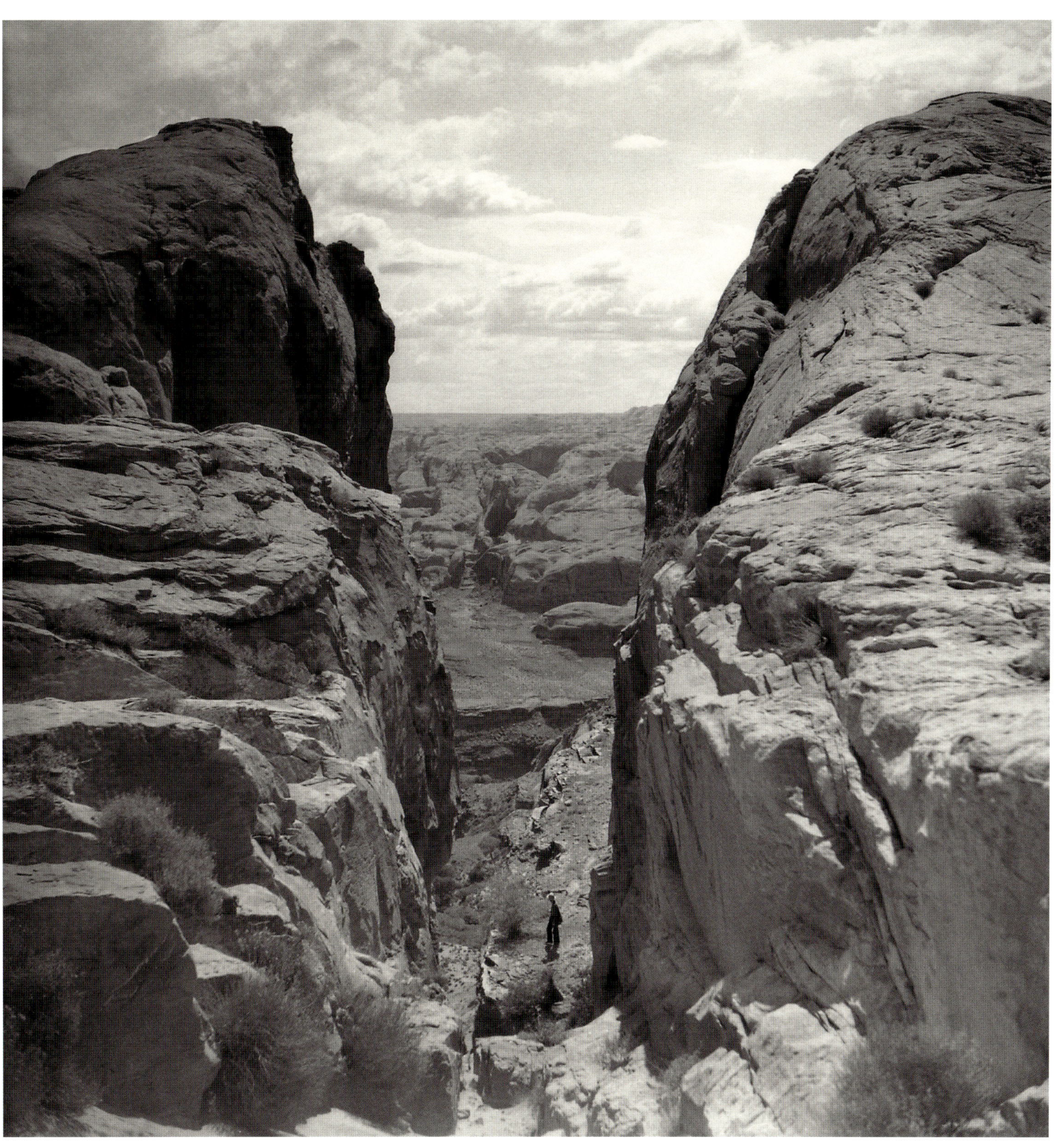

TOTEM POLE AND YEI-BE-CHAI, 1967

Two of Dad's favorite times of day to take photographs was early morning and twilight. This view of Monument Valley captures the late afternoon soft pastel-like blending of the evening sky, muting the harshness of the towering spires, while they shield the young double bareback riding Navajo sisters on their way home.

Dad would have preferred the title "Totem Pole and Yei-be-chai," because he always made an effort to honor the place names used by the Indians.

This photograph was taken for *Venture* Magazine in 1967.

Negative 1067

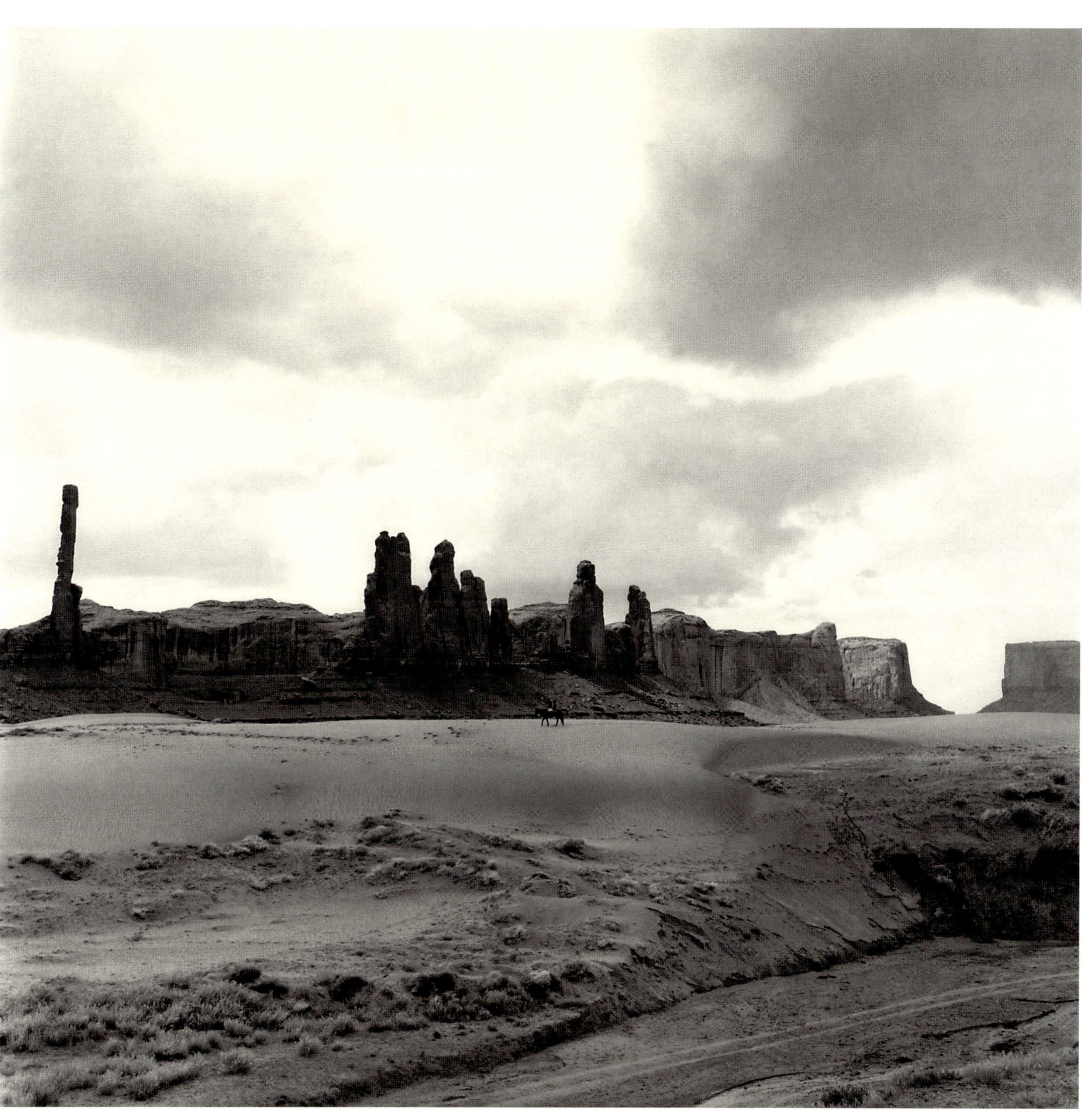

THE FENCE, 1967

Dad had an eye for the odd and the peculiar, particularly makeshift manmade edifices cast starkly against the natural landscape. In this view titled "The Fence," the depth of field melds the beauty of the valley and draws the eye to the mirage like mountains in the far distance surrounded by clouds. The location is near the Goulding's Trading Post in Monument Valley.

The post in the foreground was used to hold up the front roof of Goulding's Trading Post, while the split rail fence sits on the edge of a small cliff that drops approximately fifty to eighty feet.

Although this image has been featured in a number of fine arts exhibitions, it made its initial debut in the pages of *Venture* magazine in 1967.

Negative 1068

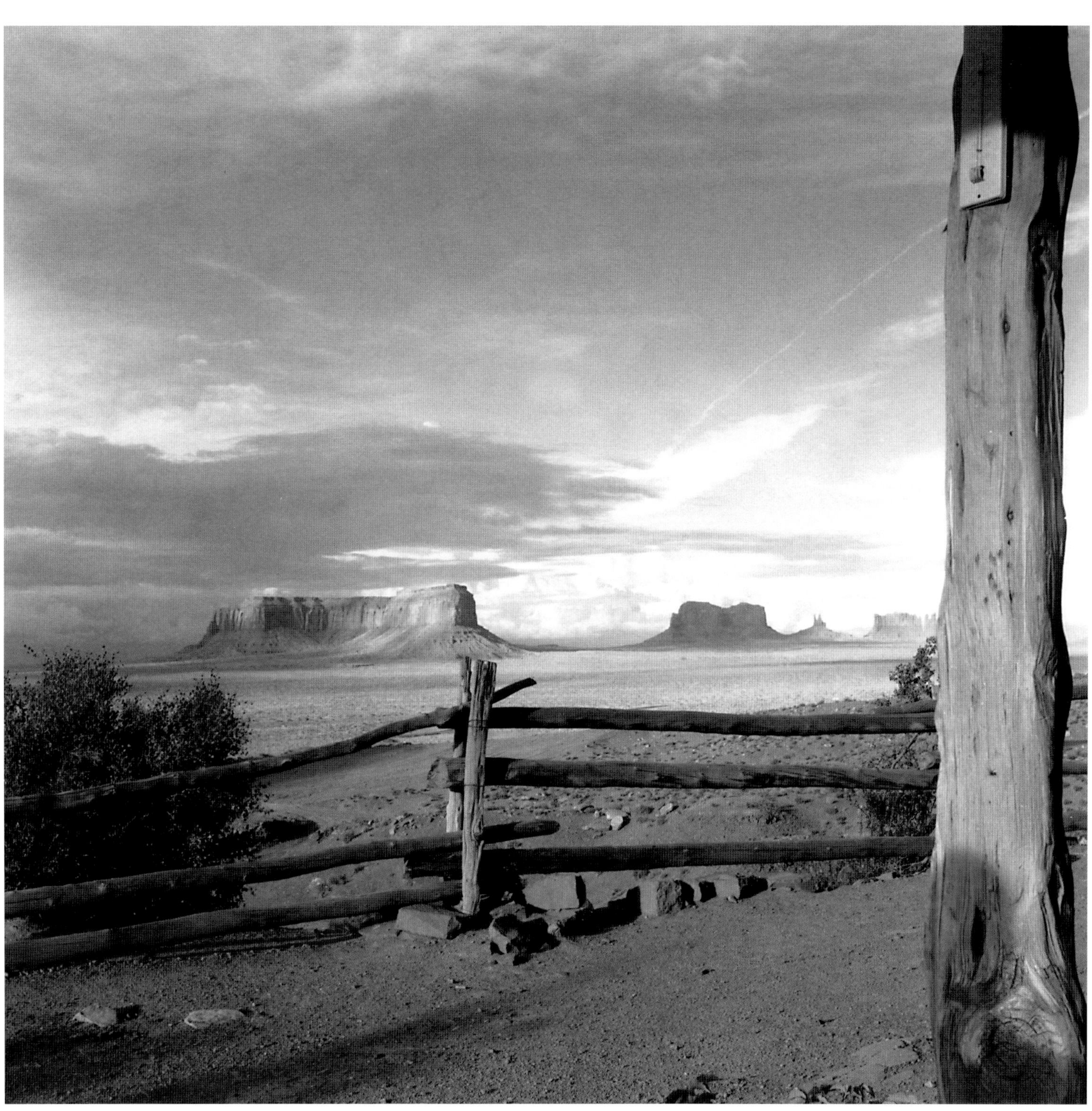

DESERT SENTINEL, 1968

One of Dad's favorite photographic motifs was to frame his subject with trees as a means of maximizing his depth of field. In this view of a Juniper tree cast against the backdrop of Monument Valley, the aging subject suggests the timeless continuity of the wild outdoors.

Although his primary focus was on the tree, his expert attention to the principles of fine art aesthetics elevates the monuments to the rank of secondary subject field.

The photograph is one of many that appeared in *Venture* magazine in 1967.

Negative 1066

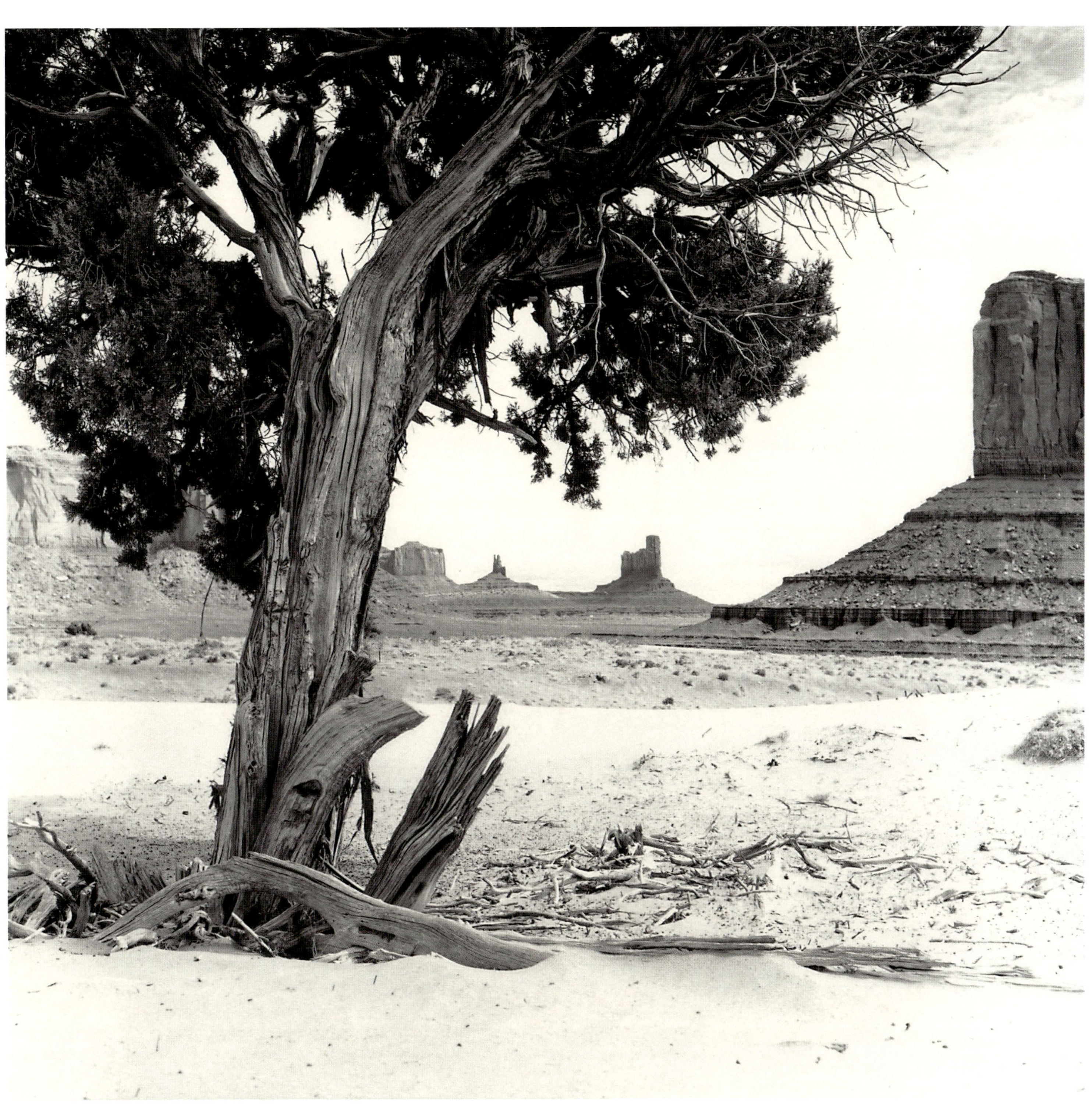

THE MITTEN, 1967

In "The Mitten," three of the most distinguishing features of Dad's photography are present in a single frame: sharp contrast, depth of field, and expert composition, a lesson he learned well from my mother. Although the primary focus is on the monument, he uses the old tree as a natural frame.

Mitten Peak stands approximately eight hundred feet above the surrounding valley and is so named because it assumes the shape of a pair of mittens when viewed from a distance. Navajos call it Big Hands and hold that these once powerful, though now still hands may someday return to rule over Monument Valley.

Almost all of the monuments and mesas in the surrounding area carry both Indian and Anglo names. "The Mittens" are often referred to as "Left" and "Right."

The photograph originally appeared in the pages of *Venture* magazine and subsequently awed audiences at various fine arts exhibitions.

Negative 1058

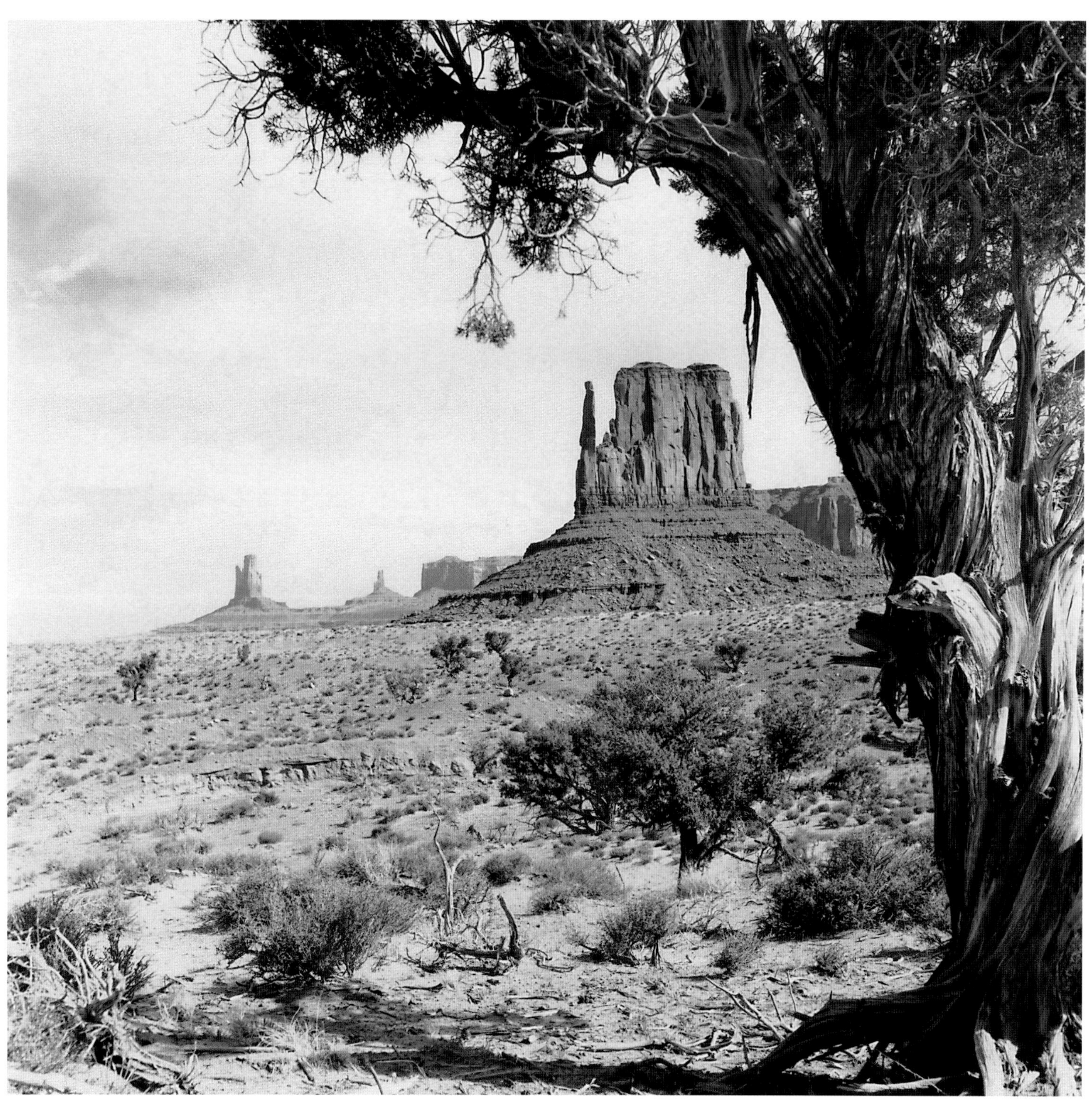

VALLEY OF THE MONUMENTS, 1967

This area in Monument Valley was the site of many noteworthy films by John Ford, starring John Wayne and Ollie Carey such as "Stagecoach" and "The Searchers." Although Ollie was not present when this photograph was taken, she was a long-time family friend, a frequent traveling companion during canyon country outings and a charter member of the Grand Canyon Hiking, Singing and Loving Club, a tongue in cheek moniker Dad used to describe the collective of family friends that commonly shared in the good times.

Dad's intent was most likely to capture the vast sweep of the valley floor and the mirror-like qualities of the clouds.

The image was another of many photographs featured in the pages of *Venture* magazine.

Negative 1036

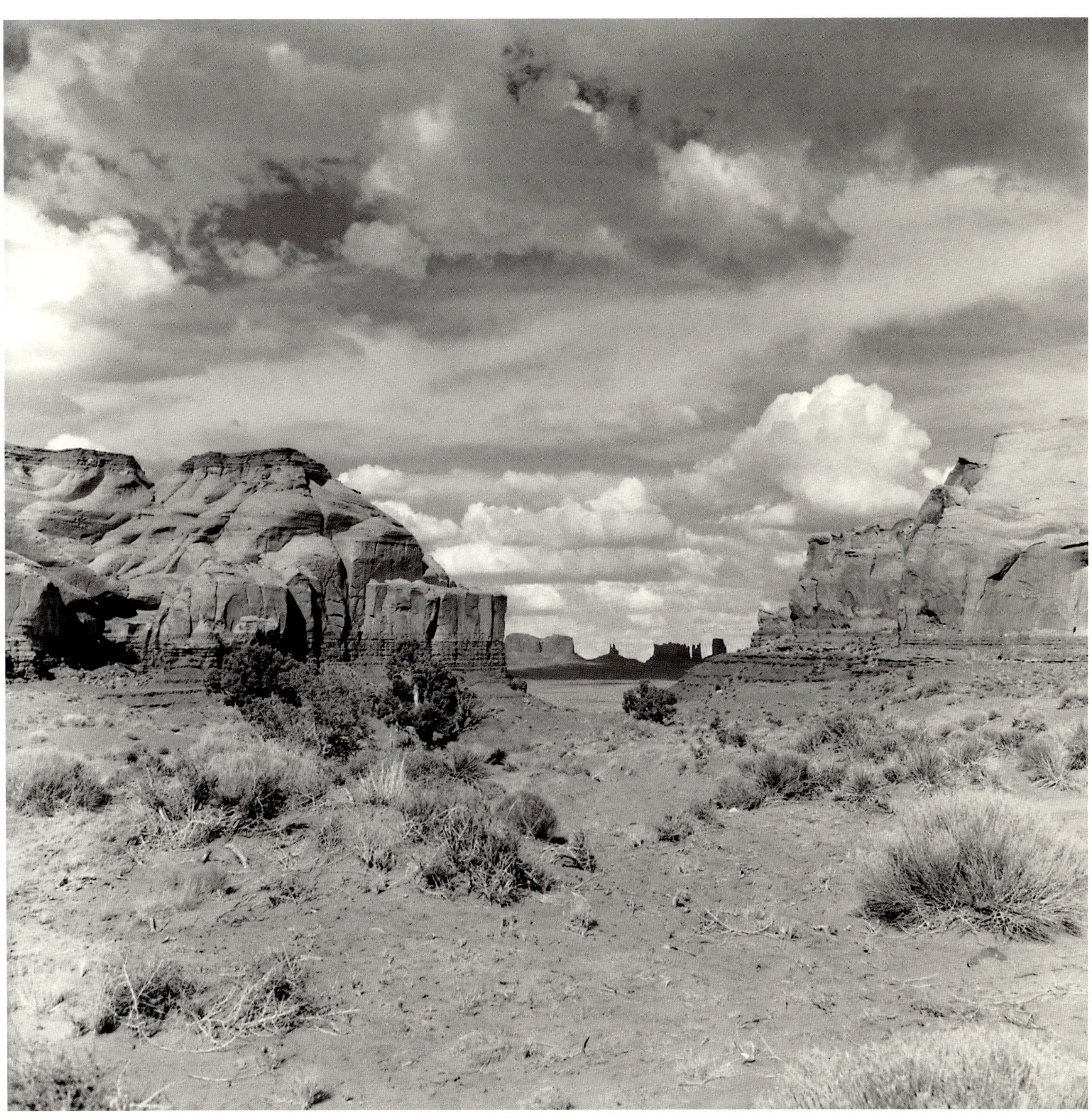

SNOWBANK, 1965

Dad was a perpetual student of nature, who found both delight and solace in her many manifestations. He also possessed an eye addicted to contrast, which means the chilly scene preserved here would have proved irresistible.

Along with his fascination for the stark contrast between the freshly fallen snow and dark water, Dad was intrigued by the dynamics of the forces of Mother Nature as they interacted with each other.

The location of the image is unknown, but the White Mountains is a likely contender for the honor.

Negative 985

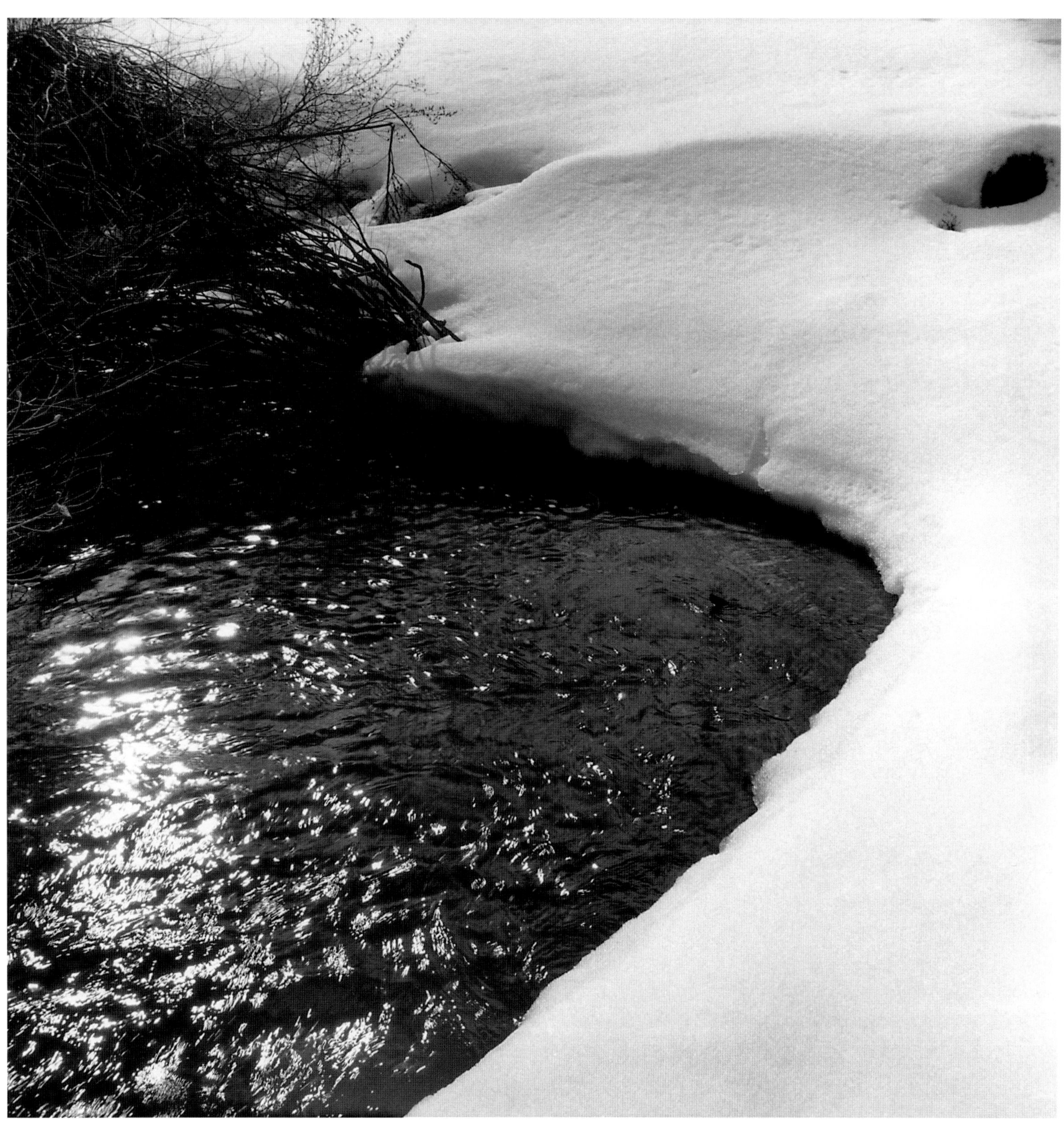

CHILDREN ON A HILL, 1950

Growing up with a Dad who was also a world-class photographer meant that the four of us often served as on-site subjects for his artistic impulse, as the subsequent view of my brother Barry, Jr. (left) and family friend Dave Peters (middle) attests. Dad appropriately dubbed the image "Children on a Hill" and eventually exhibited it in salons around the world.

The photograph emanated from one of the many "expeditions" Dad led to Indian Country under the auspices of the Y.M.C.A., after he returned from World War II. Throughout his life, he was happiest when he was teaching others about his beloved Arizona and its history. Young people were his favorite pupils, for they represented the future.

Negative 2136

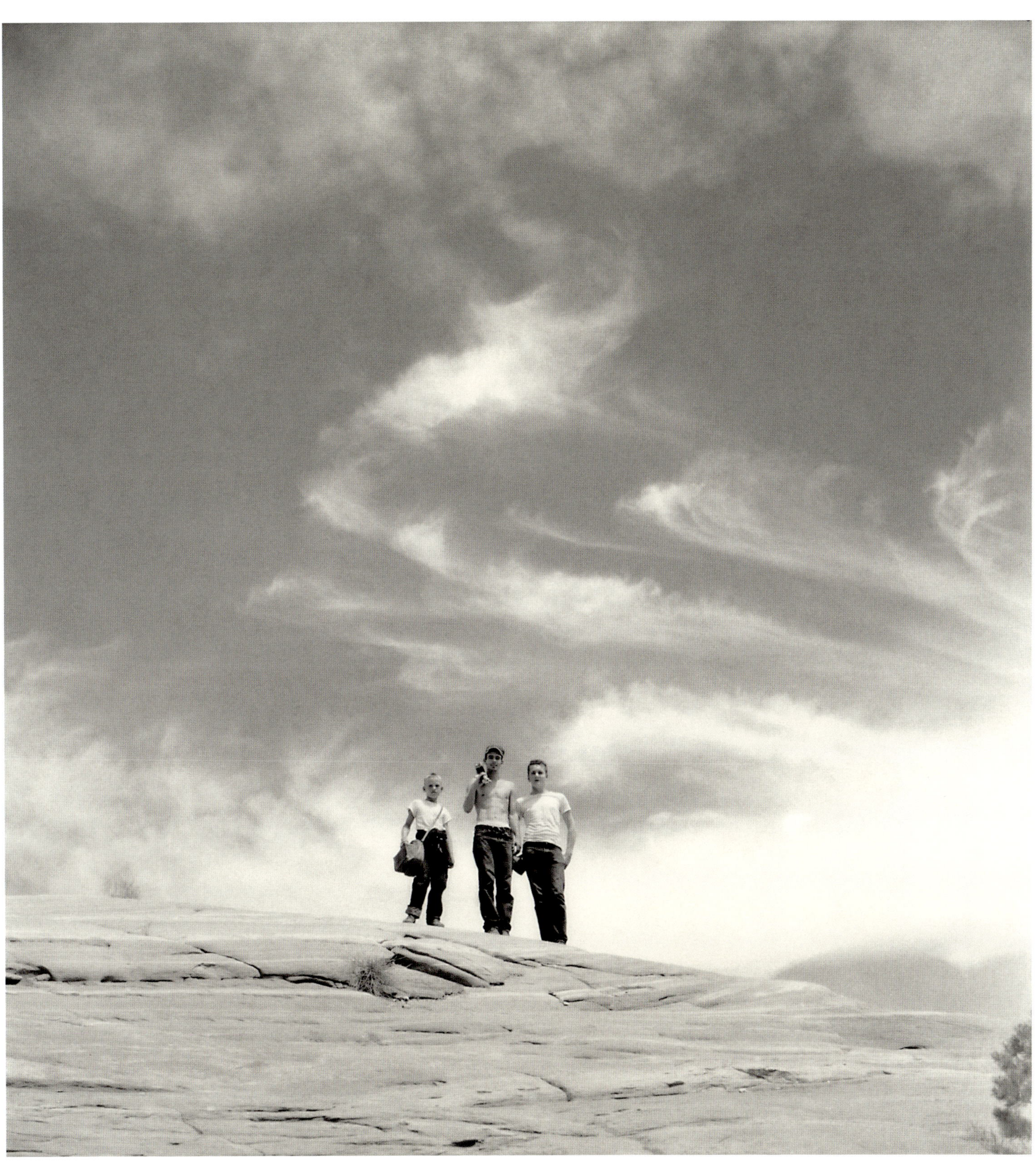

MARGARET ARCH, WHITE MESA, 1954

Dad discovered this little known arch during a wilderness excursion in the 1950s and named it in honor of my mother. At the time, it was a well-kept secret virtually exclusive to the Navajos.

As a commemoration of the friendship Dad had with the Navajos, they placed a bronze tablet near its base memorializing that relationship by officially naming it in honor of Mom.

Situated in Coconino County, White Mesa takes its name from the white walled sandstone that dominates the landscape. The natural arch is situated at the southeast edge of the mesa, where it serves as a natural bridge that spans across an erosion valley.

There are a number of these in Arizona and Dad made it a point to photograph each one he encountered along the trail.

Negative 768

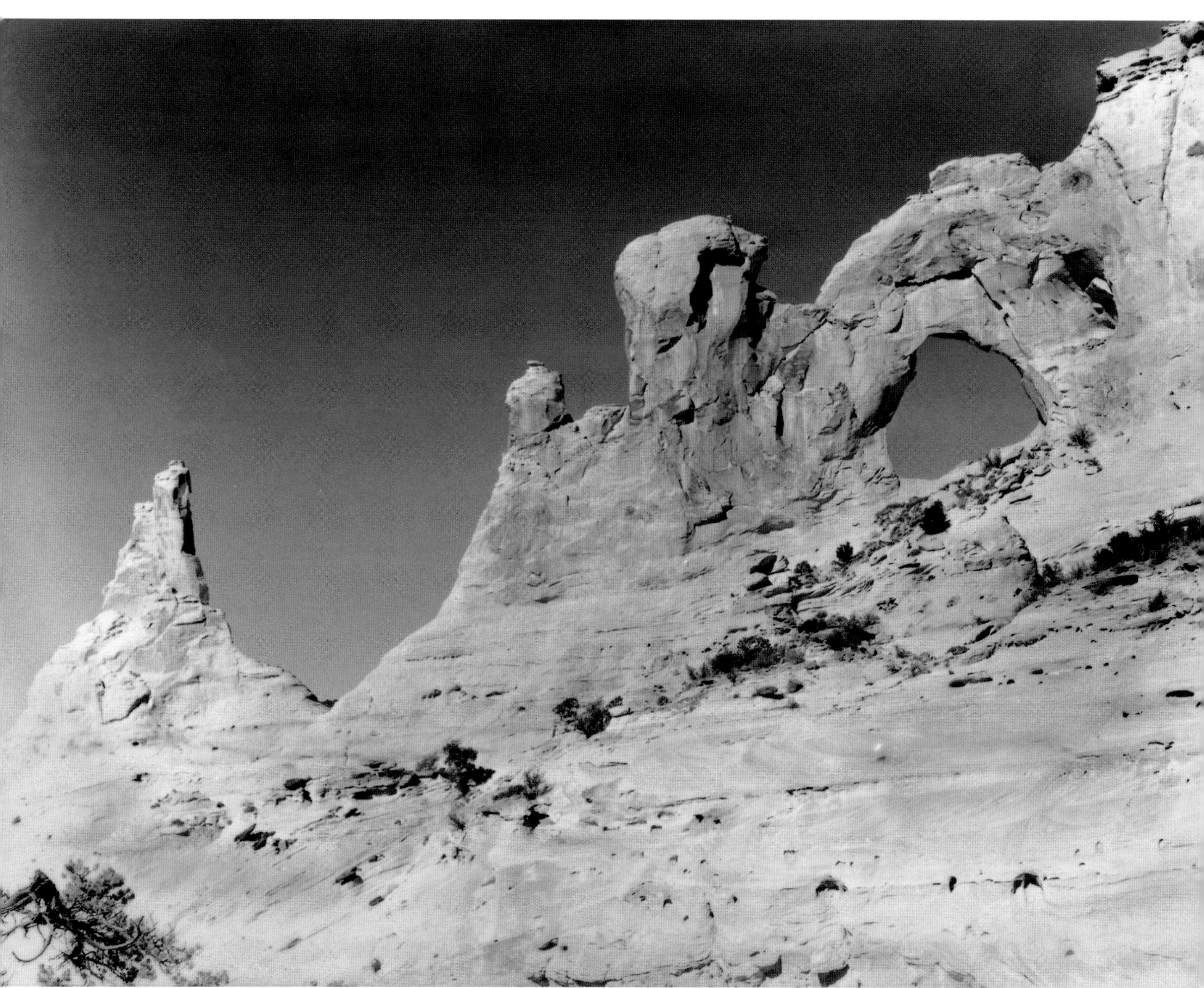

DEER CREEK FALLS, AUGUST 15, 1940

This waterfall flows cold and clear out of a crevice at the bottom of the Grand Canyon. The image was taken during Dad's first trip down the river in 1940, an eventful voyage that earned him the distinction of being the seventy-third person to run the rapids of the Grand Canyon.

In one of his official diaries of the trip, he explained that:

Deer Creek comes down from the North Rim and winds through a tortuous canyon of the Redwall Limestone along the river where it plunges about a hundred and twenty-five feet to the river level. It is situated about two hundred feet back from the river and shoots sideways out of a crack in the wall. The water assumes a fan shape as it comes down and falls freezingly and forcefully on those who venture below it. We did and were cool for a change.

Barry M. Goldwater
in *Delightful Journey*

Negative 719

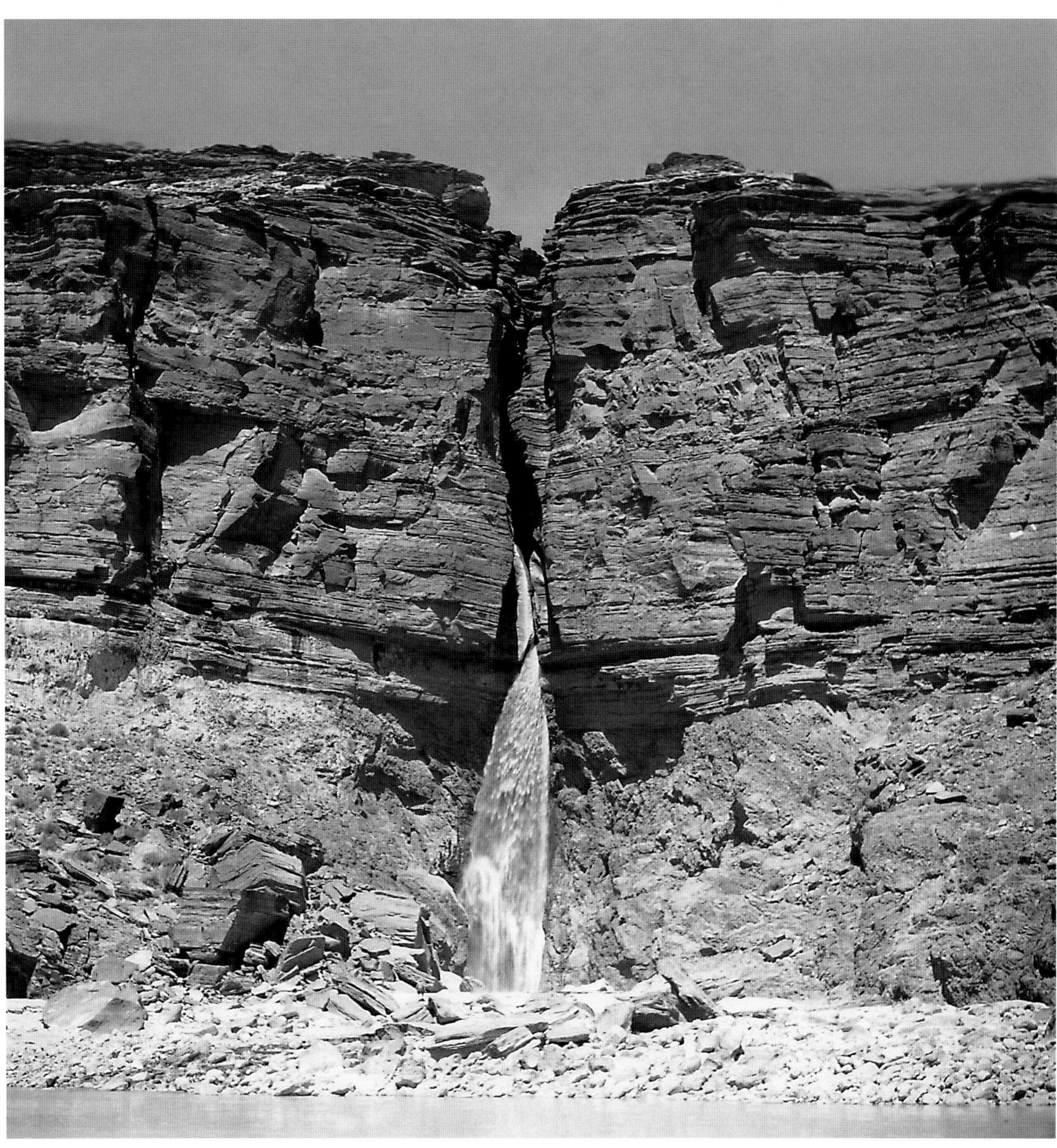

VERDE, 1951

The lush and verdant reaches of the Verde River were a frequent stop on the extended Goldwater Family wilderness itinerary. Dad would typically gather up the four of us, our cousins, friends and other neighborhood kids, set up campsite somewhere along the banks of the majestic waterway and systematically impart lessons on nature and history that reaffirmed our pride as Arizonans.

Called by the Spanish word for 'green,' the Verde runs through the counties of Yavapai and Maricopa. Various early observers called it by a variety of descriptive names. Don Antonio de Espejo called it El Rio De los Reyes (King's River), Juan de Onate preferred Rio Sacramento and Lieutenant Amiel W. Whipple opted for the Bill Williams Fork, while his guide Antoine Leroux called it Rio San Francisco out of deference to its source. Because the stream flowed past mountain ridges ribbed with multi-colored rocks starkly in contrast to its own color, the Indians simply dubbed it 'green,' thus explaining its present name.

Of the many memorable times I recall from these outings, one trip in particular stands out in my mind. The Verde campsites seemed especially cold, so I engineered an ingenuous means of keeping myself warm by putting stones under the fire and rolling them into my bedroll at night. On one such occasion, the bedding began to smolder and Dad put it out with a bucket of water. He was none too happy about the near disaster and threatened to make me sleep in the water logged debacle as an object lesson. Fortunately for me, he was just blowing off parental steam. A couple of blankets were located, a makeshift bed was set up and the rest is family history.

Negative 855X

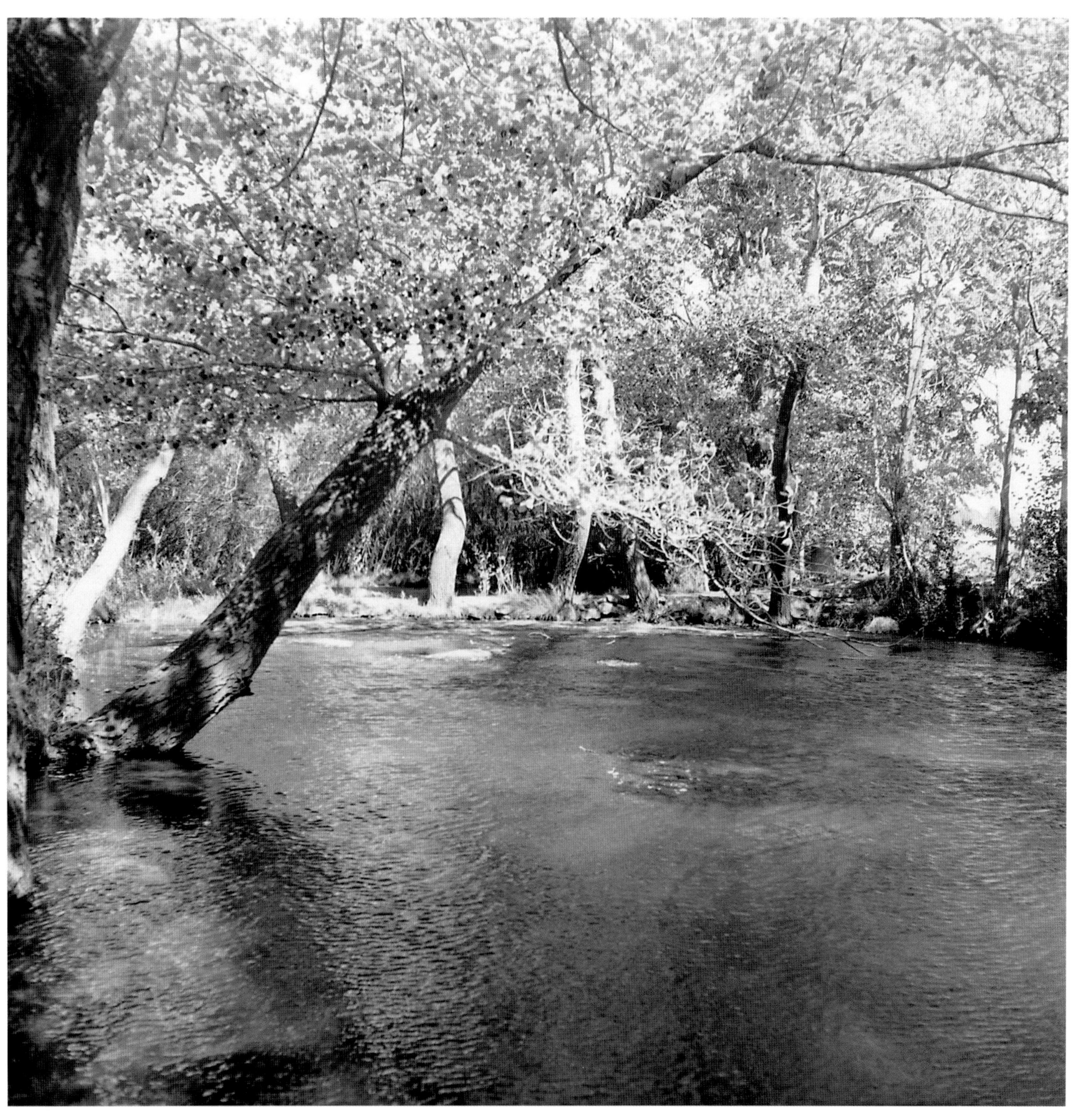

WESTWARD HO, c. 1938

Surrounded by marshmallow clouds and the arid landscape of the high desert, this was one of Dad's favorite images.

In his 1976 book entitled *Barry Goldwater and The Southwest*, he shed light on the reasons behind his preference:

> *I found these old wheels while driving north of Prescott, Arizona on the Old Williamson Valley Road one day in the late 1930s. I call it "Westward Ho" and it is one of the most popular photographs I have ever made. It has been displayed well over 60 times in various salons around the world.*

Negative 929

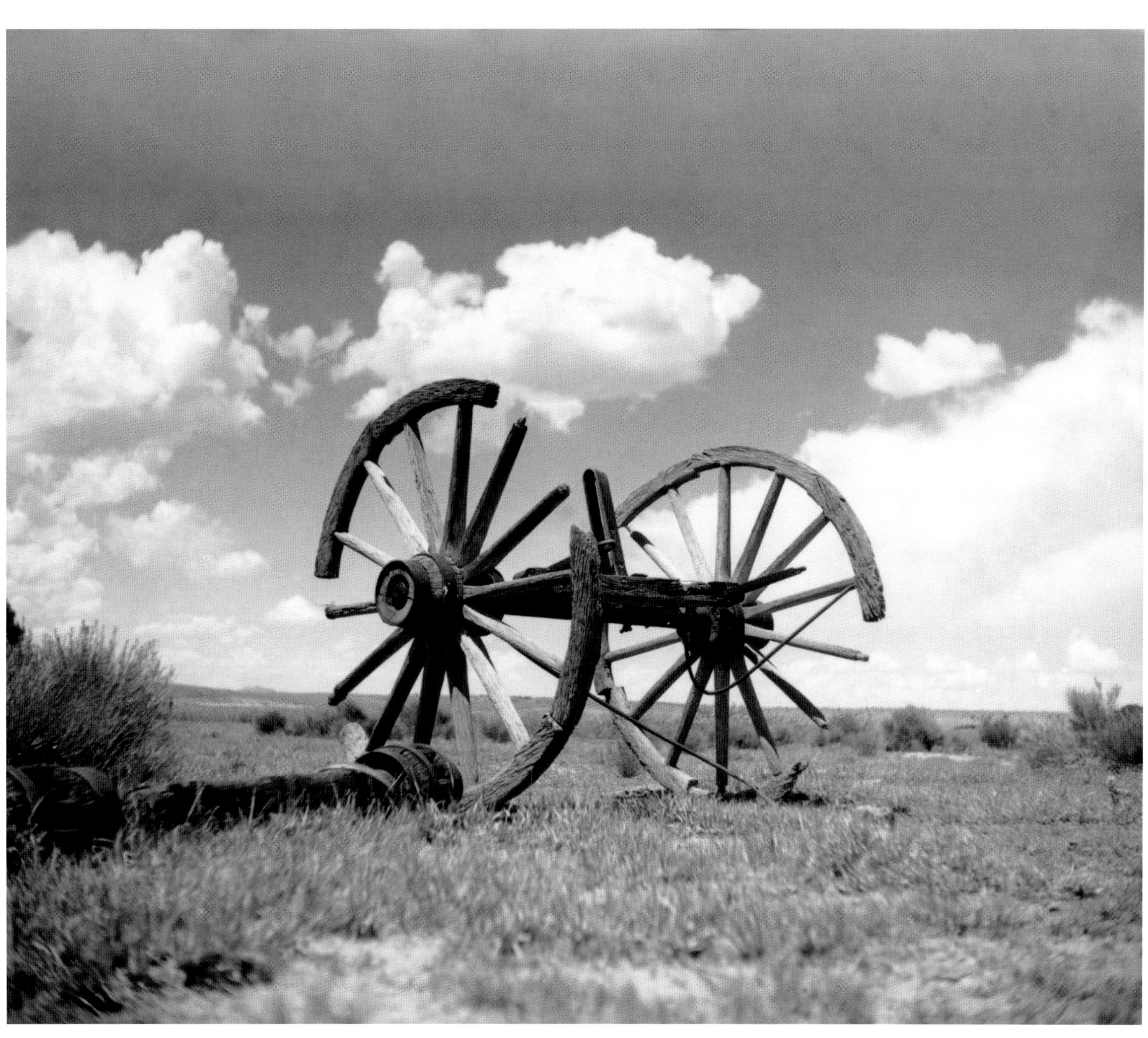

NAVAJO PONY, c. 1938

The tried and tested mount featured in this image was a favorite of Dad's for a wide variety of reasons. Let him speak for the circumstances surrounding their introduction:

> *This Navajo pony was ground tied by the hitching post at Tonalea when I saw him in the 1930s.*

Tonalea takes its name from the Navajo cognate "to" (water) and *"neheelii"* (where it sinks). Originally its location was an ephemeral sink eliminated by an earth dam storage lake. The community sits on a small hill overlooking the site. Red Lake was originally suggested as a more accessible name for the post office, but the common use of that title throughout Navajo Country prompted officials to adopt the present title as more distinctive.

Negative 932

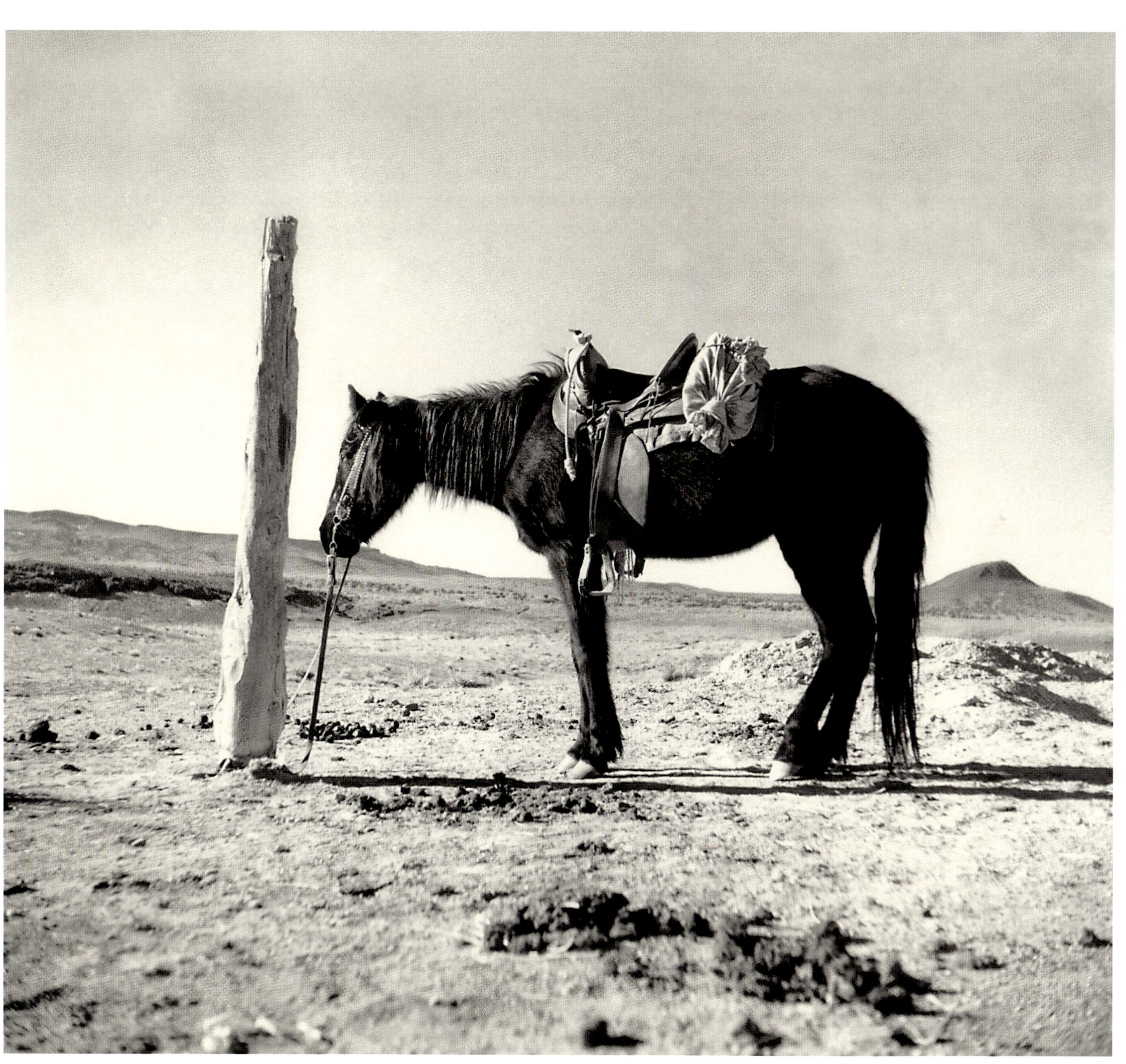

THE DESERT CORSAGE, 1936

The magnificent Saguaro Cactus is the state flower of Arizona. It is composed of a tall, thick, fluted stem column that grows from 18 to 24 inches in diameter, with several large branches, which locals refer to as arms, curving upward in a distinctive formation frequently likened to natural sentries. Its skin is smooth and waxy, while the trunk and stems have stout, 2-inch spines clustered at their ribs. When water is absorbed, the outer pulp of the Saguaro expands like an accordion, which increases both the diameter of the stem and its weight up to as much as a ton.

During the critical germination stage, the Saguaro seeks the shelter of a "nurse" tree or shrub to assure shade and moisture. Although it only grows about an inch a year in its early life, it can reach a height of 15 to 50 feet at maturity. The largest plants have five or more arms and are estimated to be about 200 years old. An average age Saguaro has about five or more arms and stands 30 feet high.

Its flowers are creamy white with yellow centers that open to about 3 inches in diameter. As the following description by Dad reveals, the blossoms only open during the cooler desert nights and close again by the next midday:

The desert corsage, a picture of two blossoming flowers of the giant saguaro taken about 1936. These flowers bloom at night and start dying as soon as the sun rises.

Barry M. Goldwater
in *Barry Goldwater and the Southwest*

Negative 1078

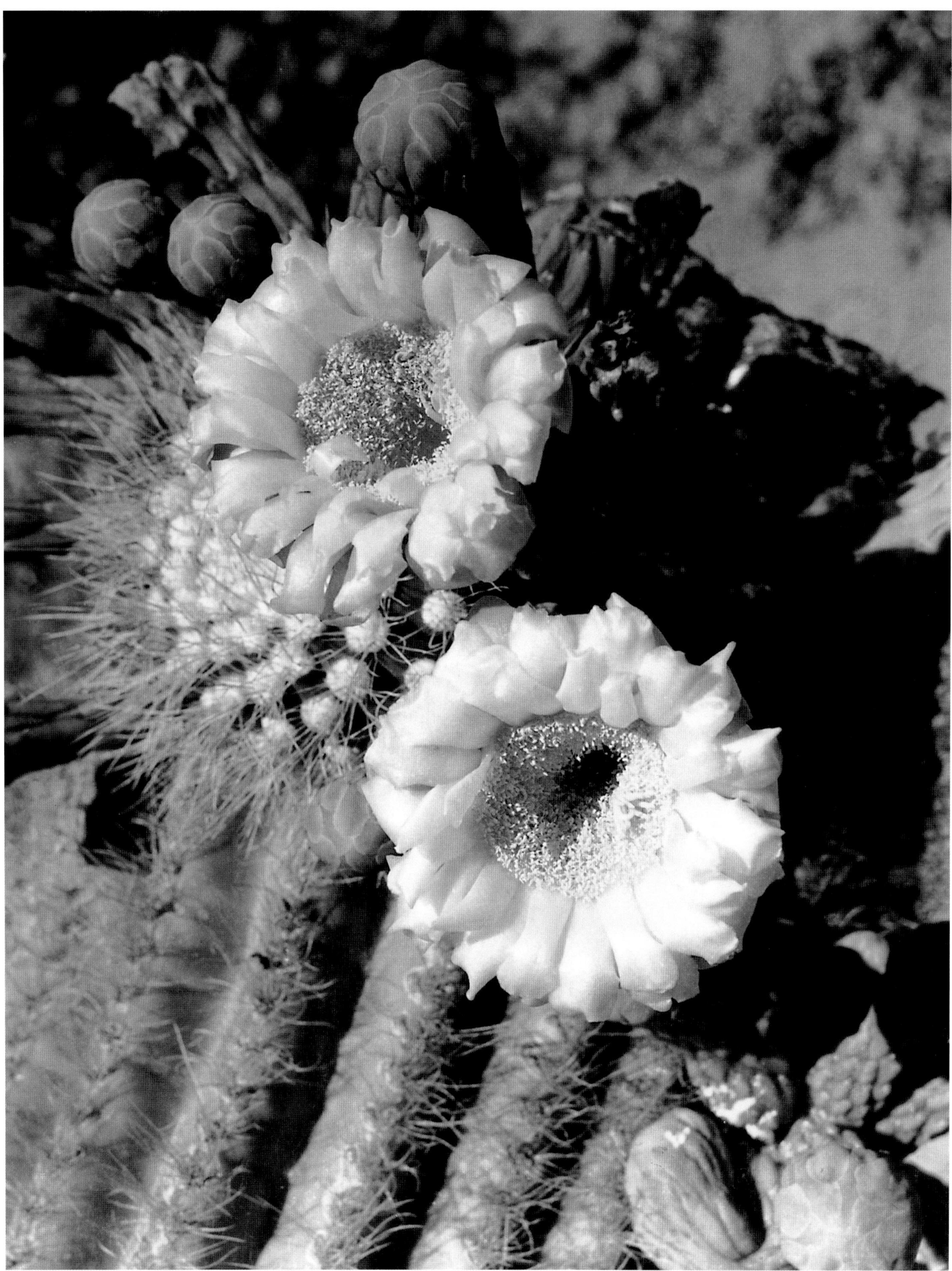

SNOW FENCE NEAR FLAGSTAFF, 1936

Dad spent most of his life trying to separate myth from fantasy and his camera always proved a reliable tool in that quest. He once wrote that:

Many people who have never been to Arizona think of it as only a land of desert. Yet, two thirds of our state is covered with forest. In fact, the largest stand of Ponderosa Pine in the world is in Arizona. When the snow falls the northern portion of our state becomes a veritable 'winter wonderland'.

The featured photograph is but one of many he took to justify his contention that Arizona was a lady with a vast and variegated seasonal wardrobe.

Negative 1080

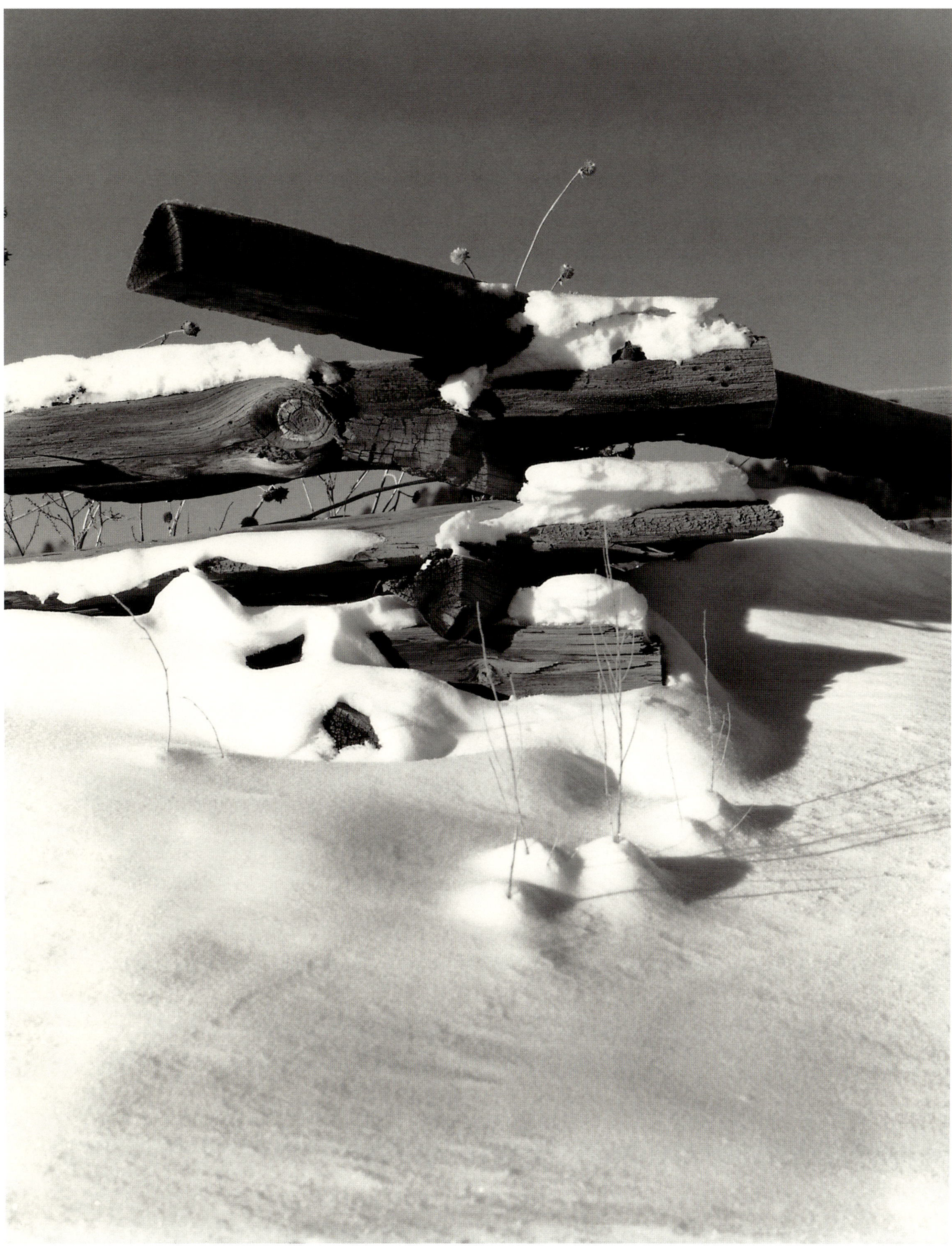

THE NAVAJO, 1938

Of all the additions to Dad's photograph collection, the present offering is perhaps the best known. He originally titled the image Charlie Potato, but protests from the subject led him to drop the specific for the more general title of "The Navajo."
Dad later wrote the following about the image:

This is one of my most successful photographs, having been shown in nearly one hundred salons around the world. The dignity of the ancient citizens of Arizona shows clearly in the features of this man. I call this photograph, which was taken at an Indian fair near Window Rock in 1938, "The Navajo."

Barry M. Goldwater

Negative 1999

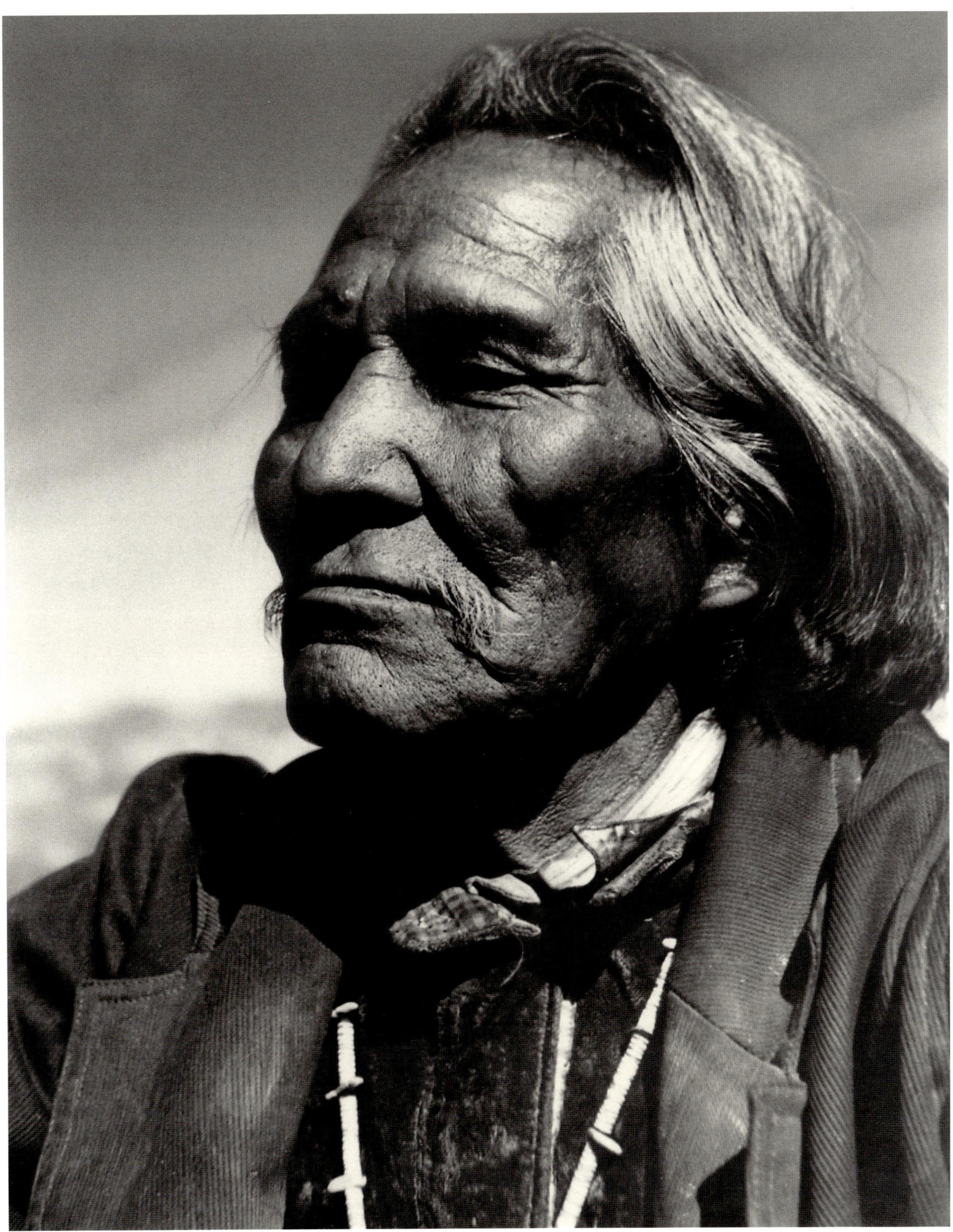

PIPE SPRINGS, WOLF HOLE, 1938

Dad possessed a fondness for picturesque scenes that conveyed evidence of the human presence on Arizona's diverse landscape, particularly those with a unique and informative history. The present offering of the site the Paiute Indians called "Yellow Rock Water" or "Yellow Rock Spring," with its handsomely crafted structure and scenic location, is a telling sample of that preference.

The written record suggests that Pipe Springs took the name in 1852, when famed pioneer Jacob Hamblin and other Mormon missionaries wagered William "Gunlock Bill" Hamlin that he could not shoot a hole through a handkerchief at fifty paces. When his best effort ended in success, the gunman upped the ante and bet his companions that he could shoot the bottom out of the pipe favored by Dudley Leavitt, who wisely placed the smoking device on a rock, which led to the name.

After the Hamlin party moved on to more hospitable climes (there was no other available source of water for a sixty mile radius), the area remained devoid of settlement until 1863, when Dr. James M. Whitmore and his brother-in-law Robert McIntyre established themselves in a dugout on the east side of a small hill located near the spring with the intention of raising cattle. They were ultimately slain by the Indians on January 8, 1866.

In April of 1870, B.P. Winsor bought the property from Mrs. Windsor and the Mormons formed a livestock cooperative called the Winsor Cattle Livestock Growers Association. The featured structure, which was colloquially known as The Castle, was constructed over the springs in an effort to keep the Indians from poisoning the water supply. The structure housed the first telegraph office in Arizona, which was established in 1871.

Although a combination of overgrazing and drought eventually devastated the area, the sturdily crafted fortress is rumored to have served as a safe house for practicing polygamists on the run from federal authorities. On May 31, 1923, the Pipe Springs National Monument of forty acres was set aside as an means of educating future generations on how pioneer Arizonans lived.

Negative 2443-C

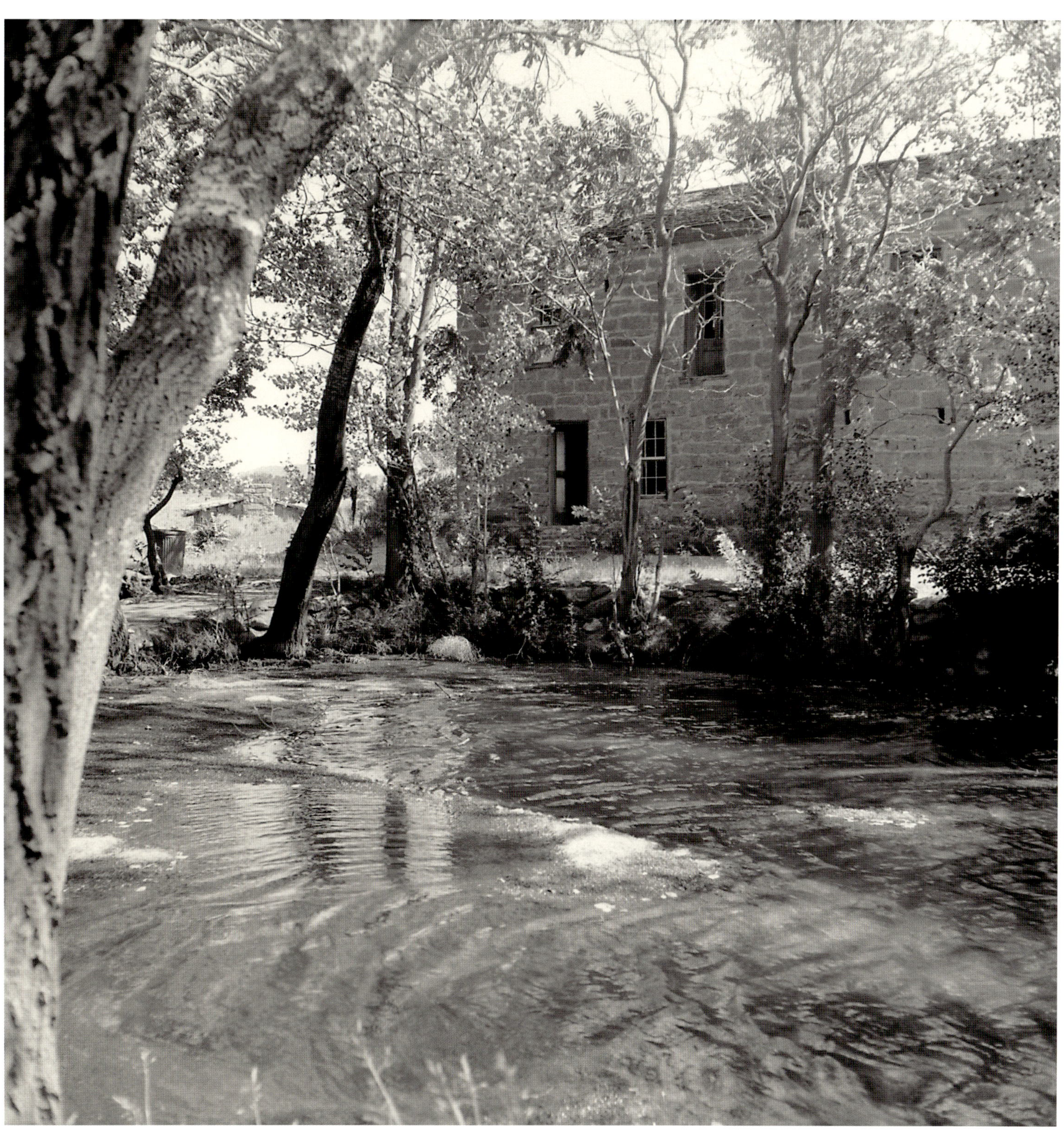

THE SHEPHERDESS, 1946

Over the years, several of Dad's photographs graced the pages of *Arizona Highways*. He enjoyed a long and productive friendship with the magazine's editor, Raymond Carlson, who was prone to assign him photographic tasks that ended up making history for more reasons than their content.

The adjoined image emanated from a request Carlson posed to Dad in late February of 1946. He wanted Dad to photograph Navajo girls herding their sheep in the snow, but Dad objected on the basis that the snow season had already passed. Two weeks later, he flew to Rainbow Lodge and woke up to a freshly fallen snow and the sound of sheep bells tinkling in the distance. He quickly got dressed, grabbed his camera and set out in search of the sheep herd, which he located and photographed in both black and white and color.

When the magazine issued its first all color issue in 1946, a color image from this series served as the cover. After Dad's passing, a reporter for the *Arizona Republic* went in search of the youthful subjects. A copy of that story and other related information is contained within my collection at The Arizona Historical Foundation.

Negative 762

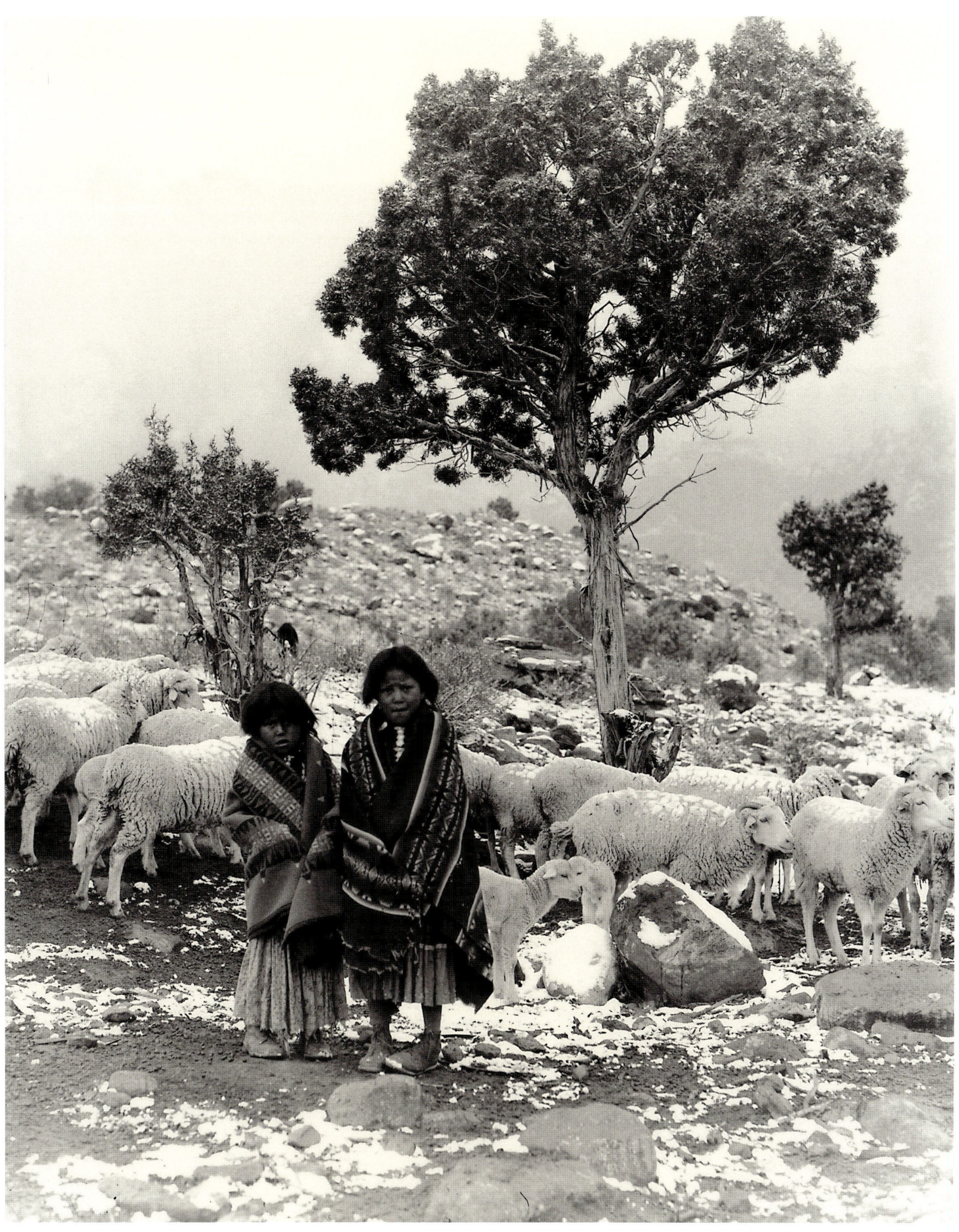

ROAD TO RAINBOW, 1938

While Dad was flying cargo missions over The Hump during World War II, Mom arranged for Dad to become a partner in the Rainbow Lodge, located at the head of the trail leading down to Rainbow Bridge near Navajo Mountain. Built by S. I. Richardson around the turn of the 20th Century, the lodge was situated in one of the most remote and picturesque regions of Navajo Country, where some of the Dine were alleged to have hidden out to avoid the Long Walk and subsequent imprisonment at Fort Sumner during the 1860s.

Richardson's intent was to use Rainbow Lodge as a point of demarcation for intrepid tourists intent upon exploring the virgin reaches of the northern canyon regions. Once a trail was built that connected the area to existing trails to the west in 1924, Richardson blasted out Redbud Pass and built a twelve mile shortcut to Rainbow Natural Bridge, a stunning sandstone edifice that stretches 309 feet high, 279 feet across and 40 feet in width. He ultimately turned the lodge over to his brother Hubert, who hired Stanton and Ida Mae Borum and W.W. and Katherine Wilson to run it. Bill Wilson was related to Sam Wilson, a former Goldwater's store manager.

Mom purchased Dad a half interest in the concern as an anniversary present. Although his schedule prohibited him from spending as much time there as he would have liked, he invested time and money toward improving the lodge, including the construction of 2,000 foot runway, the installation of a walk-in icebox, a five-kilowatt generator and a half dozen one room cabins, which he hired Del Webb to build.

Along with its status as a favorite hangout for my parents and their friends, Rainbow Lodge and its rugged surroundings, including the primitive road featured here, proved a favorite subject field for his photographic pursuits both during his tenure as owner and beyond.

Negative 715

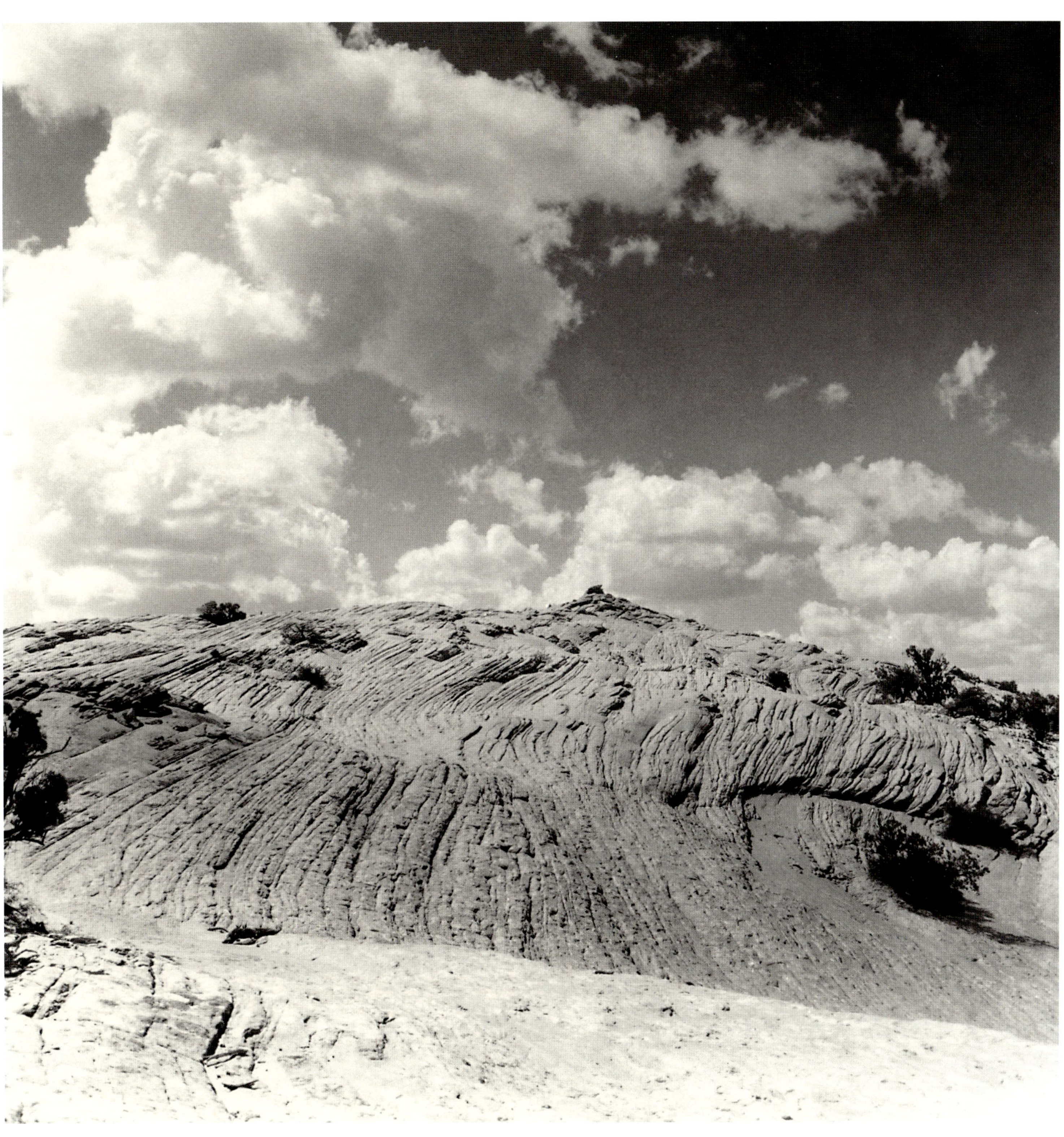

DRIFTWOOD, 1965

Of the many frames Dad shot of natural formations, few are as revealing of the influence of Edward Weston upon his work as those captured during a 1965 trip into the Grand Canyon.

The subtleties of texture and tone in an old piece of driftwood caught between the crevices of rock enabled him to create his own style of visual poetry that commands more than a cursory glance to appreciate.

Although few of these images ever appeared in his many publications, they are among his most provocative photographs, if for no other reason than their mirror like ability of the complexities that lay beneath his studied view of nature in all of her many dramatic expressions.

Negative 917-B

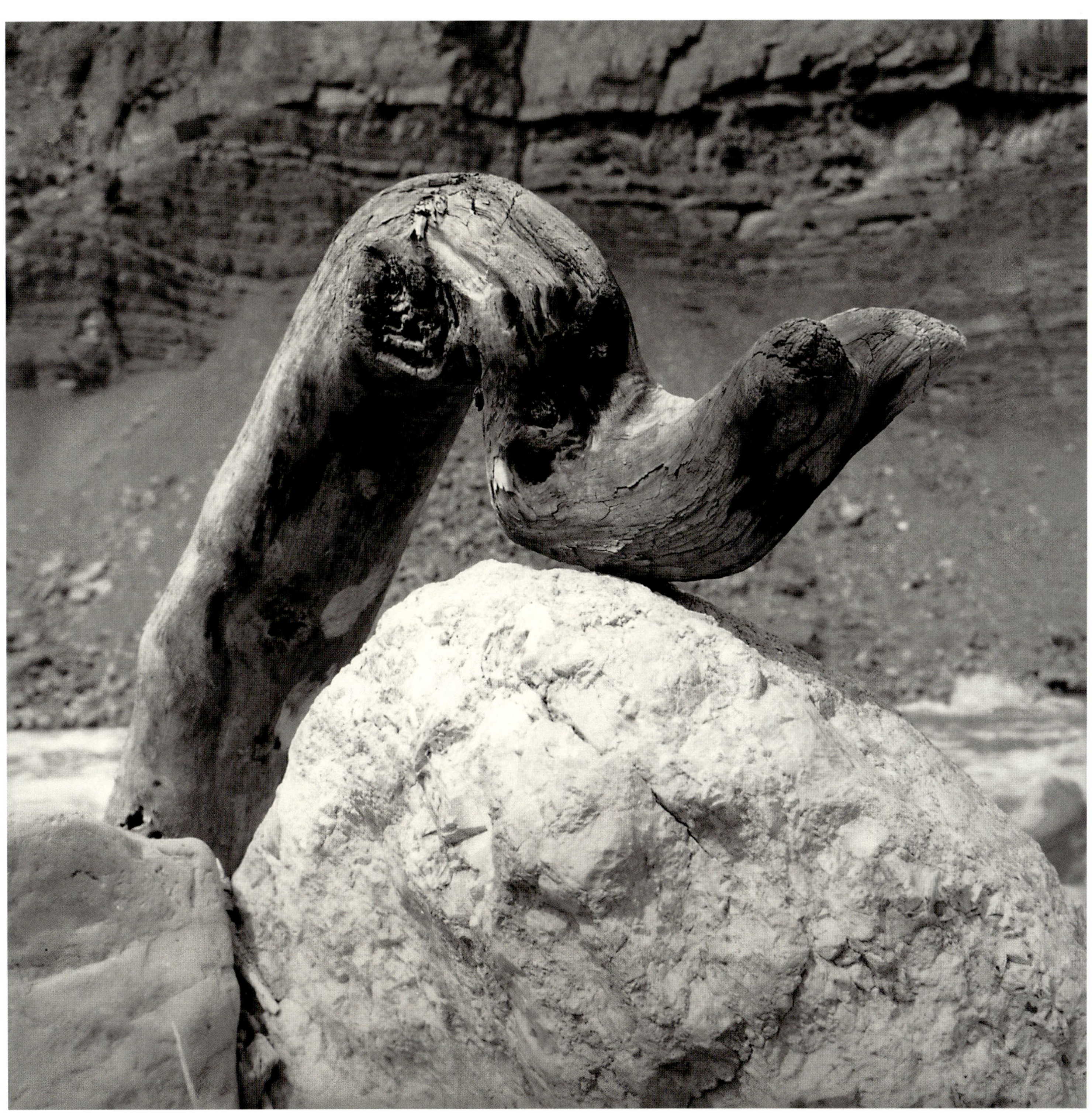

FALLEN FRIEND, 1965

On more than one occasion, Dad claimed the Grand Canyon as his mistress. The love affair began in youth and continued unabated to the end of his life. Among the many sources of his fascination was the timeless nature of the mysteries the Seventh Natural Wonder steadfastly revealed such as the clear and concise relic of a tree, with enough rings to suggest that it had nobly weathered the hands of time for decades, if not for centuries.

The superbly composed view serves as an aesthetically pleasing reminder that nature carries its own rhyme and rhythm, which humankind need not necessarily understand to appreciate.

Negative 959

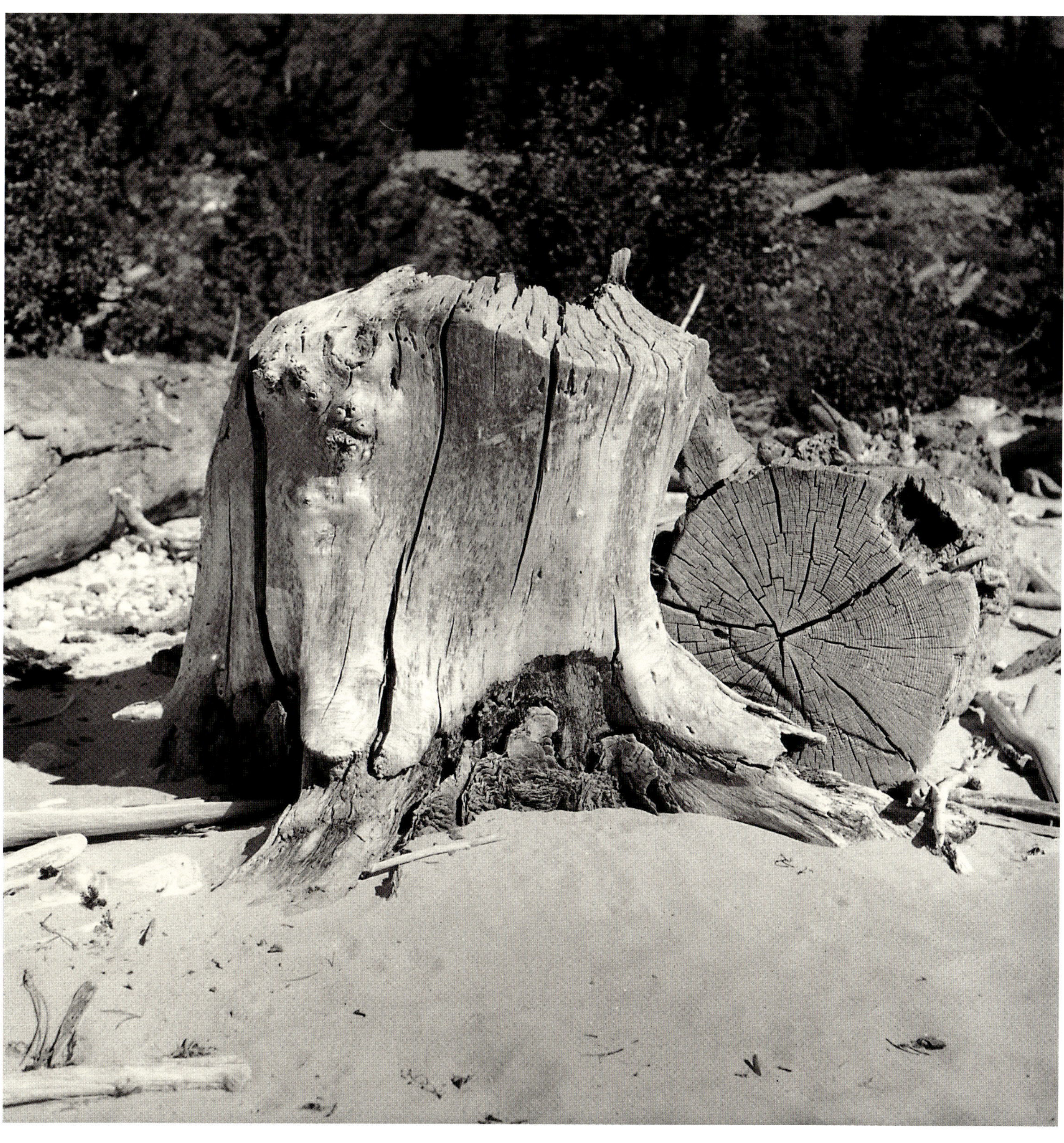

OLD HUALAPAI INDIAN SCOUT, 1938

Light, shadow and the intricacies of the hands of time across the face of a Native elder were favored elements of Dad's Indian photography. Sometimes his subjects were strangers whose acquaintance he made through a haphazard introduction in the wilderness or during his tenure as partner in Rainbow Lodge. As often, they were childhood friends from the Phoenix Indian School, who welcomed him into their homes as a trusted friend, who behaved as though he understood the meaning of the word.

In his second autobiography, he posited that he had

probably spent more time with Arizona's Indians than any other white man...they were kindred spirits...After years of developing friendships, I began to understand Indian ways, needs and causes...They'll always be my brothers and sisters.

Negative 867-X

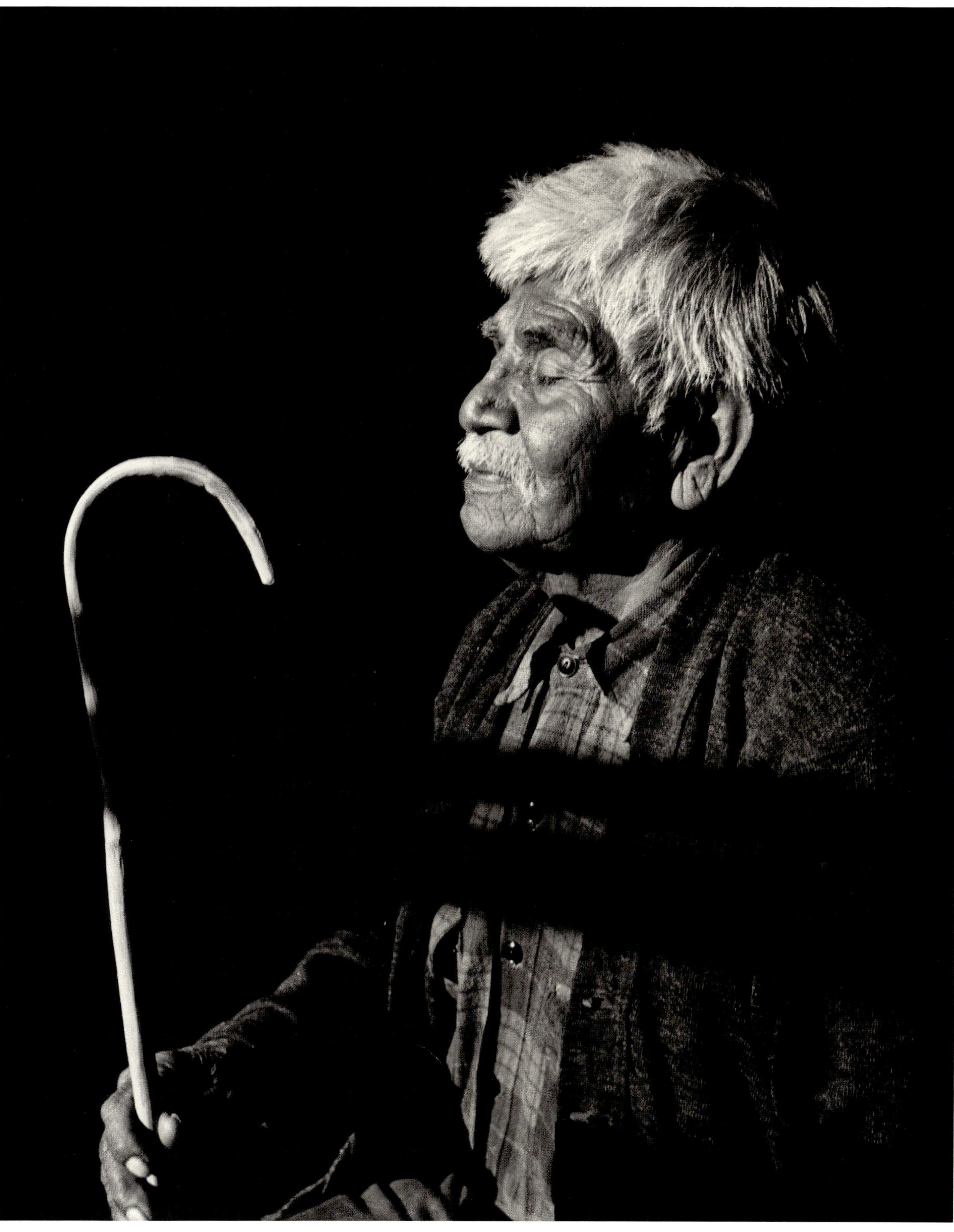

FOREST LAKE, 1937

Located in Navajo County, this place is known to the Navajo's as *Debebekid*, or 'sheep lake,' a name that is also applied to other areas within the region.

By 1968, it was more commonly known as Forest Lake, primarily because it was the only body of water that boasted trees.

Negative 1047

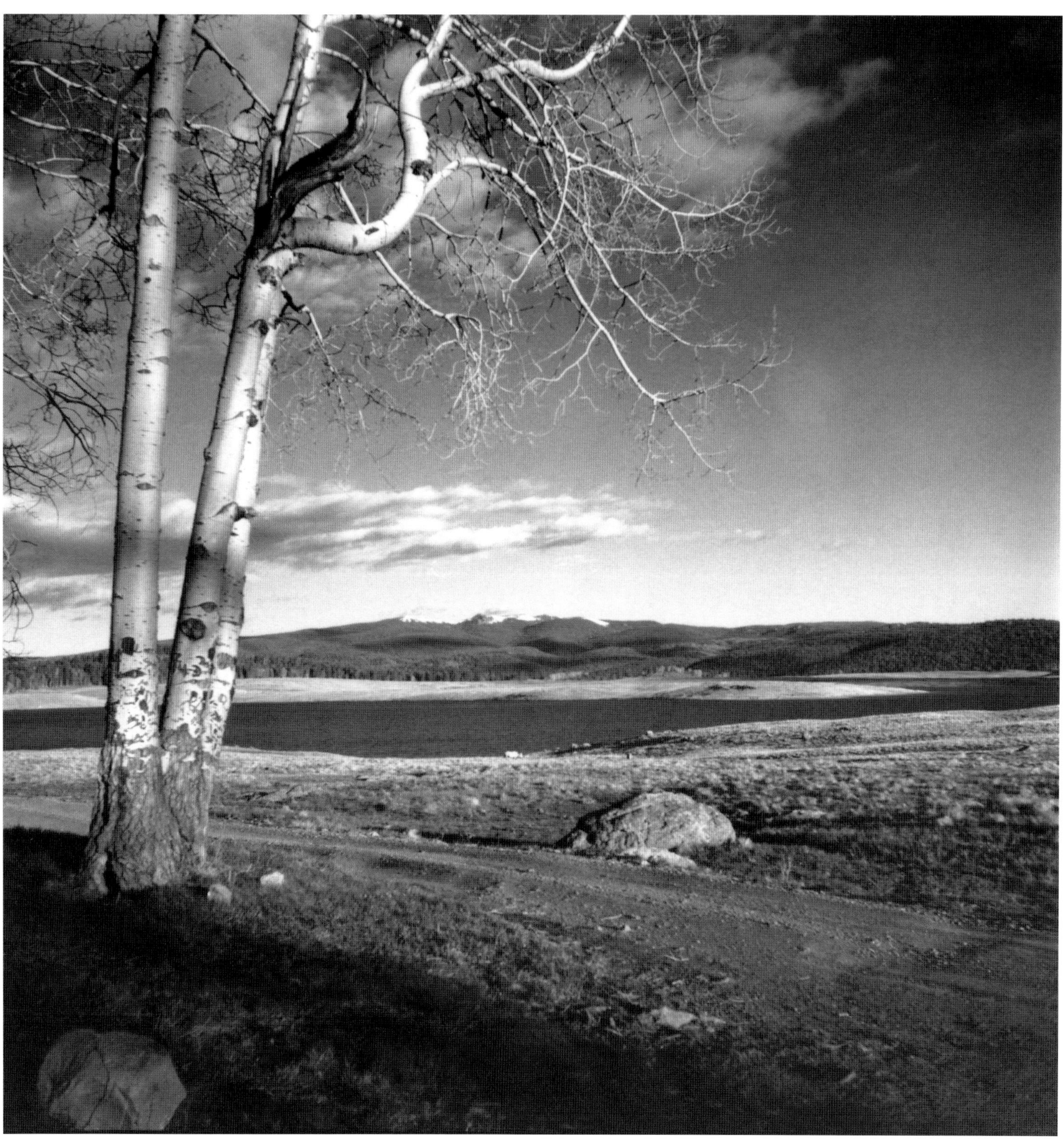

HELL ROARING CANYON, JULY 12, 1940

Captured on the fated river trip wherein Dad became the seventy-third person to retrace John Wesley Powell's second aquatic reconnaissance down the Green and Colorado Rivers, this slice of the Arizona landscape is typical of the rugged terrain Dad was prone to frequent at every opportunity at his disposal.

Hell Roaring Canyon is a large tributary of Labyrinth Canyon on the Green River, located above the junction of the Green and Colorado Rivers.

Dad was on the Green River when he captured the present frame.

Negative 872X

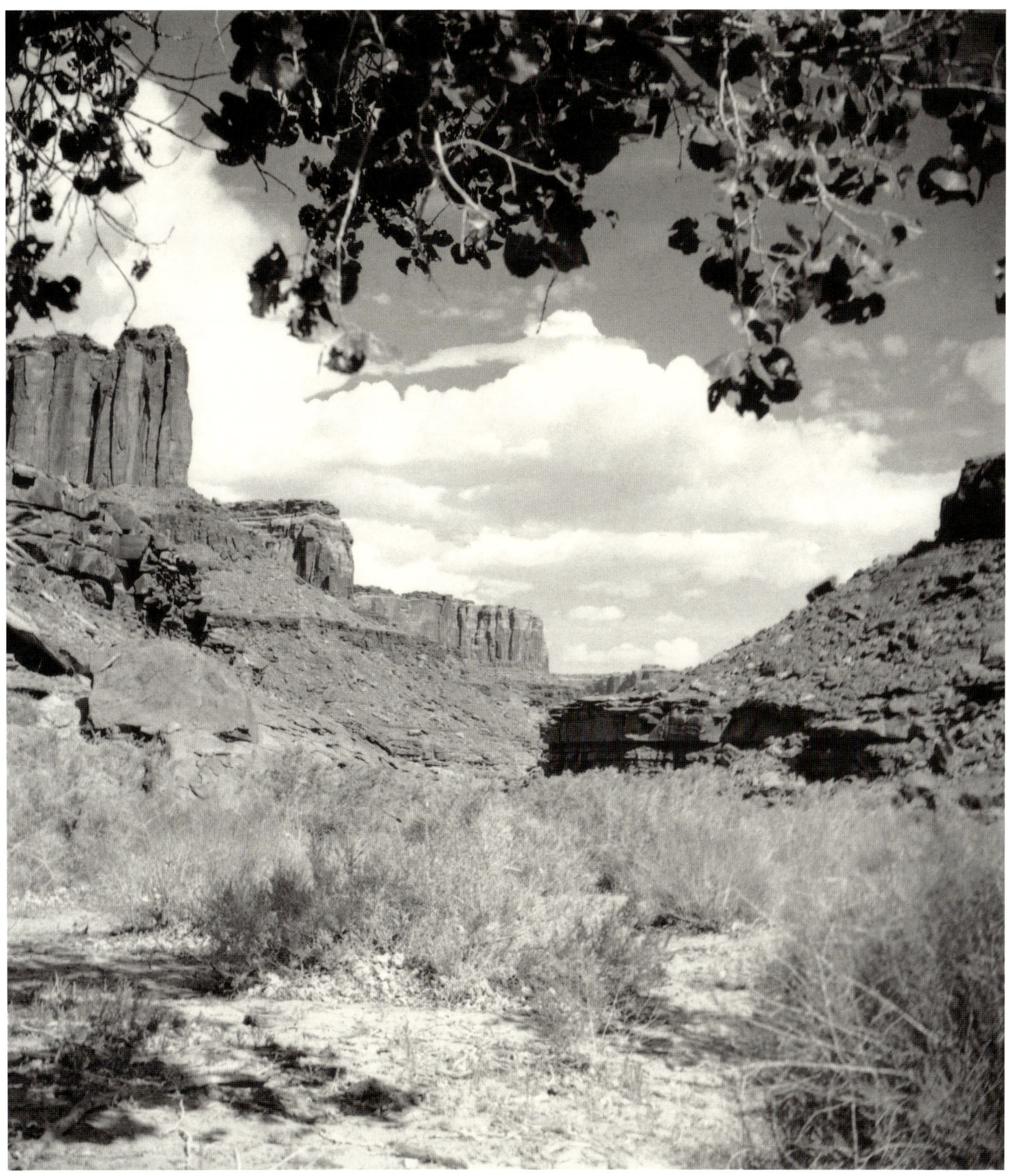

SPIRES, WHITE MESA, 1936

Located in Coconino County, this white wall sandstone mesa dominates the landscape. Among its many scenic features is a natural arch located on the southeast edge of the mesa that spans an erosion valley.

Dad's fascination with geology and archeology repeatedly enticed him back to this north central Arizona location. The nearby ruins of Keet Seel, Betatakin and Inscription House were strong drawing cards.

On the many flights to and from Rainbow Lodge, he would fly low over the terrain, spotting ruins and arches and then mark the location on his aviation maps. Later we would drive to the area and hike into his discoveries.

Negative 1079

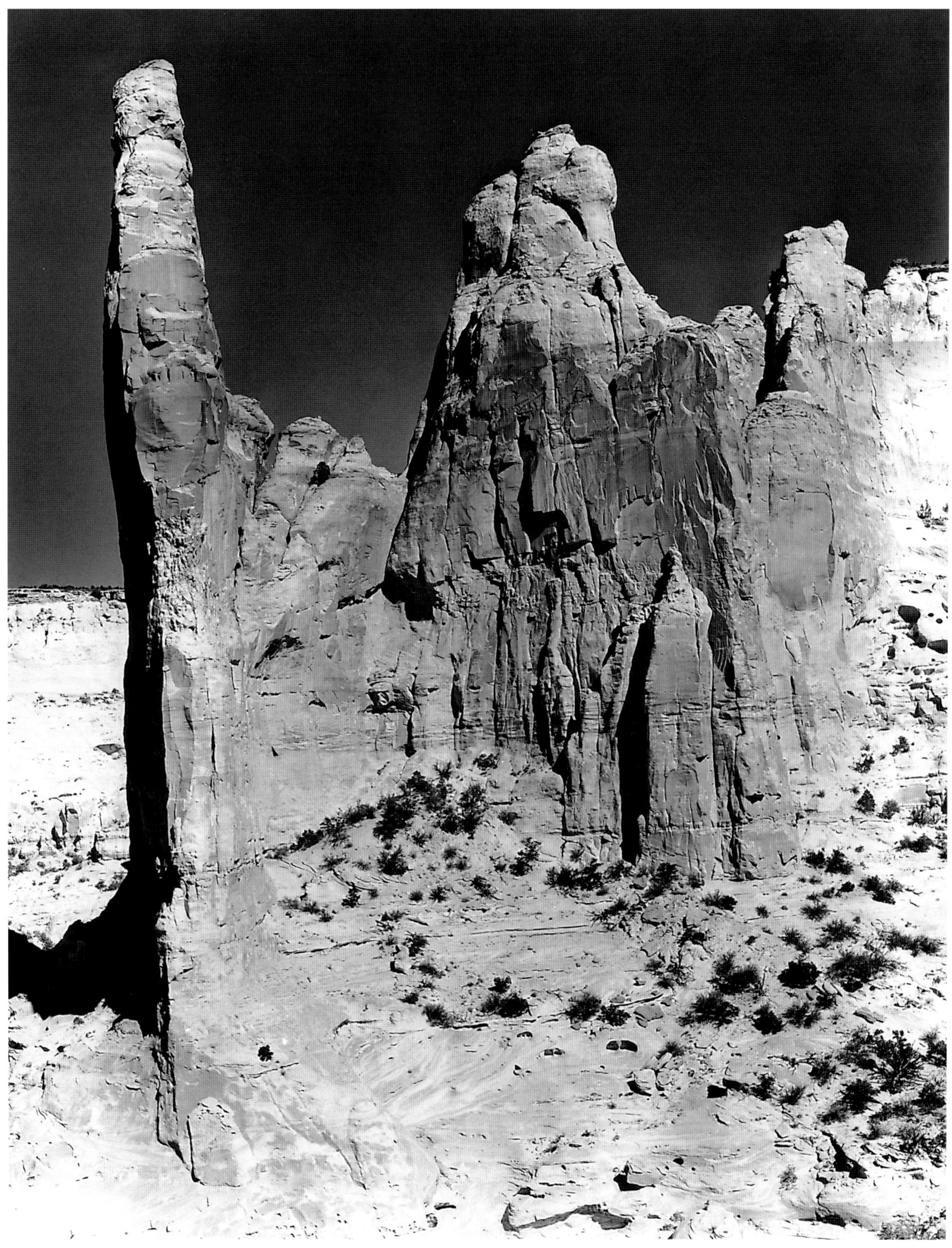

COCHISE STRONGHOLD, 1965

The name affixed to this picturesque place in Cochise County is a bit of a mis-nomer, because it implies that the legendary Cochise and his Chiricahua followers were limited to a single location. In reality, the Apaches had several such sites they commonly used to avoid detection or capture by the United States Cavalry.

Located within the Dragoon Mountains in the southern part of the state, the tree-lined setting is named in honor of one of the most respected and feared Indian chiefs in all of U.S. history. Cochise spent his early years raiding Mexican territory, but enjoyed good relations with the Americans until he joined other chiefs in an 1861 visit to Lieutenant George Bascom in Apache Pass to deny his band's rumored role in the recent abduction of a white child. Instead of honoring the Indian leaders flag of truce, the young, inexperienced military officer placed his guests under arrest, when they steadfastly refused to admit their guilt in the incident. The chiefs plotted and executed an escape that left one dead and four captured and unceremoniously hanged. Cochise managed to escape, despite the fact that he was shot three times.

In the intervening years up until his death on June 8, 1874, the angry chief conducted a ceaseless campaign against the Americans as vengeance for the death of his comrades. Military authorities managed to capture him for a time in 1871, but he again managed to escape accompanied by an estimated two hundred followers. Cochise remained on the run for a year, before capitulating in 1872, when the Chiricahua Reservation was officially established.

Negative 991

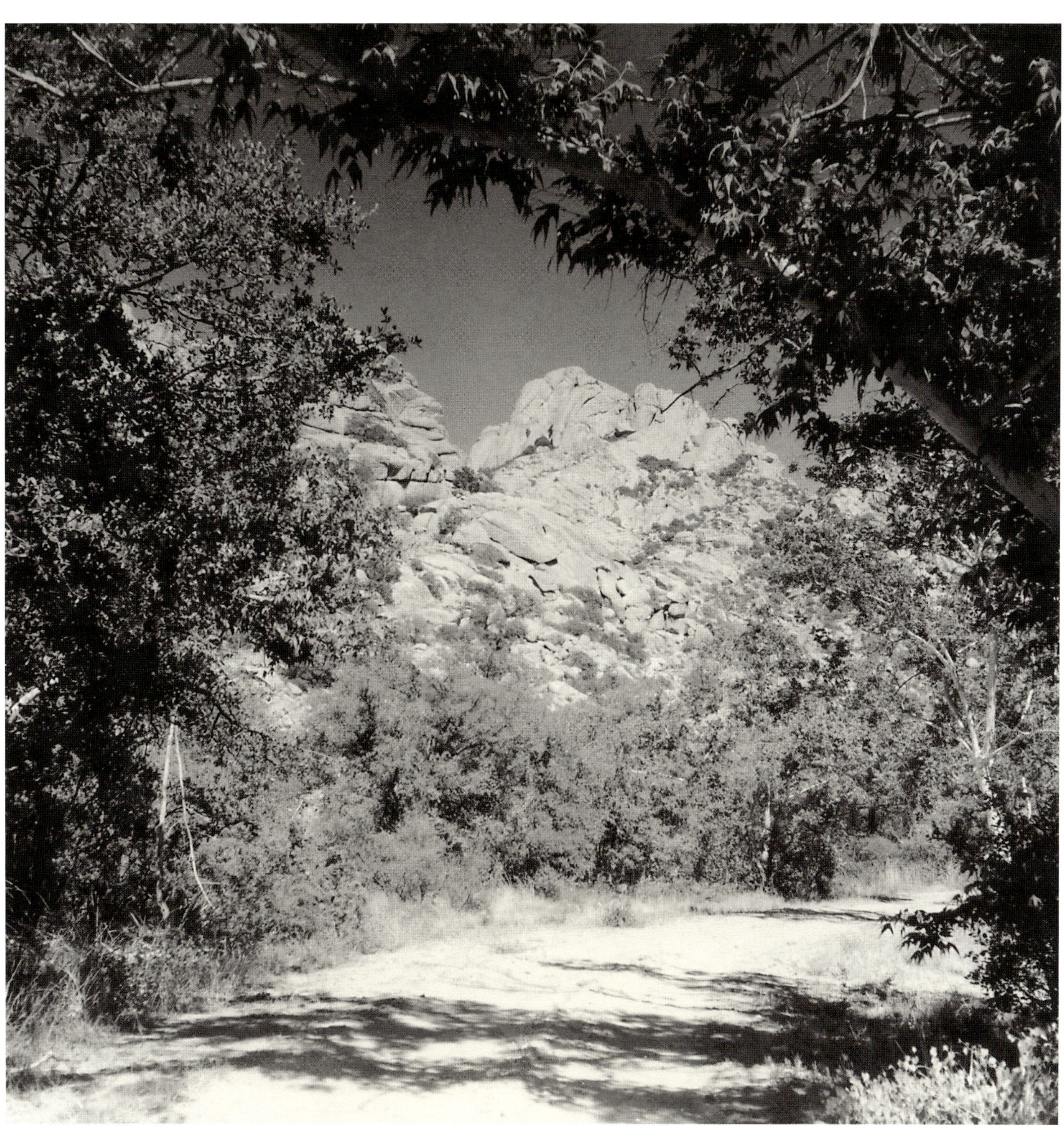

CHURCH ROCK, 1938

Situated south of the entrance to Monument Valley on the Navajo Reservation, this approximately 7000 foot high basaltic lava plug rises abruptly from a spare valley floor. Its name emanates from its uncanny resemblance to a church steeple.

The Navajos call it *Agathla*. It is also known in some circles as *El Capitan*.

Negative 717

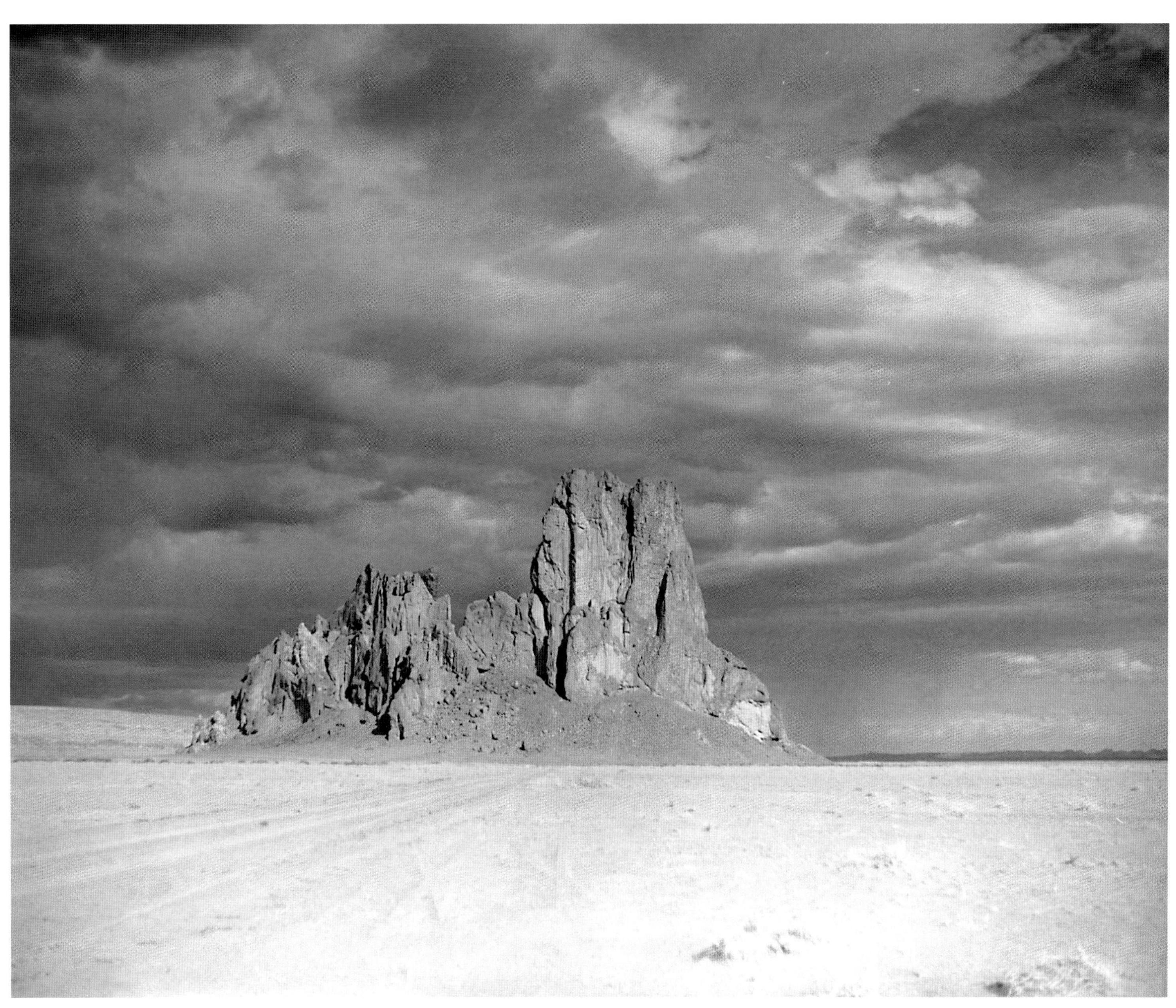

THE OLD ONE, 1938

The elderly lady in this frame represents one of the many Indians Dad photographed during his frequent trips to the Navajo Reservation. Dressed in the traditional velvet shirt and full skirt of her time and place, she was scouting for medicinal roots when the two met in the wilderness.

Dad later recalled that she proved a reluctant subject, but various expressions of the series of photographs he captured of her face and form proved highly popular on the exhibition circuit.

Negative 782

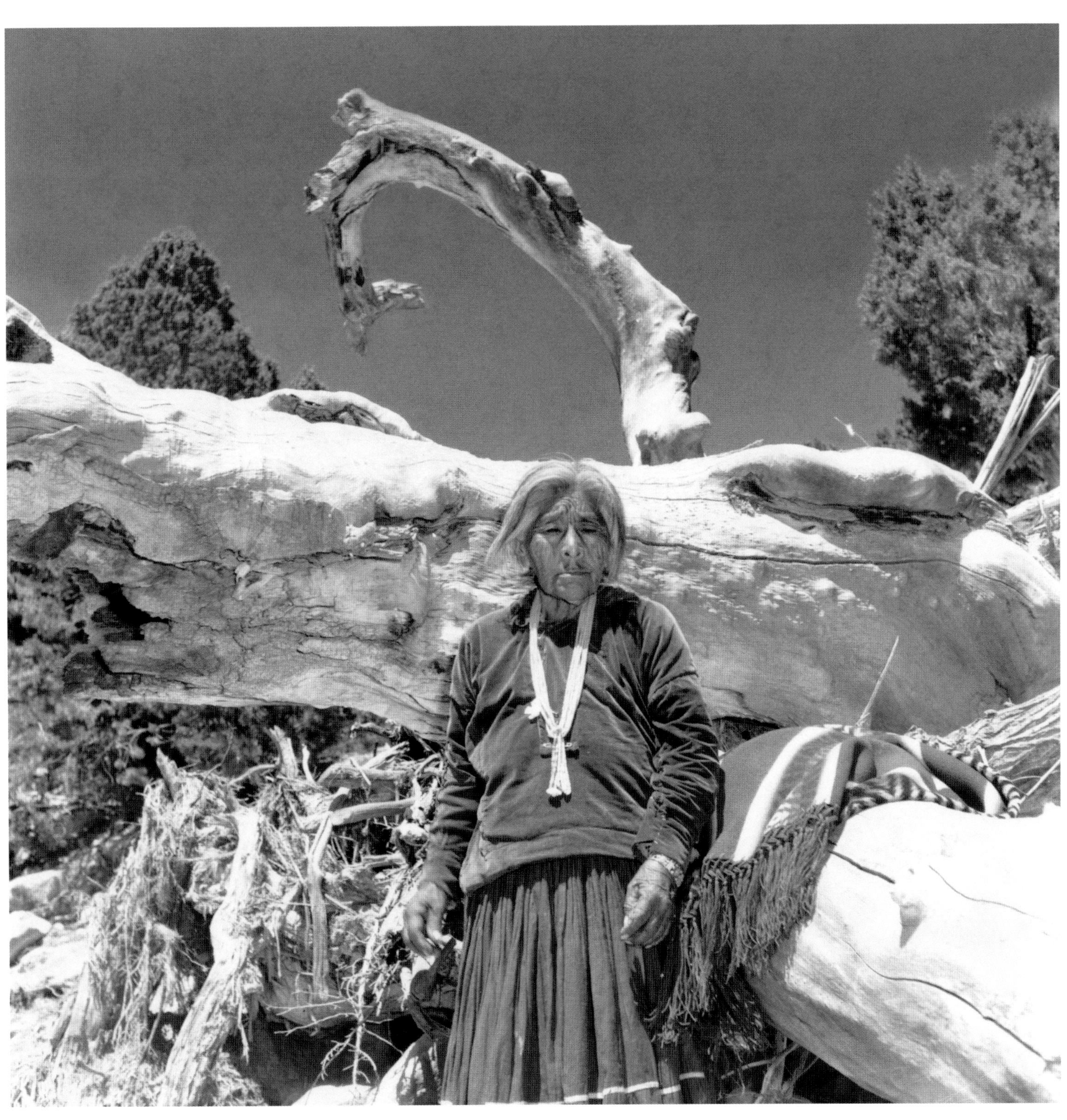

CABIN AT OLD MINE IN GLEN CANYON, JULY 24, 1940

This cabin is built tightly against a red sandstone cliff so that the cliff forms one wall. The other three walls are of rock with the cracks filled with mud; a dirt floor and a roof of iron and canvas complete the picture. Inside are a stove, two tables, and three cupboards; and an oil-drum heater stands in one corner. The latter seemed unnecessary until we read on the calendar in the cabin that ice came down the river one day in the winter, and that it had been snowy and blustery.

The mining equipment is all good and in first-class condition, showing that a great deal of money had been spent here. Their gold log, though, does not show a particularly good return.

Barry M. Goldwater
in *Delightful Journey*

Negative FPGD-29

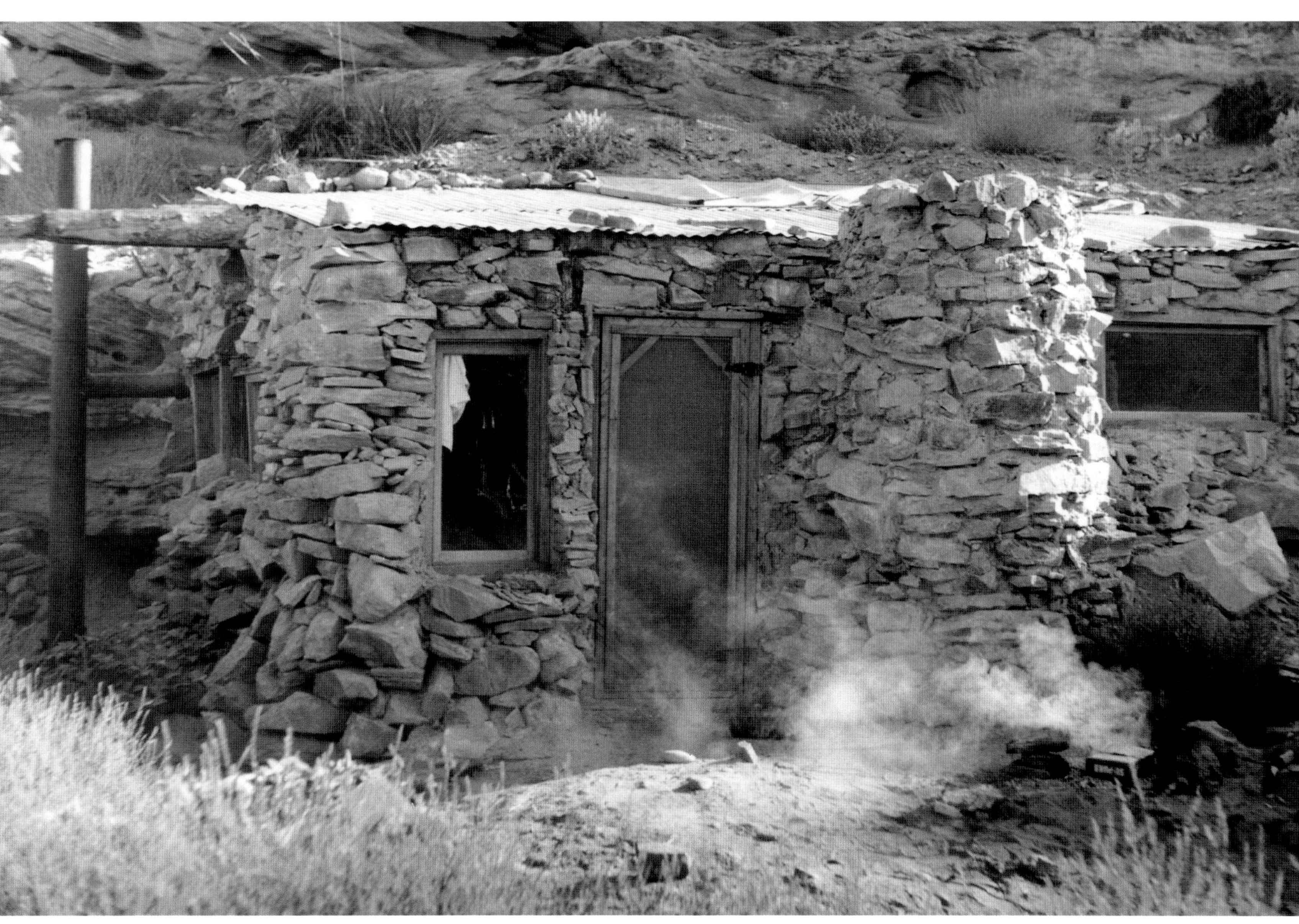

BEDROOM, DARK CANYON, JULY 18, 1940

We are seated here on the solid limestone that forms the bed of this creek. Hugh is making Mormon tea, sometimes called Brigham tea, from the ephedra plant. The Mormons have it nearly every night. We dined on spaghetti and meat balls and apricots, out of cans: and all that remains to close this fine day and allow us to retire to our beds of sand is for night to draw her blankets over the top of the canyon that towers nearly a thousand feet above us.

Barry M. Goldwater
in *Delightful Journey*

Negative FPGD-19

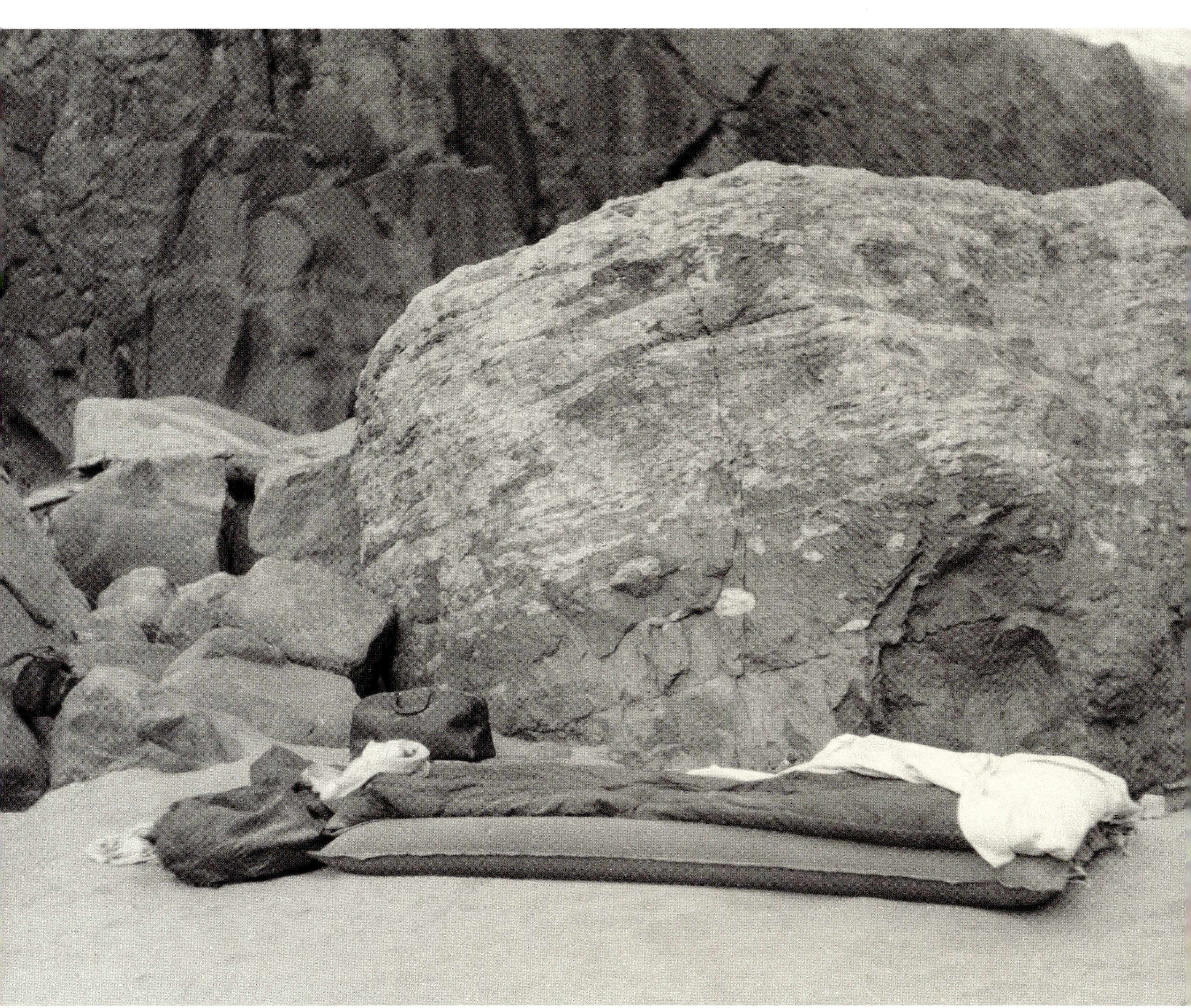

JOURNEY'S END, SEPARATION CANYON
AT THE HEAD OF LAKE MEAD, AUGUST 22, 1940

On August 22, 1940, the fateful river journey that inadvertently made Dad's name a household word throughout the state and region came to an end. Mom and my sister Joanne were there to greet the nine-member party at the culmination of the dramatic adventure, which Dad described with the sanguine resolve of a man both proud and humbled by his lofty achievement:

Skin that was white is now dark brown, but God knows what a bath will do to these tans. Levis that fit snugly at the beginning hang loosely over hips that are strangely thin again. Hands that were soft are hard and calloused. A face that was covered with inch-long whiskers is now clean-shaven. (The shaving operation involved scissors and two razor blades and a clogged drain in the hotel bathroom.) A body is tired and aching from exposure and work. A man has come home from doing something he had longed to do for a long time. He has seen the waters flow through canyons, the waters that flowed by places his forefathers built.

Barry M. Goldwater

Negative FPGD-90

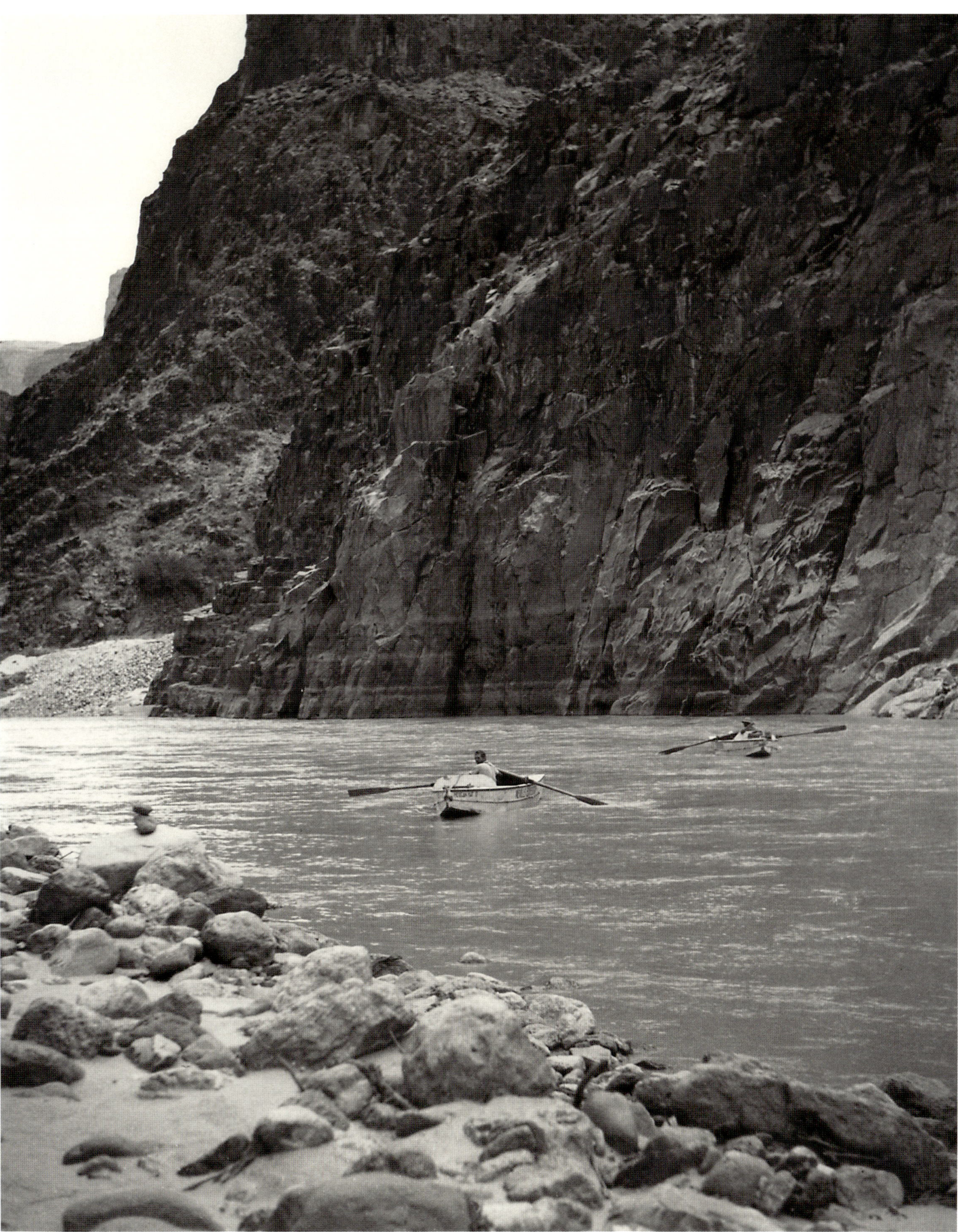

BOWKNOT BEND, LABYRINTH CANYON, JULY 12, 1940

Situated in the Labyrinth Canyon of the Green River, Bowknot Bend is appropriately named. The first great bend stretches five miles in length, before sweeping back to a point within a quarter mile of the starting point. A second great bend follows that extends nine miles, then verges back to a point within six hundred yards of the beginning bend. The overall configuration is that of a figure eight, which stretches approximately fourteen miles in length.

John Wesley Powell is credited with ascribing it with its present moniker, although Dad discovered evidence during his 1940 river voyage with the Neville Expedition that he had at least one visitor that preceded his visit. In his published diary of the eventful excursion, he recorded that "Just as the river enters the smaller knot, below and slightly to the right of center, is the May 16, 1836 inscription of Denis Julien, at Mile 72.6 left bank." Similar inscriptions were found as far south as Cataract, which further piqued Dad's historical curiosity.

Intrigued by the identity and background of the intrepid explorer, Dad set his sights on learning more about his past. These investigations led him to the writings of Charles Kelly, whose July, 1933 article in the *Utah Historical Quarterly* revealed that D. Julian had been a trapper and guide for the 1831 Robidoux Expedition and may have made as many as three trips to the region.

Through the force of his own imagination and keen abilities to calculate the odds, Dad offered his own assessment that Julian may well have "become the first modern victim of the rapids of the Colorado."

Negative 776

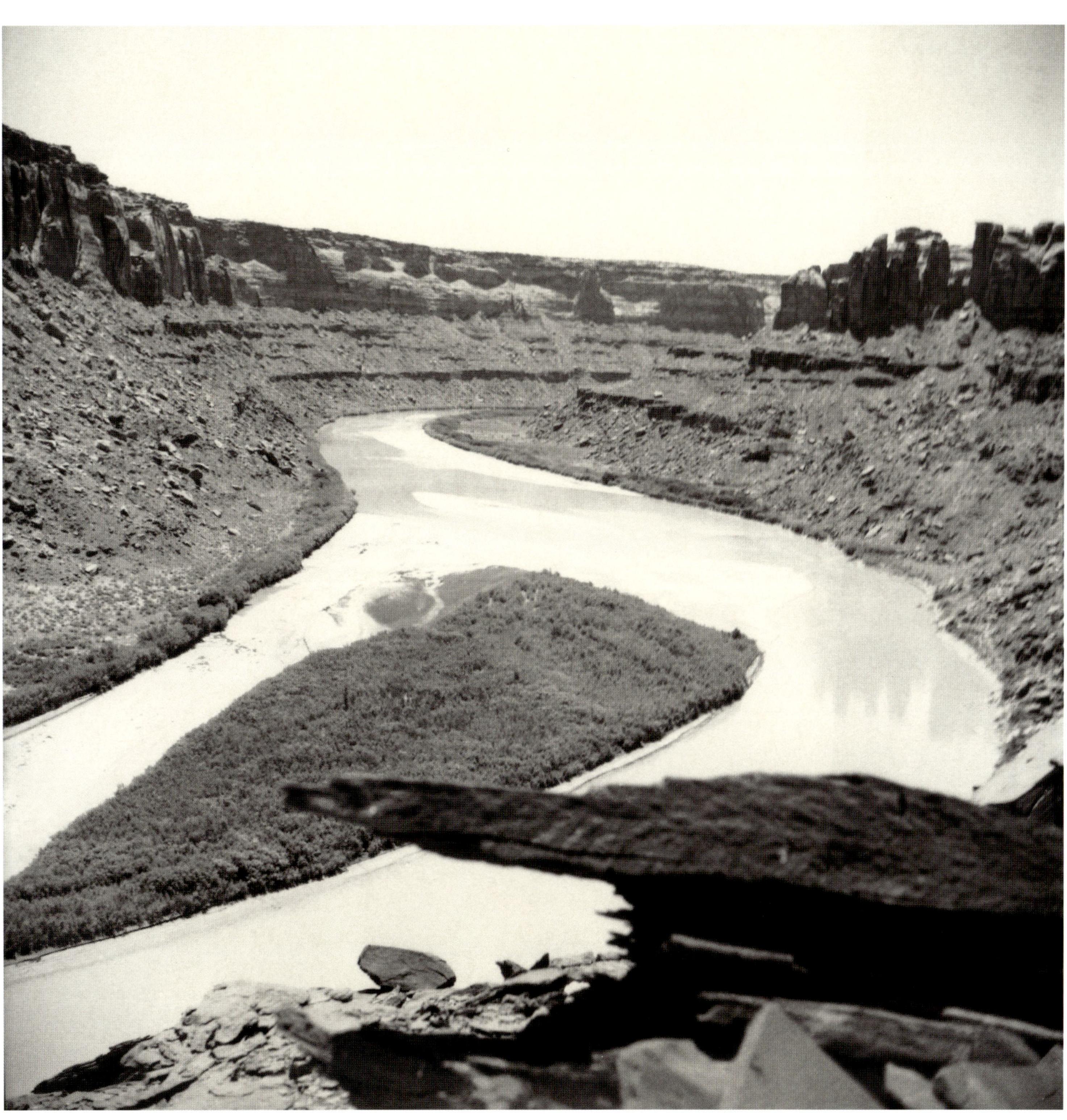

NAVAJO ELDER, 1967

Because Dad spent so much time in the northern part of the state, Hopis and Navajos served as his most frequent Native subjects. He respected their ways and customs to the extent that he made a deliberate effort to record their historic transition to modernity, often with mixed emotions. Later in life, he acknowledged that he "liked the Navajo reservation in the 1920s and 1930s when the Indians looked liked Indians," but he was hesitant to begrudge the transition for it meant a better life and greater opportunity for the Indians.

The distinguished face of the Navajo man featured here is one of many contextual character studies he engineered of Native faces across time, distance and unprecedented socio-economic and political change.

Negative 1088

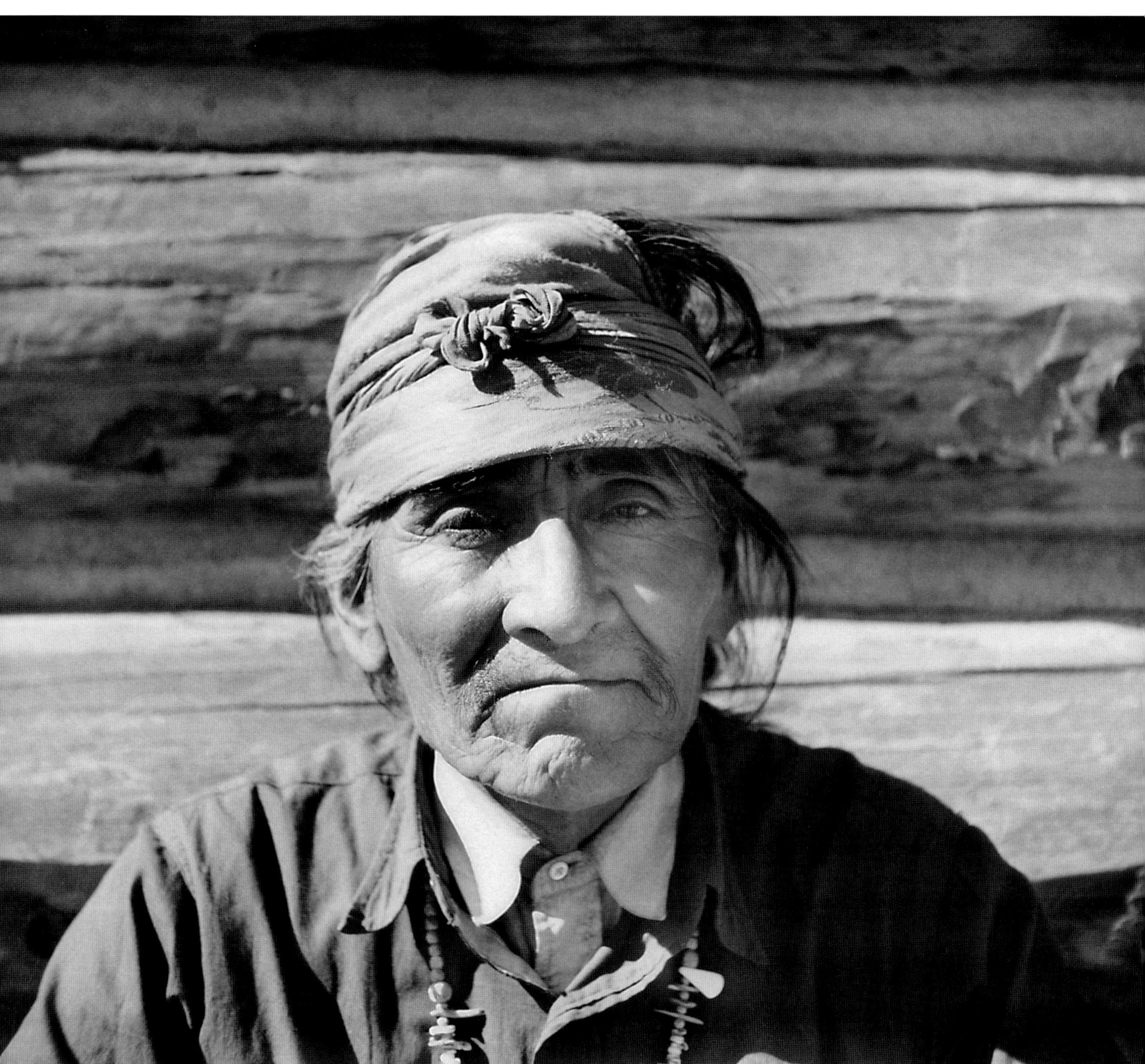

CHEMEHUEVI WOMAN, 1938

Native artists and artisans were favorite subjects in Dad's photography, primarily because of the intense appreciation he had for the discreet nature of their creative expressions. As the featured character study of the Chemehuevi basket maker reveals, he was particularly fond of capturing the artist in the act of making art both as a collector and amateur historian intent upon preserving Arizona as it existed during his lifetime.

The Chemehuevi people are indigenous to the Mohave Desert in California. They moved to the right side of the Colorado River after Charles D. Poston was appointed the first United States Indian Agent for Arizona in 1863, onto lands near present day Parker, which were left vacant when the Maricopas moved eastward.

Since the establishment of the Colorado Indian Reservation in 1865, they have shared the allotted lands with Mohaves, Hopis and Navajos. Their livelihood comes primarily from rental fees garnered from California based agro-business.

Negative 728

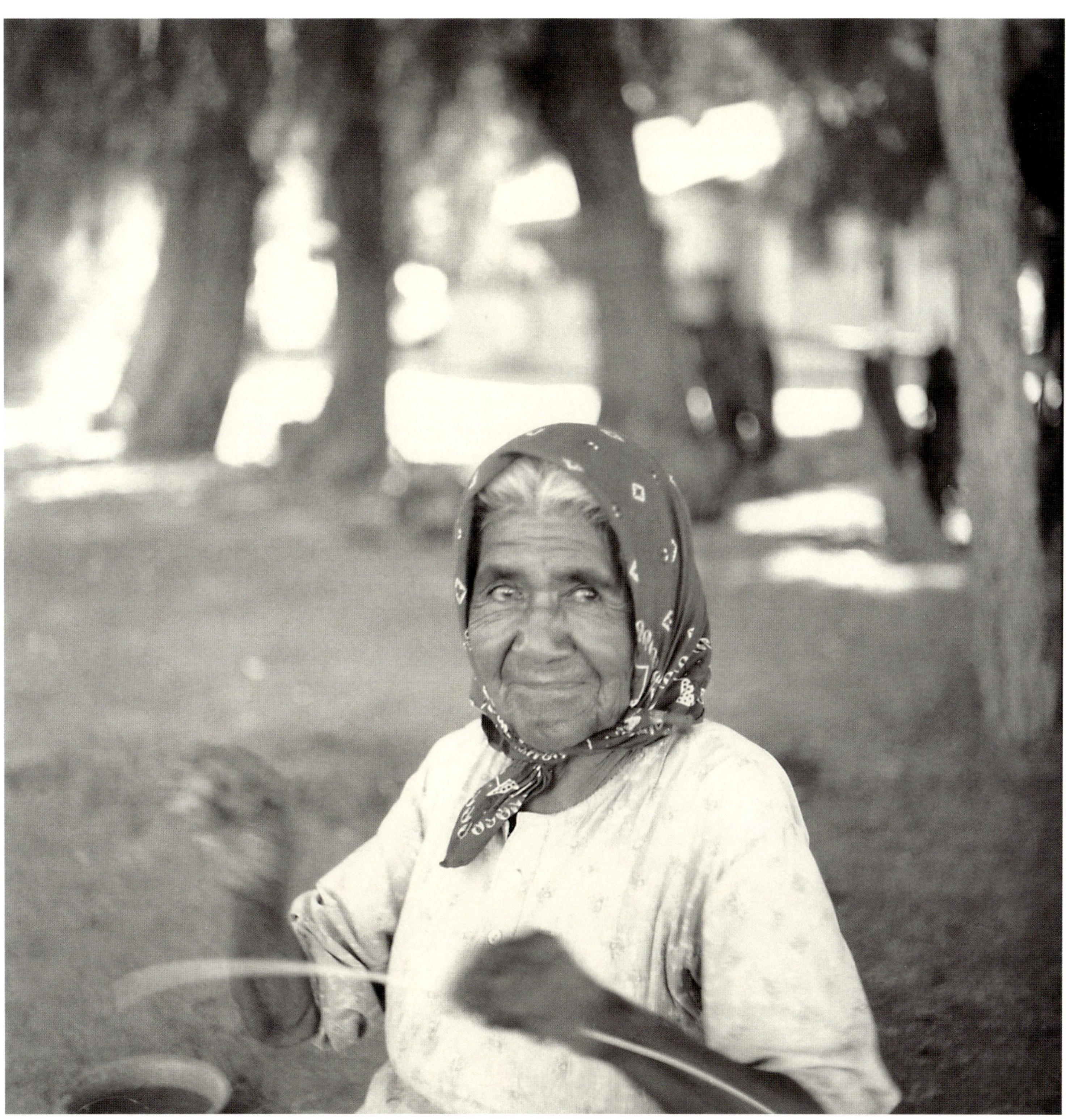

CENTURY PLANT, 1948

Throughout his life, Dad was a devoted scholar of all things Arizona, including its flora and fauna. He knew enough to seek out and recognize the unusual like the famed Century Plant, which lives up to thirty years or so, flowers and then dies.

A native of Mexico, agave plants are sometimes called "century plants." This unique agave is a short-stemmed perennial with a tall, thin stalk that grows from 10 to 14 feet high and boasts gray-green, spiny leaves that extend 10 to 18 inches in length. Agave plants enjoyed a variety of uses among the Native Peoples, including food, fiber, medicine, weaponry and soap. Sap from the young flower stalk on some varieties of agave can be fermented and distilled into tequila.

Century Plants are typically found along washes and dry, rocky slopes in both the Sonoran and Chihuahuan Deserts. Large amounts of water are required for it to produce the small, white flowers seen growing from the spiny stalks extending from its basal rosette.

Negative 773

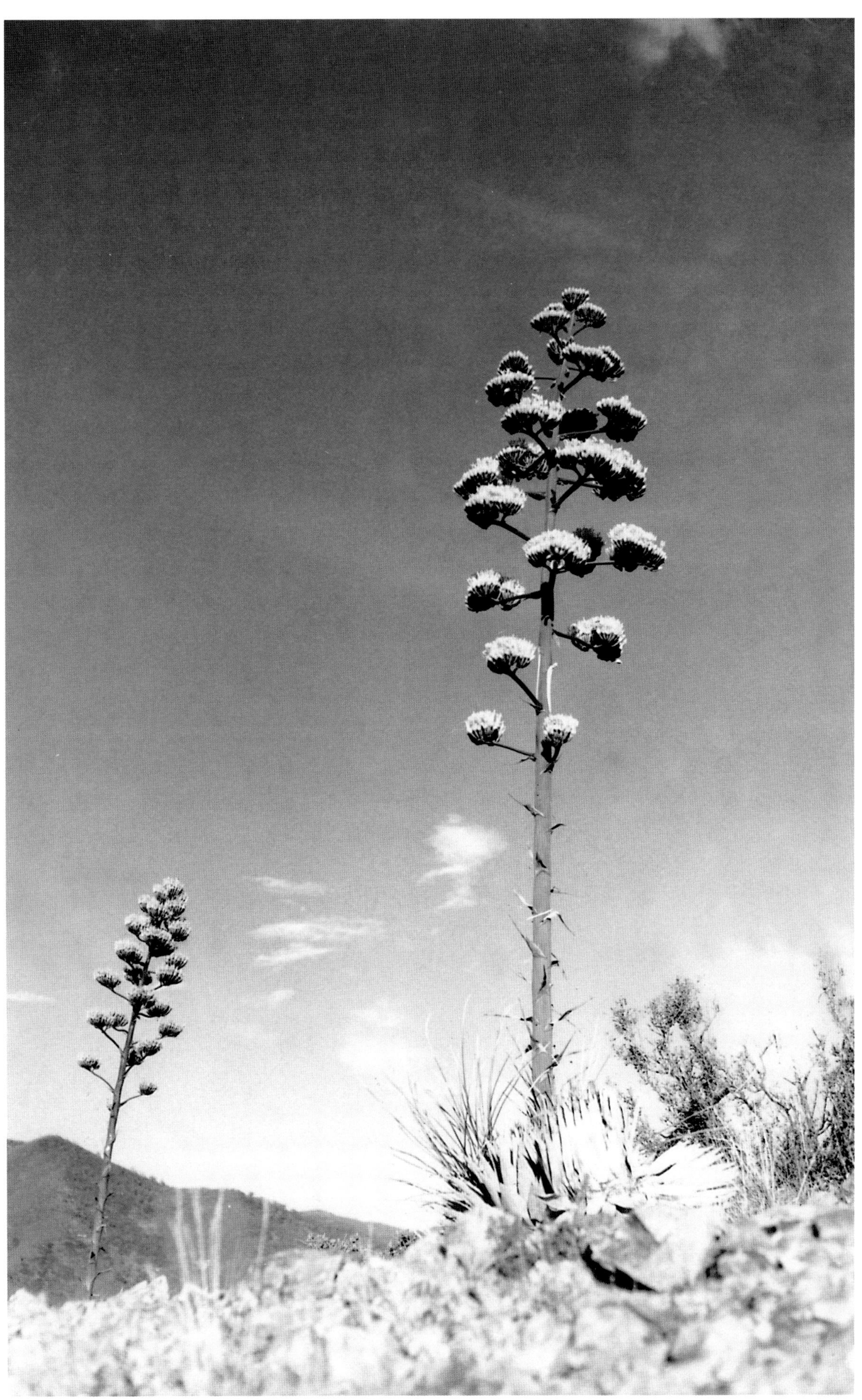

HOPI CHILD, 1959

This little bucket of fire was the daughter of Mr. Potter, a Hopi who lived in the Grand Canyon at the Indian shop. The one right across from El Tovar. When she would see me coming, she would run up to me and want me to take her picture.

Barry M. Goldwater to Evelyn S. Cooper
Summer, 1987

Negative 859X

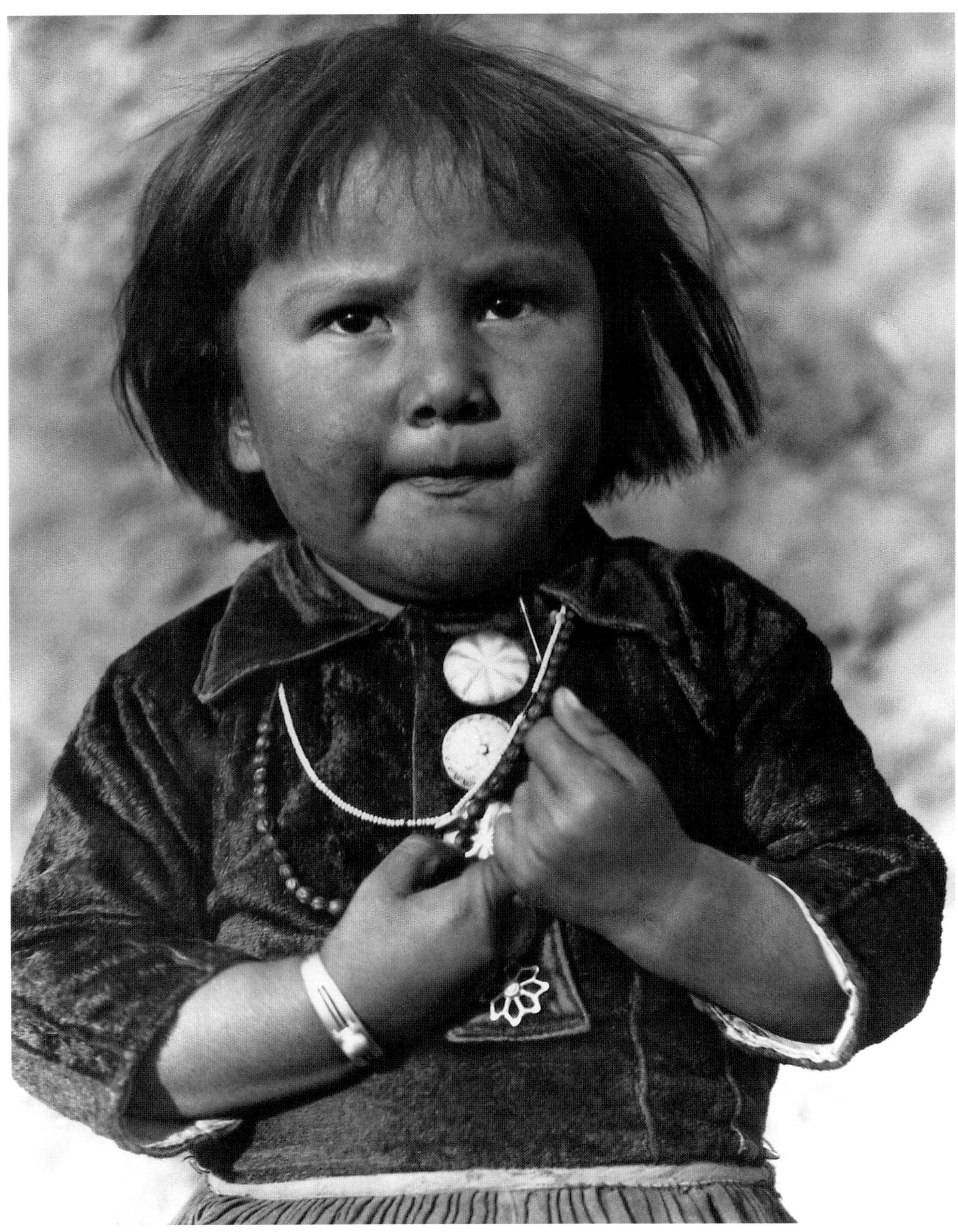

SUNDUST FAMILY PORTRAIT, 1959

This is Sally Sundust and her four children. I knew her from the Indian School. The boy in her lap fell off of a wagon and the wheels ran over his legs. I drove her down to the hospital at Tuba City, 90 miles away. She didn't have the faith in white doctors that I had. She liked medicine men. The next night, or two nights, she got a horse and got the kid out of the hospital and rode him all the way back up there on horseback.

I later flew that boy and his mother down to Phoenix and had a good friend of mine here—a doctor—look at him and see if there was anything he could do. Years later, I ran into that boy on the reservation and he was all crippled up.

Barry M. Goldwater to Evelyn S. Cooper
Summer 1987

Negative 1097

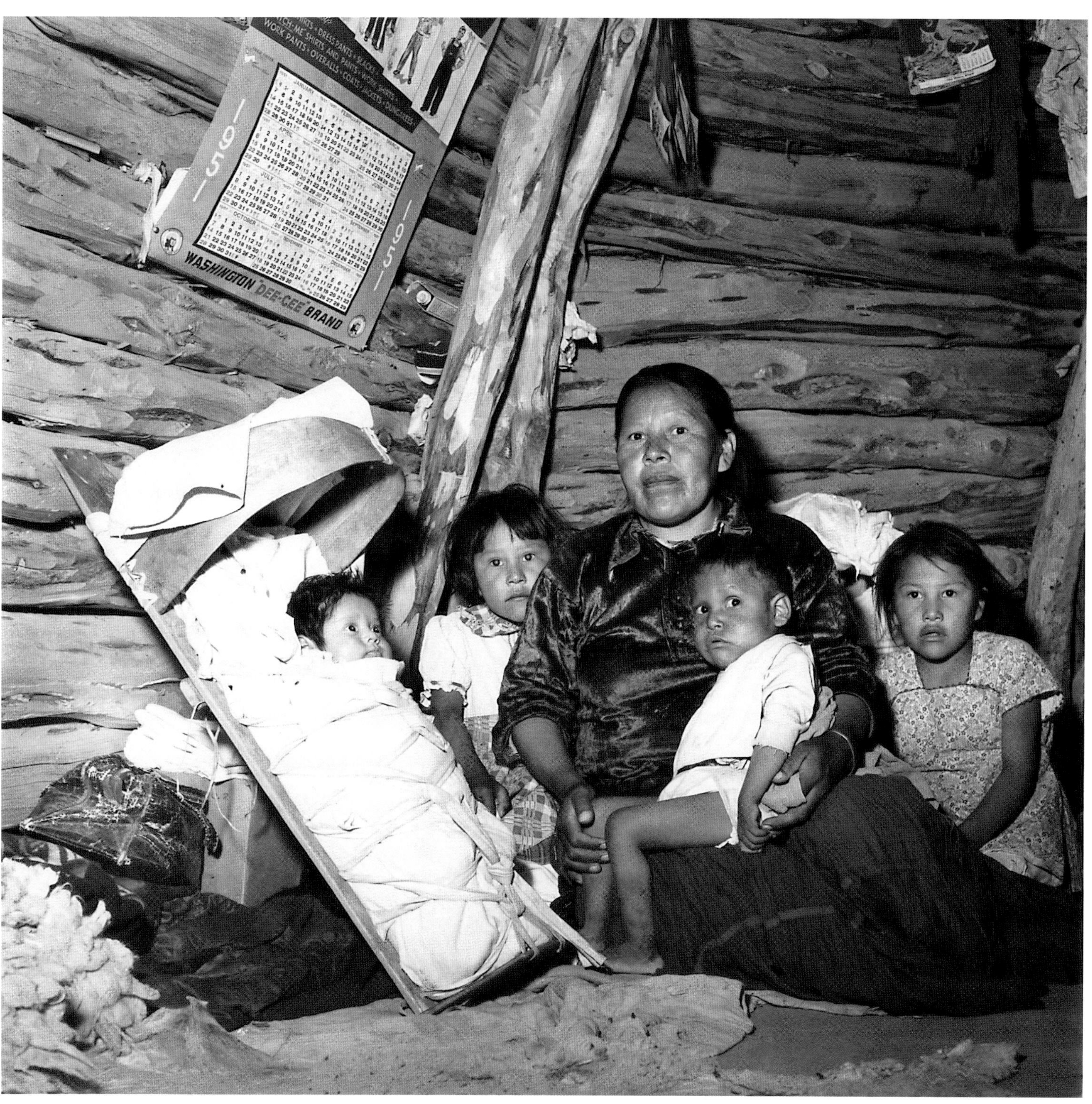
DRESS PANTS • SLACKS •
MATCH-ME SHIRTS AND PANTS • WORK SHIRTS •
WORK PANTS • OVERALLS • COATS • JACKETS • DUNGAREES
1951
JANUARY
FEBRUARY
MARCH
APRIL
MAY
JUNE
JULY
AUGUST
SEPTEMBER
OCTOBER
NOVEMBER
DECEMBER
WASHINGTON "DEE-CEE" BRAND

THE CHIEF, 1948

This man is a Navajo who lived up in the Paiute country, which is north of Navajo Mountain. This is one of my favorite pictures. When I do it from the proper negative, there's more down here and you get the face of this little girl in the background. I just call it "The Chief."

Barry M. Goldwater to Evelyn S. Cooper
Summer 1987

Negative 79319

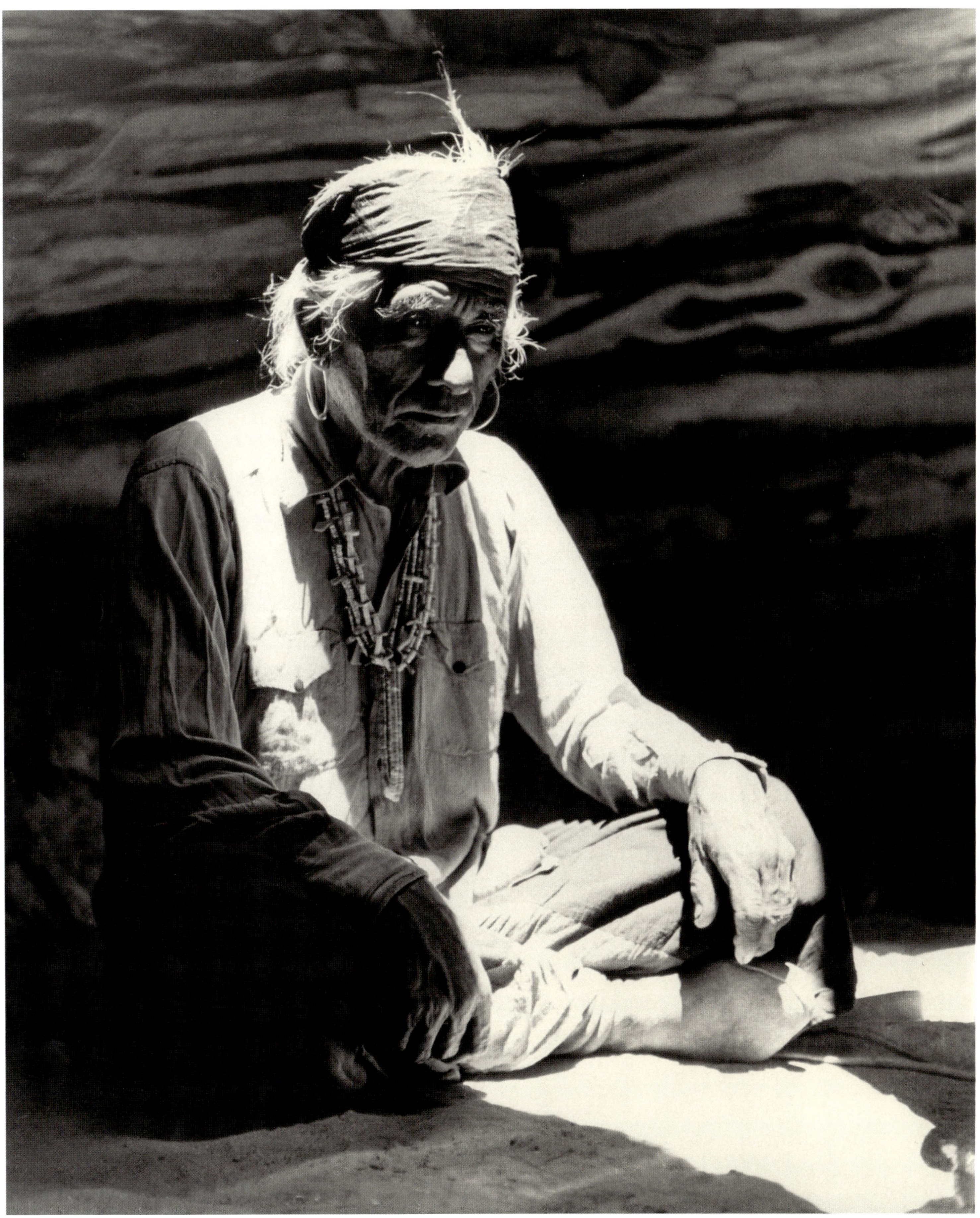

NAVAJO MAIDENS, 1956

I call the girl on the right the spinner, because she has a spinning wheel in her hand. She spins the raw wool into threads the other girl will use to make the rug with. This was taken up on the Navajo Reservation.

Barry M. Goldwater to Evelyn S. Cooper
Summer 1987

Negative 53

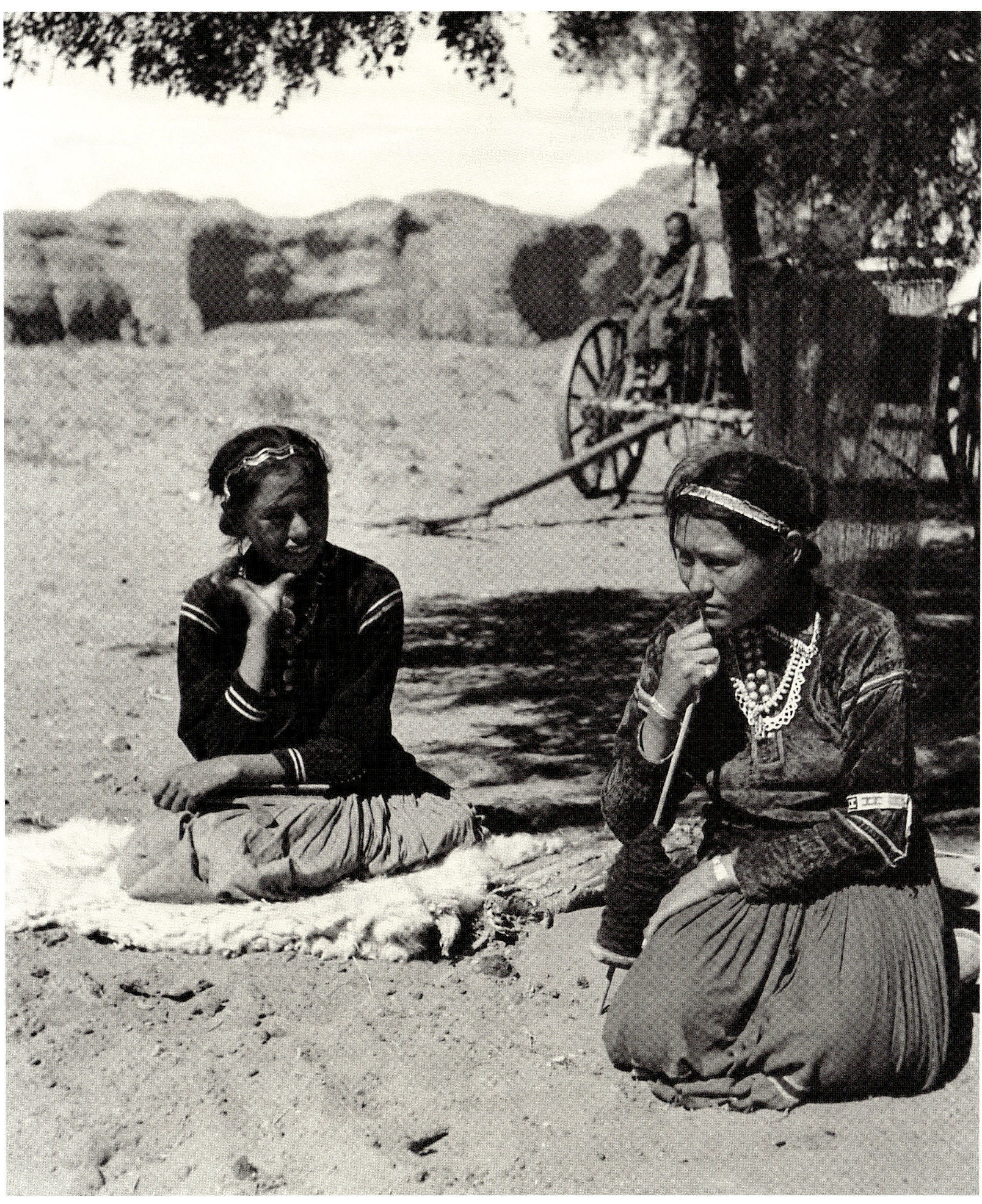

WATERWAY, 1954

Detail was a facet of Dad's photography that tended to stop short of his willingness to take the time to record on the spot the date and location of his negatives. The present image is offered as a symbol of the confusion that omission often engenders.

When my daughter Anna printed many of the negatives contained in this volume, she used the identification Dad recorded on the sleeve of the negative. After studying the present image, I have serious reservations about the accuracy of the cited location of "Tapeats Creek," a noisy waterway that rushes into a gorge in the Grand Canyon.

Because the photograph itself is a study in fine aesthetics, we decided to include it here as an example of both Dad's artistic skill and disinterest in saying in words what he felt was best conveyed in two dimension.

Negative 775

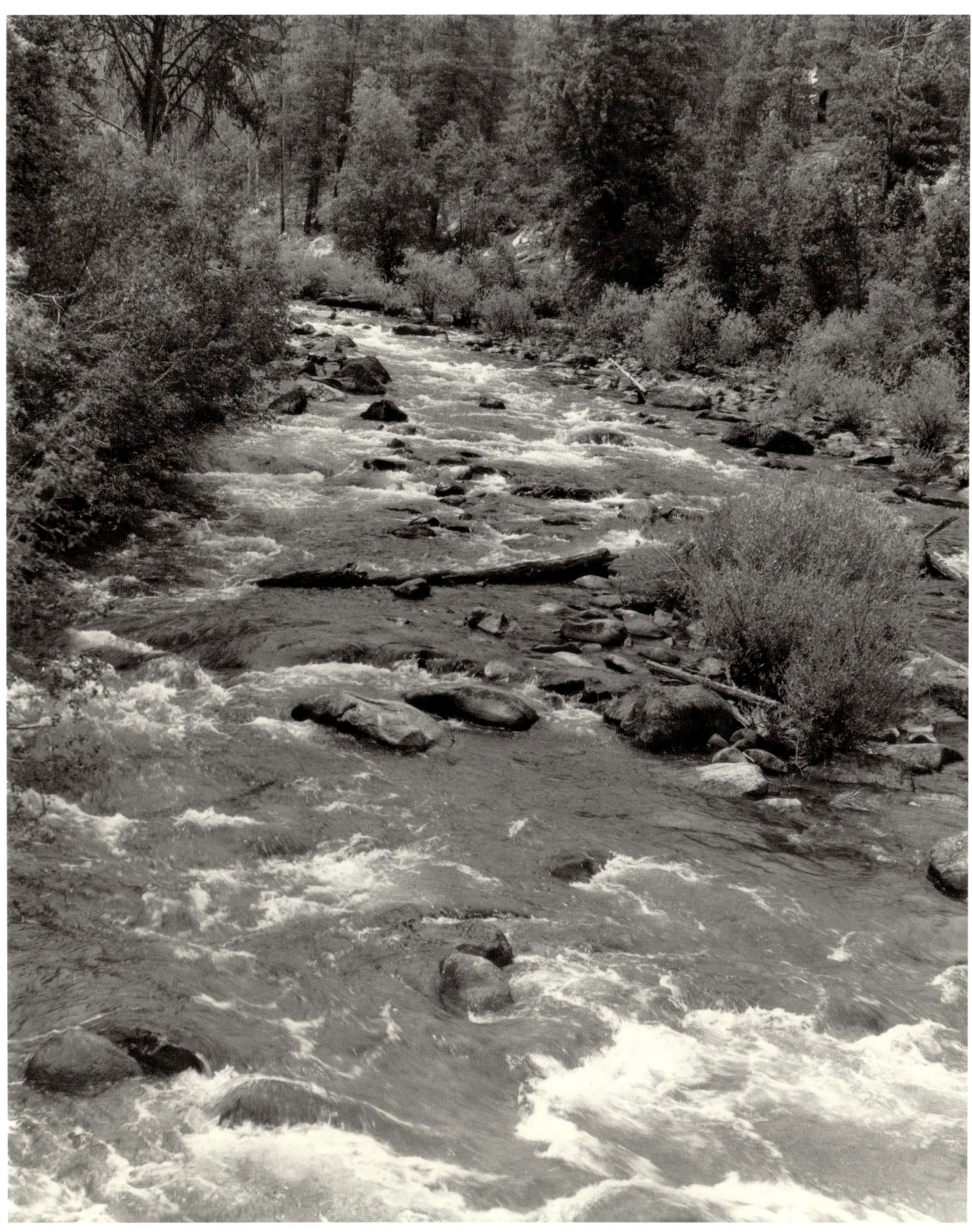

WHITE MESA, 1967

Situated in Coconino County, White Mesa is the proper name given to a white wall sandstone mesa that boasts an elevation of approximately 6800 feet.

Its namesake is rumored to be a controversial Arizona Argonaut named James White, who claimed to have navigated the Grand Canyon on a raft in 1837, several years prior to John Wesley Powell's maiden venture. According to his colorful tale, his traveling companions (Capt. C. Baker and Henry Strole) forfeited their lives on the trip. White felt sure he would have suffered a similar fate were it not for his personal ingenuity in engineering an escape from the canyon. Learned opinion classes White's story as more fabrication than fact, since he lacked either evidence or eyewitness testimony to lend credence to the daring deed.

Although White Mesa's distance from the Grand Canyon may raise questions about James White as the man behind its name, the captivatingly scenic nature of the setting leaves little doubt that it is one of Arizona's most aesthetically engaging natural jewels.

Negative 1084

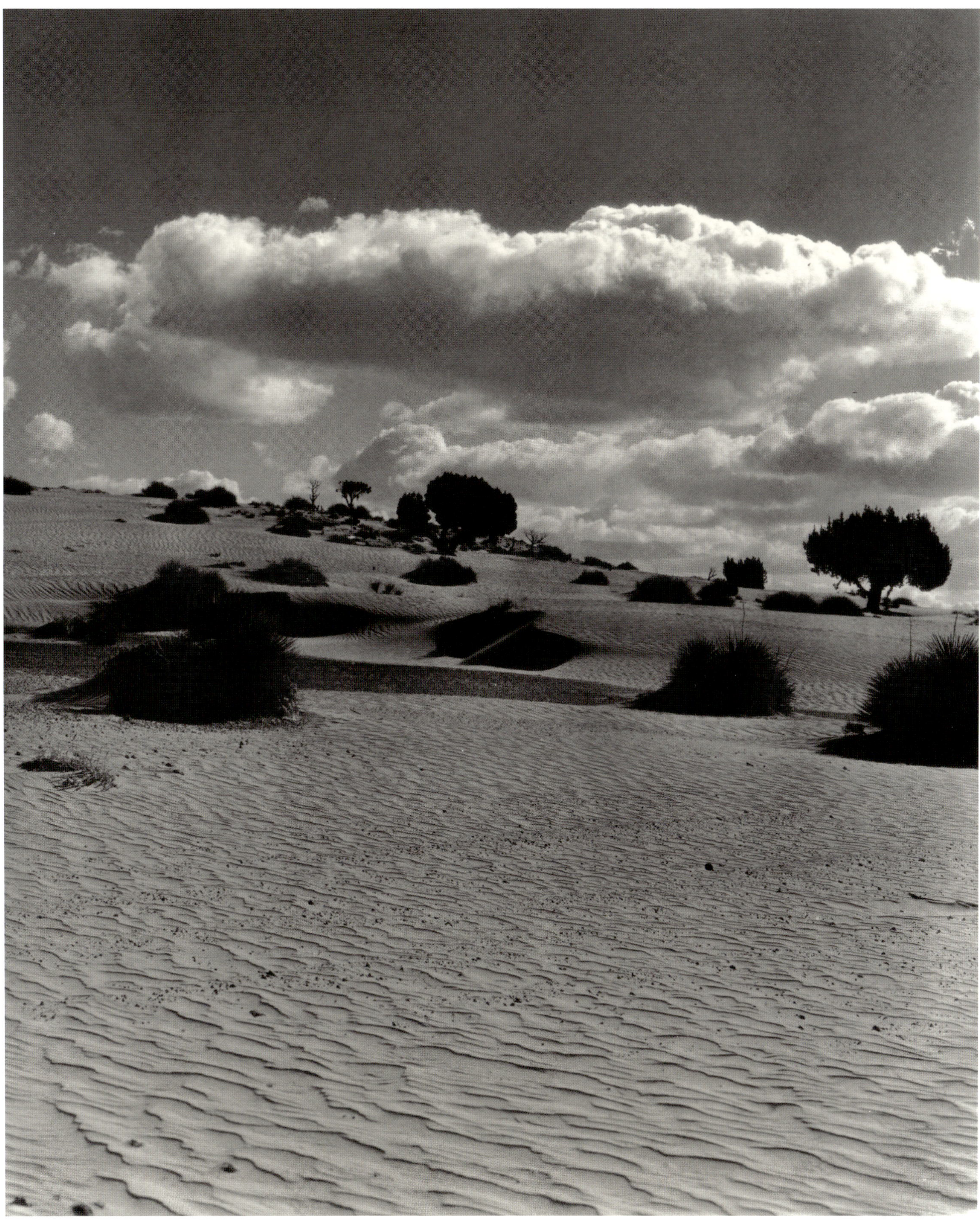

SAN FRANCISCO PEAKS FROM MORMON LAKE, 1967

The magnificent San Francisco Peaks have served as a magnet to photographers since the camera first came west in the middle decades of the 19th Century and Dad proved no exception. Because he took the time to learn the history through both Indian and mainstream eyes, he was a walking repository of lore, legends and scientific facts about the area, which he generously shared in both words and pictures.

Situated in northern Arizona in the midst of extinct volcanic activity that extends across an area of about three thousand square miles, the San Francisco Peaks consists of three mountains, Agassiz, Fremont and Humphreys, which range in elevation from 6,000 to 12,000 feet. The mountains hold a special place in the beliefs of both the Navajo and Hopi, particularly the latter, who view the range as the home of their spirits.

The present name was conferred in 1629, when members of the Franciscan Order then stationed at Oraibi named the range in honor of their founder, St. Francis of Assisi. During the Spanish Era in southwestern history, they were called by a variety of names: explorers Farfan and Quesade called them Sierra Sinagua in 1598, Father Garces opted for Sierra Napoc (maybe a phonic attempt at Navajo) during his 1776 canvas of the area, Sierra de los Cosninos (also believed to be Indian inspired) and Sierra Cienega, the name used on a number of early Spanish maps.

Dad's chosen vantage point in the featured image is Mormon Lake, so named for early settlers to the region, who planted a dairy and sawmill on the west side of the critical watering hole in 1878. It was used as a grazing area for the hundred or so cows the Mormon settlements of Sunset, Brigham City and St. Joseph jointly purchased to stock the dairy.

By 1900, the drainage channels for the grazing field had become clogged, which caused water to collect into a shallow lake that extended about four miles long and three miles wide. During drought cycles, the lake literally disappears, which may explain why General James Henry Carleton alone chose to include it on early military maps of the area.

Negative 1096

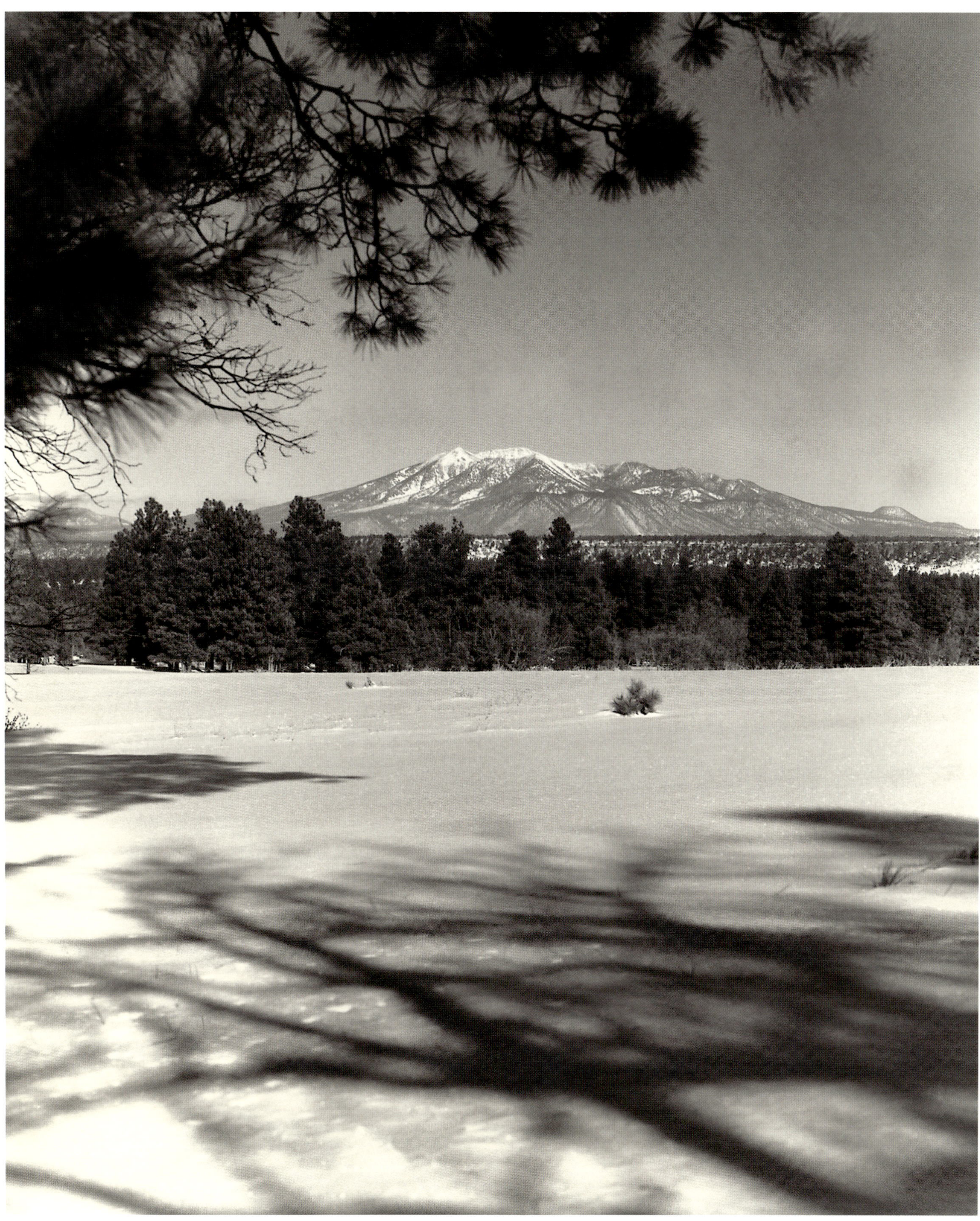

SNOWFALL, SAN FRANCISCO PEAKS, 1957

In this intimate view of the San Francisco Peaks following a snowfall, Dad captured the drama explicit in a blanket of moisture spread across an otherwise arid terrain.

Evident in the frame are several of his favored motifs such as clouds, contrast and the stark and compelling geometrics unique to the unsullied reaches of Arizona's natural landscape.

Taken from a vantage point somewhere in the vicinity of Lake Mary, the image carries its own brand of reverence.

Negative MPG-01

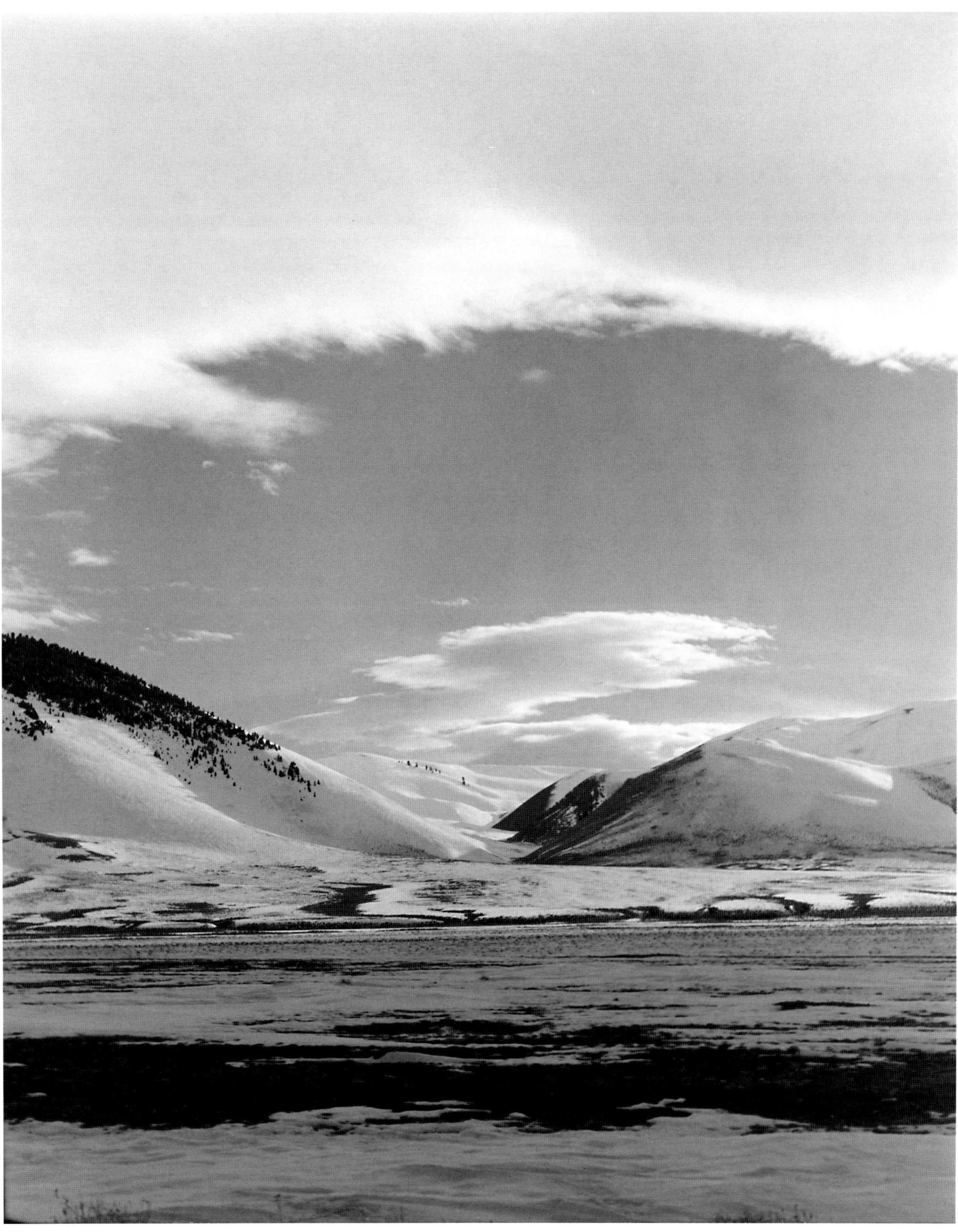

JEGINI YAZZIE BEGAY, 1949

Indians were second only to the landscape in Dad's photographs of Arizona for reasons ranging from personal acquaintance to historic significance. Because he spent so much time in the canyon country to the north, Navajos and Hopis command a starring role in his canon.

Dad selected faces on the basis of his own personal aesthetic, which meant an express favoritism toward dignified faces imbued with the special dignity laid only by the hands of time. Because he was hyper aware of the manifold changes Indians faced in modern times, he was especially sensitive to human subjects, whose dress and demeanor symbolized that difficult transition.

Despite our best efforts to the contrary, we were unable to locate biographical information on Jegini Yazzie Begay, nor did Dad leave a written account explaining their association. The mainstream suit next to traditional jewelry and hairstyle suggests that sitting probably emanated from some haphazard encounter on the Navajo Reservation either within the subject's Hogan or at a trading post, maybe even Rainbow Lodge.

Negative 876X

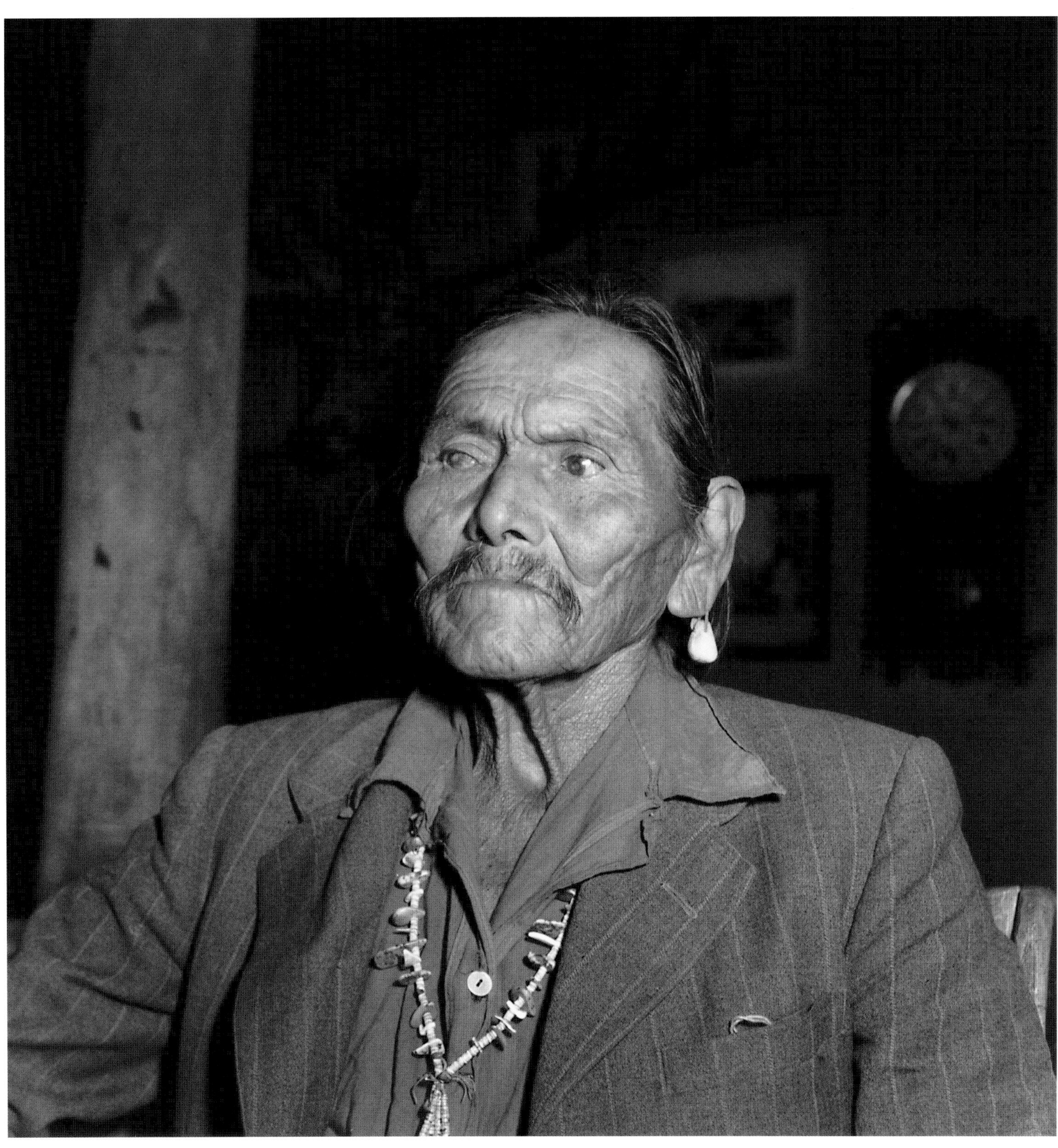

THE POWER OF ADVERTISING, 1948

Of the many trips Dad took down the Colorado River, the 1940 Neville's journey proved the most significant in a historic sense. He earned his laurels as the seventy-third person to retrace John Wesley Powell's second river expedition and made what is believed to be the first feature length, documentary film shot in Arizona. Anxious to share his achievement with others, he toured the state showing the film to sell out audiences, a venture that helped set the stage for his rise in politics.

The featured photograph was taken outside the Wickenburg Way Theatre and is included here as an example of the various promotional techniques he used to publicize the highly popular tour.

Negative 1338X

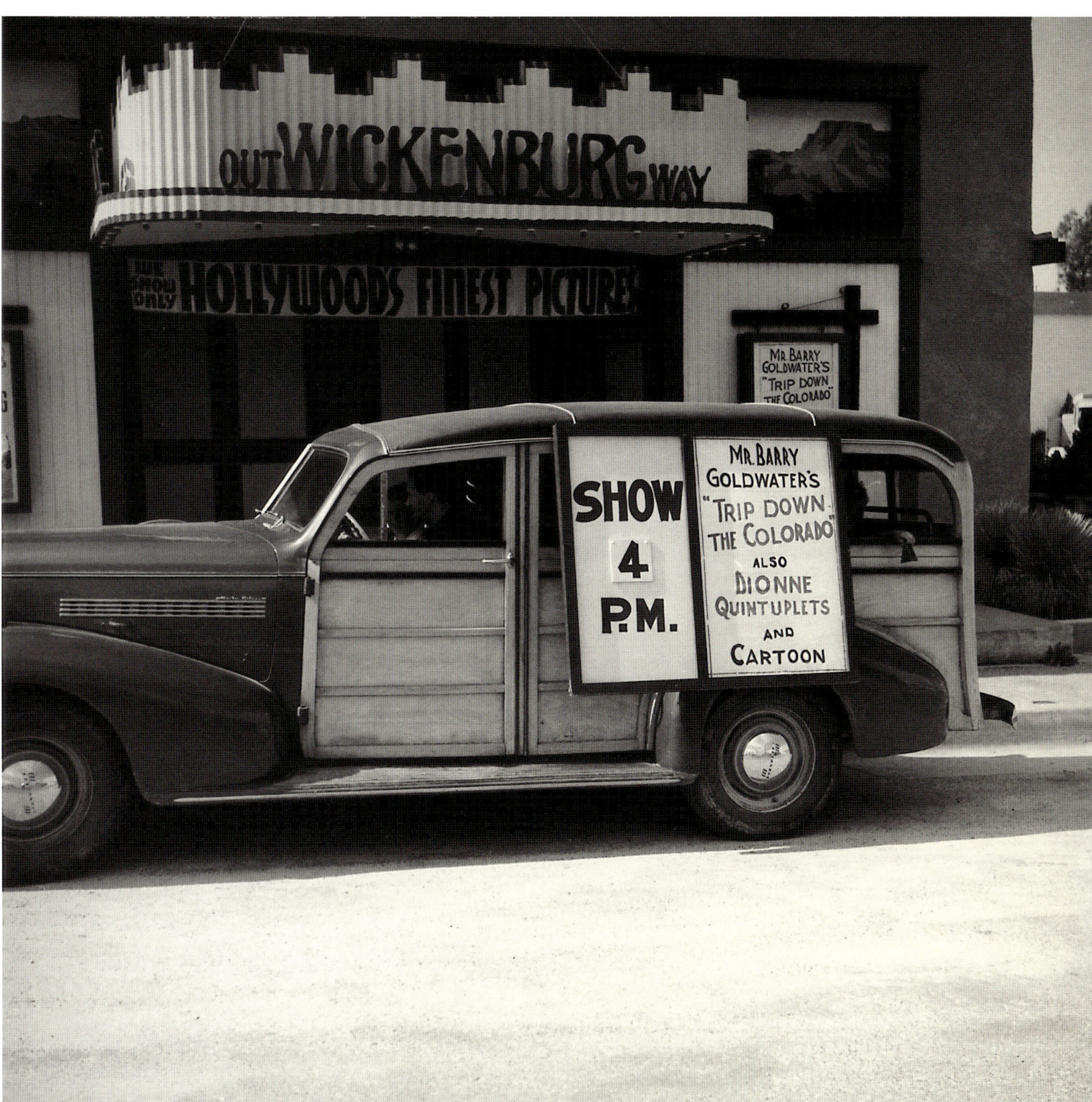

out WICKENBURG way
THE SHOW ONLY
HOLLYWOODS FINEST PICTURES
MR. BARRY GOLDWATER'S
"TRIP DOWN THE COLORADO"
SHOW
4
P.M.
MR. BARRY GOLDWATER'S
"TRIP DOWN THE COLORADO"
ALSO
DIONNE QUINTUPLETS
AND
CARTOON

THE HOPI, 1949

It was a Hopi custom that the chief rarely ever spoke publicly on important matters. A promising young brave always did so. If anything went wrong, it was the brave's fault. If things went right, the chief was praised...

My interest in the Hopi began when I started collecting their unusual Kachina carvings while still in my teens. These first dolls were purchased with nickels and dimes, as well as in trade for different objects. Kachinas are religious symbols that represent the earth, wind, and other spirits. The Hopi are pantheistic.

Barry M. Goldwater
in *With No Apologies*

Negative 858X

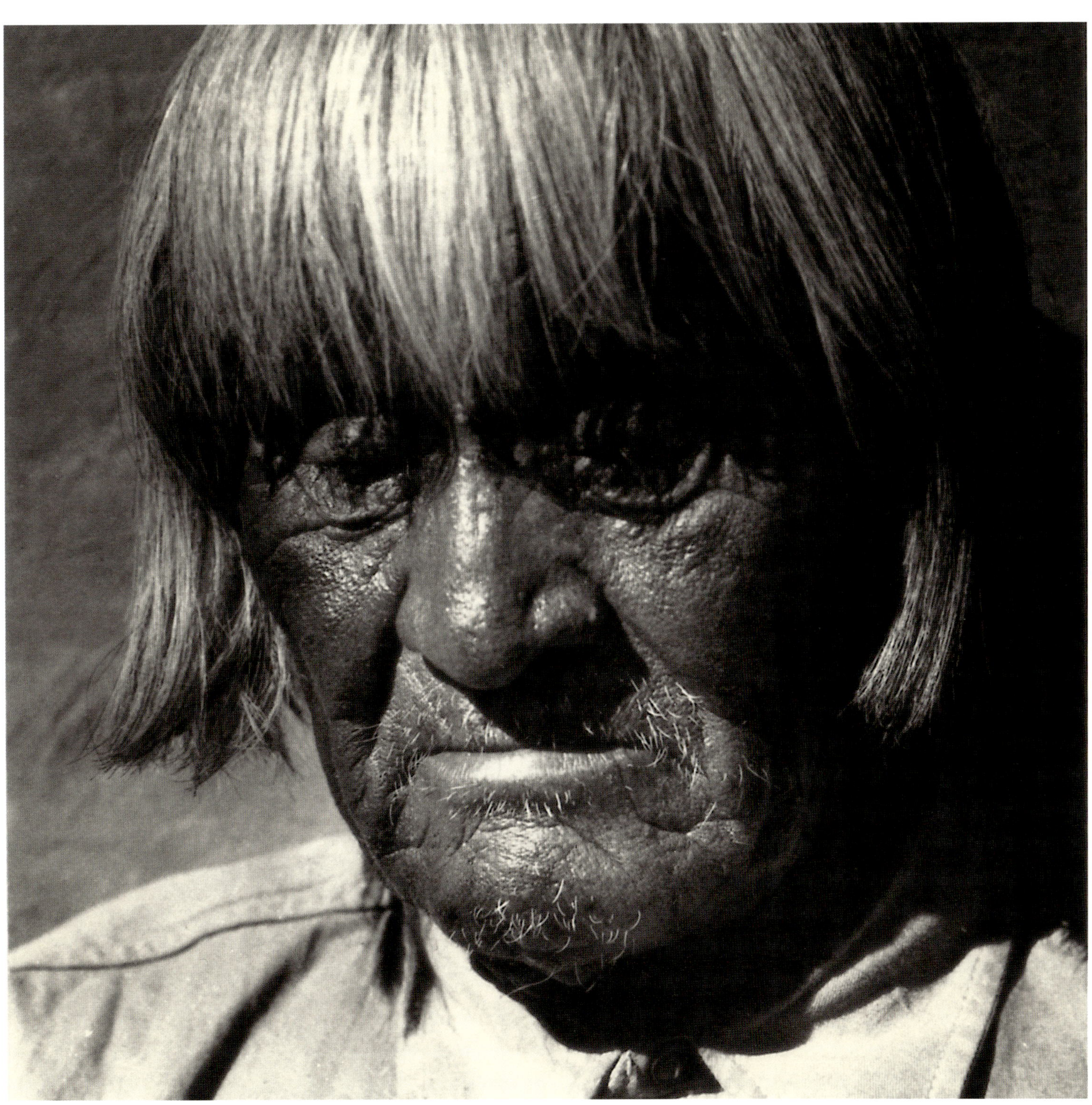

Dad had an eye for the picturesque, whether natural or manmade. He particularly fancied scenes that offered a combination of the two such as this stunning view of the windmill located near Pipe Springs in the vicinity of Wolf Hole.

The name Wolf Hole is rumored to have been conferred by Major John Wesley Powell, because he translated the Indian word for coyote as wolf. Drought and years of overgrazing have left the land nearly barren, but in bygone days Pipe Springs played a pivotal role in the development of the region. The first telegraph line in northern Arizona ran from Kanab to Pipe Springs.

Negative 2443-A

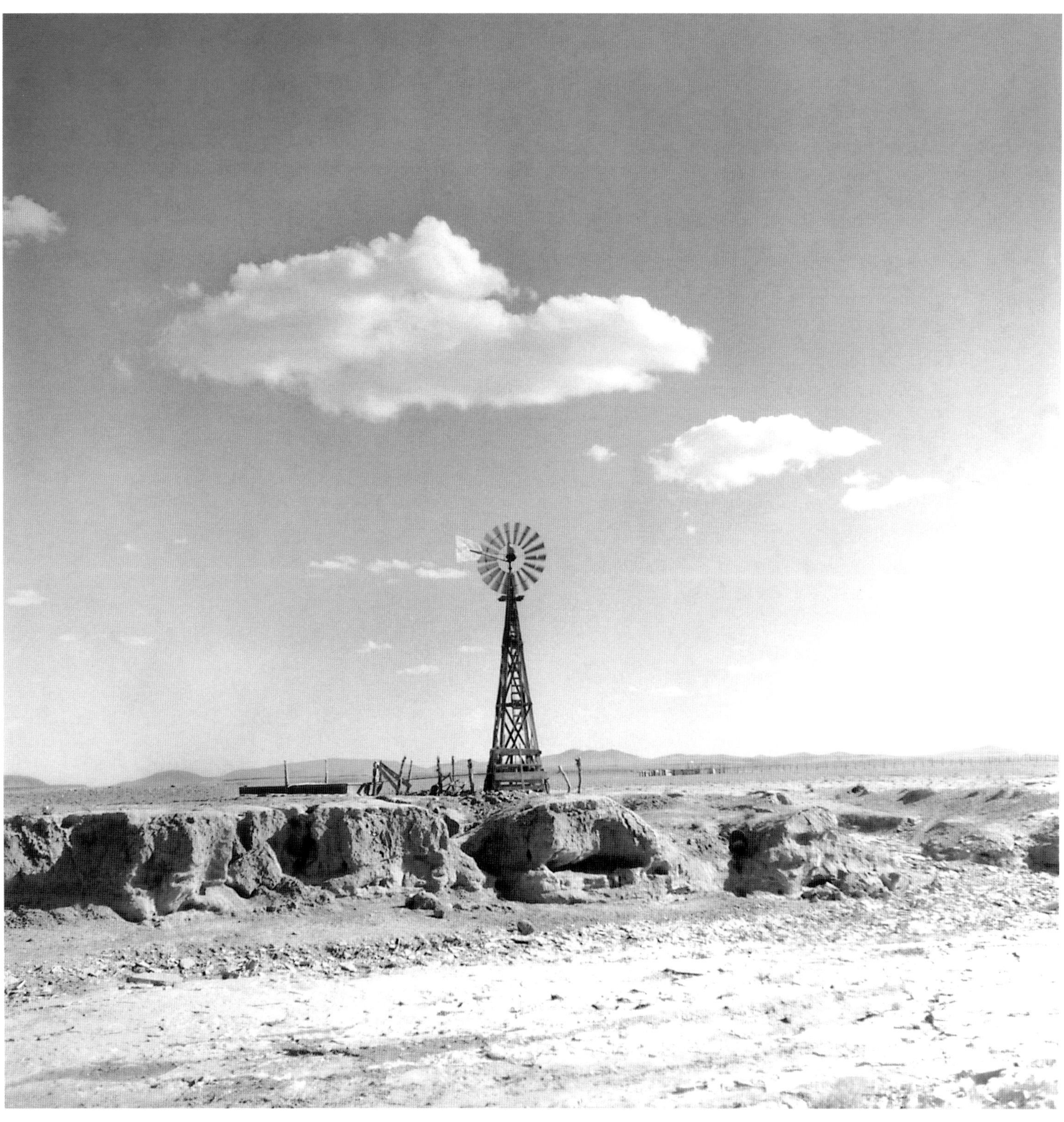

MAURICE AND ROSEMARY KNEE, INFORMAL PORTRAIT, 1967

During Dad's frequent excursions into the northern part of Arizona, he often traveled in the company of other mainstream residents who shared his fascination for the people and places that continue to lure a worldwide audience of tourists to the state annually.

The Indian jewelry clad couple featured here against the unique skyscape of Monument Valley are Maurice and Rosemary Knee, who were long time family friends. Rosemary was the sister of Mike Goulding, who helped start the Goulding's Lodge, which served as setting for the photograph. They were fun people to be around, as well as gifted linguists. Both spoke fluent Navajo, which is arguably one of the most difficult languages for non-Natives to master.

Negative 1033

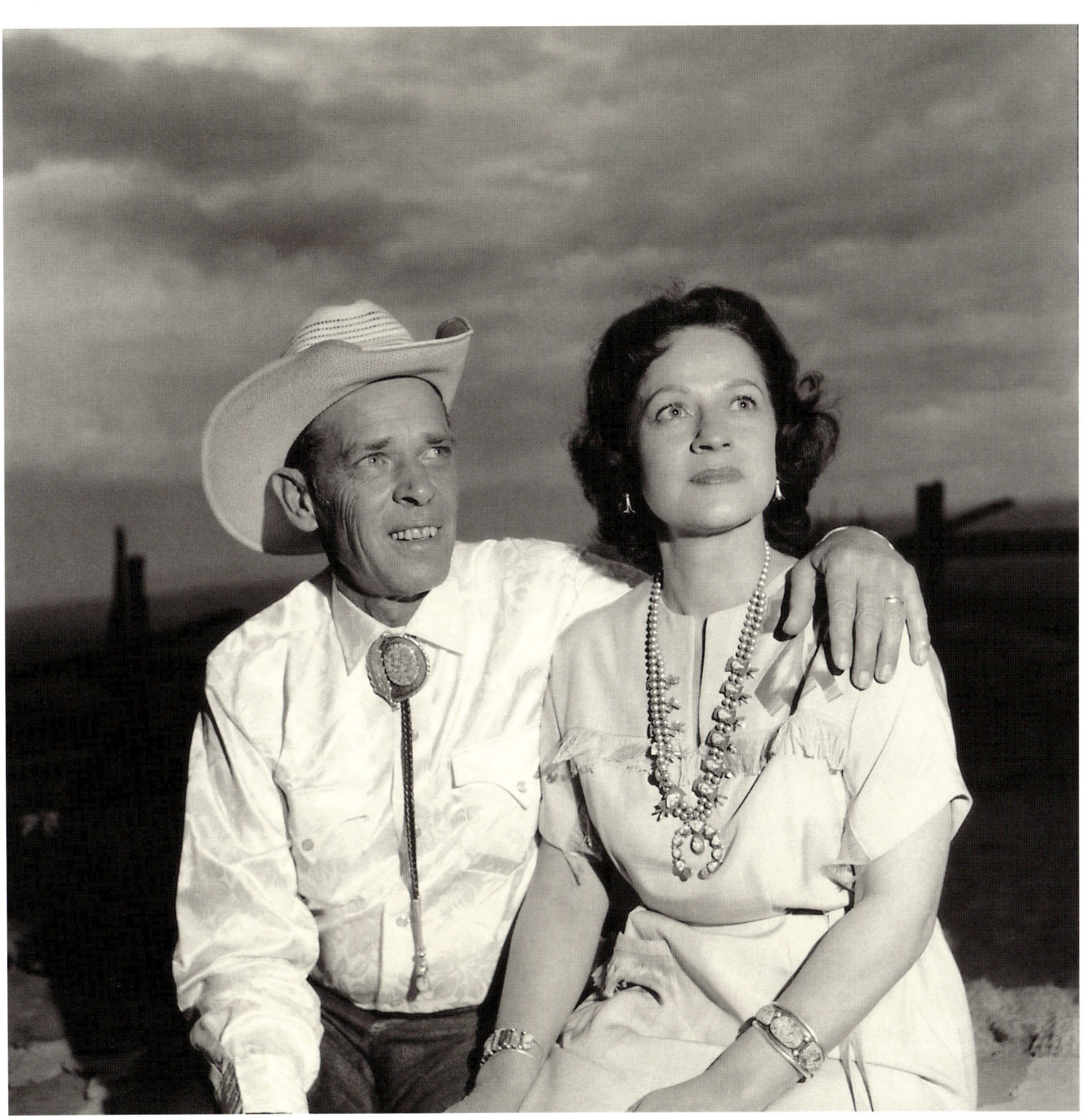

NAVAJO MAN AT SPRING, 1959

Reflecting the pride and dignity of the Navajo people, Dad continually strived to capture character traits as well as location. This photograph was taken against the sandstone cliffs of Canyon de Chelly in northeastern Arizona and is considered one of Arizona's premier canyons.

Its history includes one more example of man's inhumanity to man when in 1863, Colonel Kit Carson sent a detachment of soldiers under the command of Captain Albert Pfeiffer into the Canyon resulting in the surrender of the Navajos and their subsequent relocation to Bosque Redondo, New Mexico.

Negative 807

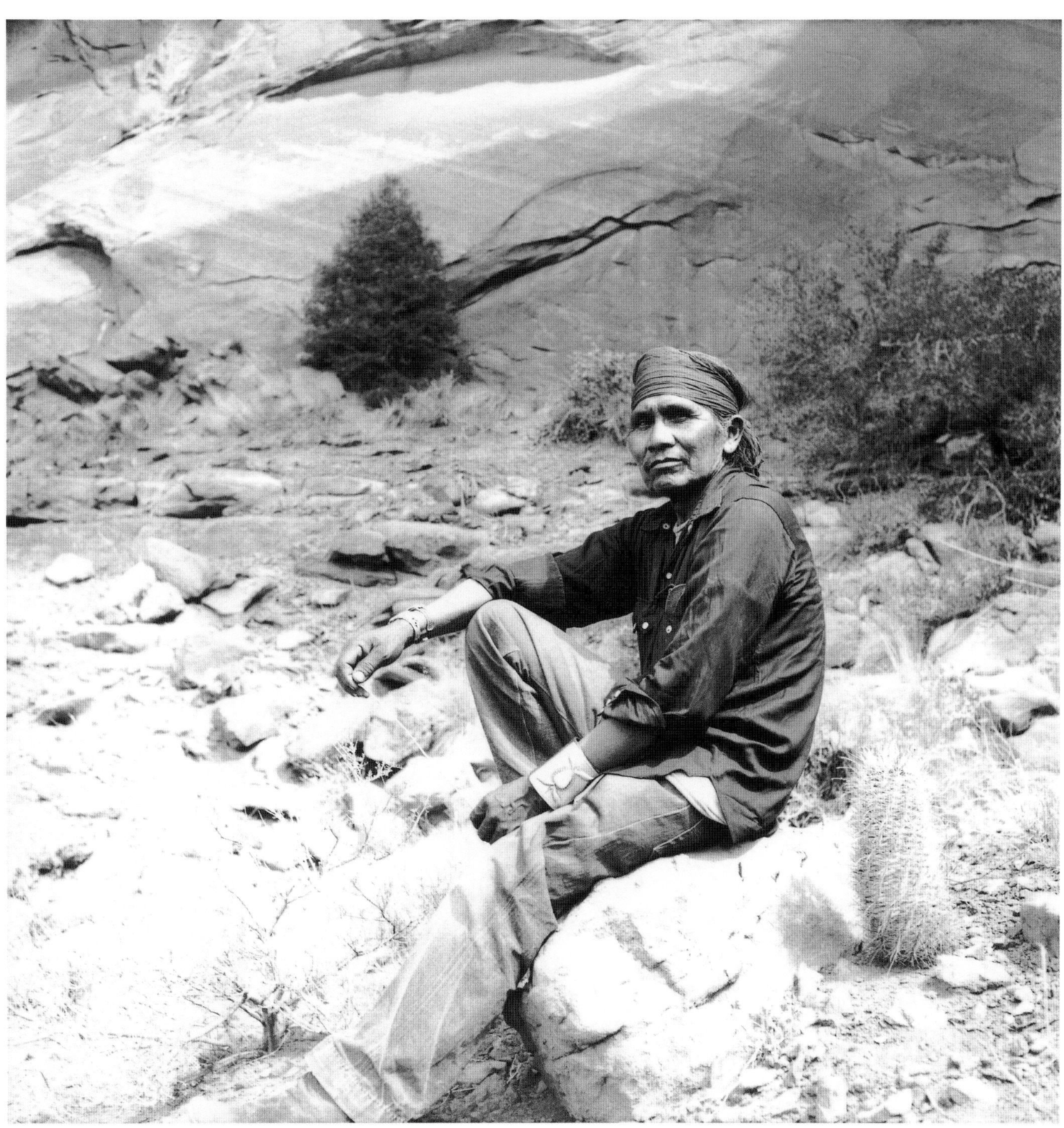

WEAVER'S NEEDLE,
SUPERSTITION MOUNTAINS, 1938

Popular legend holds that famed scout Pauline Weaver served as namesake for this unique natural configuration, but an equally pervasive volume of lore credits the title to the fact that the rock formation resembles a needle formerly favored by weavers.

Weaver's Needle (elevation 4525') is situated within the Superstition Mountains, which are perhaps best known as the home of the famed Lost Dutchman's Mine. The Pima Indians have a legend centered upon a great flood, the foam of which caused the broad white streak in the limestone extending for several miles along the face of rough and treacherous range located east of Phoenix.

Because of the legend, the Spanish referred to these mountains as the Sierra de la Espuma, or "mountains of foam." Their current name probably emanates from the valley dwelling tribes who viewed the mountains as a place of bad medicine, since it was alleged that those entering them never returned. The real culprits may have been Apaches, who typically watched from the peaks and ambushed any soul daring enough to enter the mountains. When the United States cavalry engaged in two skirmishes with the raiders and returned to tell the tale, most of the fire was taken from the fear. Rumors of a mythical mother lode in gold soon generated another round of folklore in which Weaver's Needle inevitably played a part.

An early rumor held that a Mexican lover, fleeing the wrath of his sweetheart's angry father, took refuge in the Superstitions and discovered a large gold deposit. In order to take advantage of the find before the land was transferred to the United States as part of the Gadsden Purchase, he returned to Mexico and led his entire village to the area to assist him in the digging. When every member of the party was loaded with gold, the motley miners headed home, only to be ambushed and killed by Apaches. All four hundred men were killed, but two small boys survived, grew to manhood and returned to the area with a partner in 1870. They had barely begun to dig when a Dutchman with a long white beard murdered them for the mine.

During the ensuing years, countless would-be miners attempted to retrace the Dutchman's trail, eight of whom reputedly died by his hand. He passed away in 1884 without revealing details of the mine except to one neighbor, who was unable to follow his directions, thus earning the mine its present name.

As an interesting sideline, the so called Dutchman was a prospector named Jacob Waltz, who allegedly worked at the Vulture Mine in Wickenburg, until he was fired for 'high grading' ore, a popular euphemism for stealing.

Negative 2438A

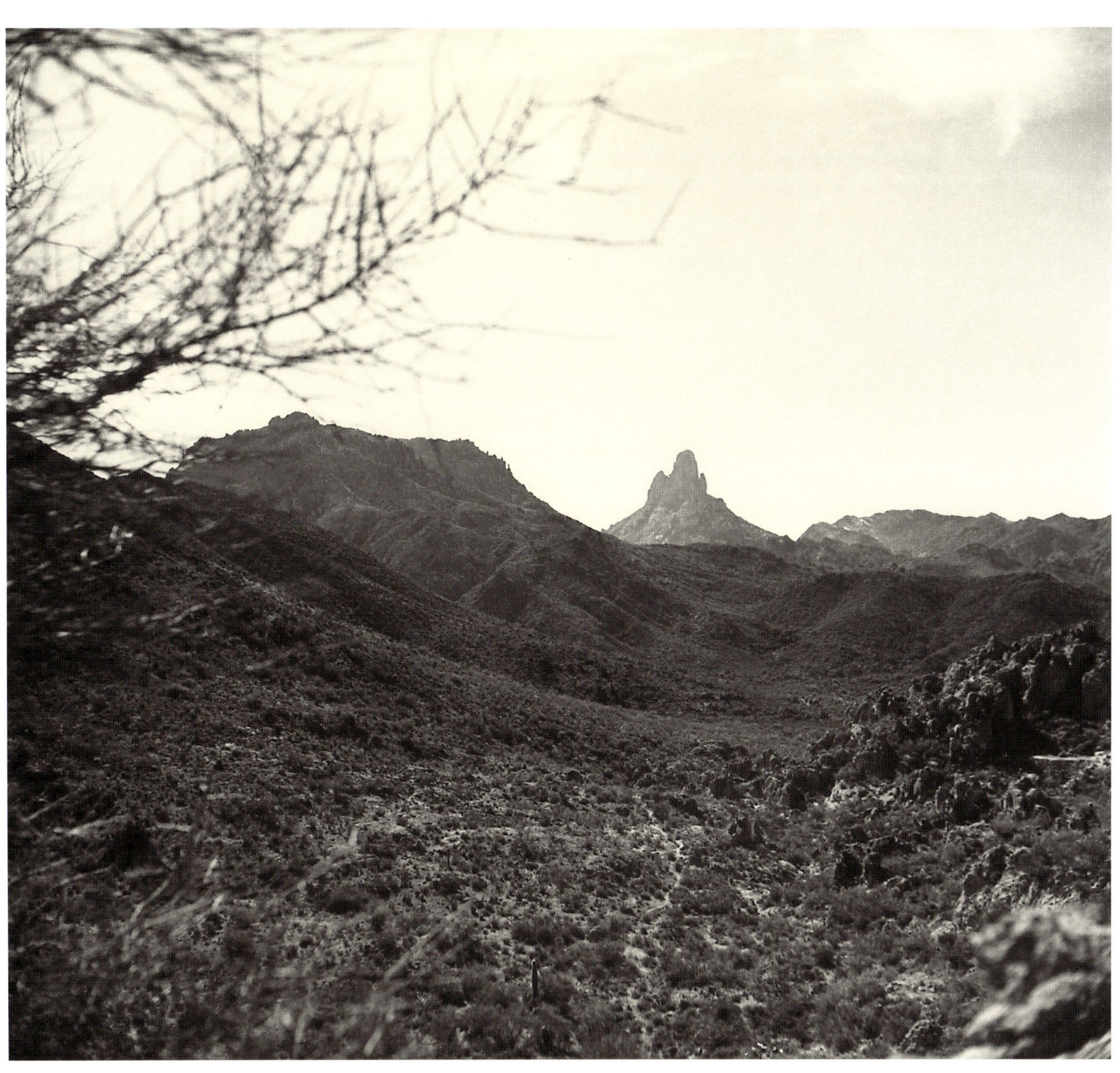

ROOSEVELT DAM, 1936

In the wake of the devastation wreaked by a severe drought in 1890, Phoenix city fathers and central Arizona farming interests decided that a water storage system was the only plausible answer to their woes. They joined ranks and founded the Salt River Valley Water Users' Association, which immediately petitioned the federal government to construct a dam on the Salt River, under the auspices of the National Reclamation Act of 1902.

After considerable political haggling and a full litany of unforeseen construction problems, the Roosevelt Dam was finally dedicated on March 18, 1911 by its namesake, President Theodore Roosevelt, who sagely predicted that Phoenix would forthwith transform into, "one of the richest agricultural areas in the world."

Negative 134

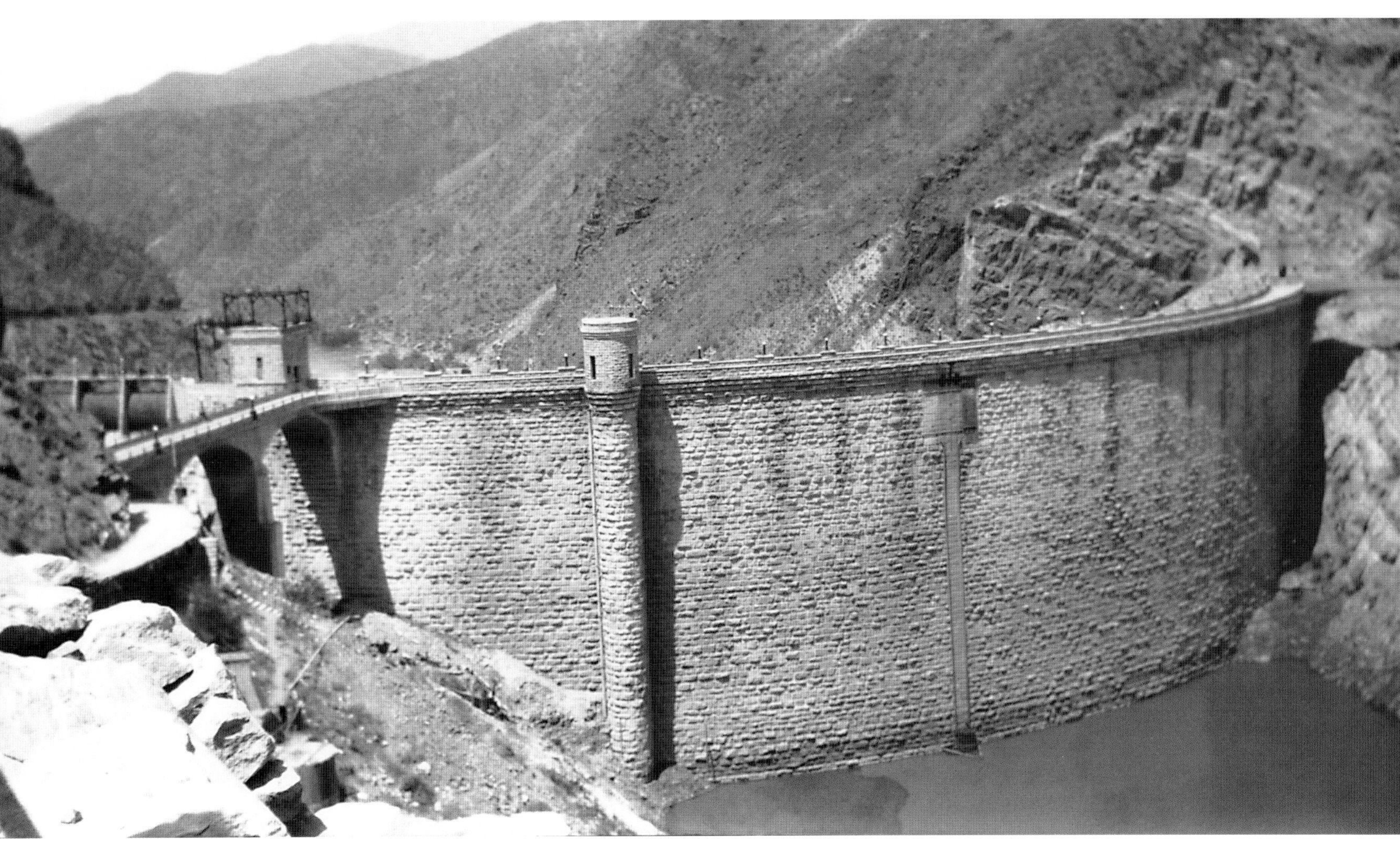

LANDSCAPE, 1959

Dad always viewed Arizona as a fickle mistress always in the midst of a costume change. She gives and takes away with equal frequency, but the end result is usually breathtaking to behold.

The featured landscape scenic is a study in that puzzling dichotomy, as witnessed by new growth next to fallen trees and verdant foliage jutting out of otherwise spare terrain. Clouds hovering overhead and the mountain jutting conspicuously in the background were trademark elements in his visual quest to record Arizona as it existed during his lifetime.

Although the actual location is unknown, the tree stumps suggest that it may have been taken in Pinal County, since Ironwood trees were commonly used to make coke to use in the copper smelters.

Negative 843X

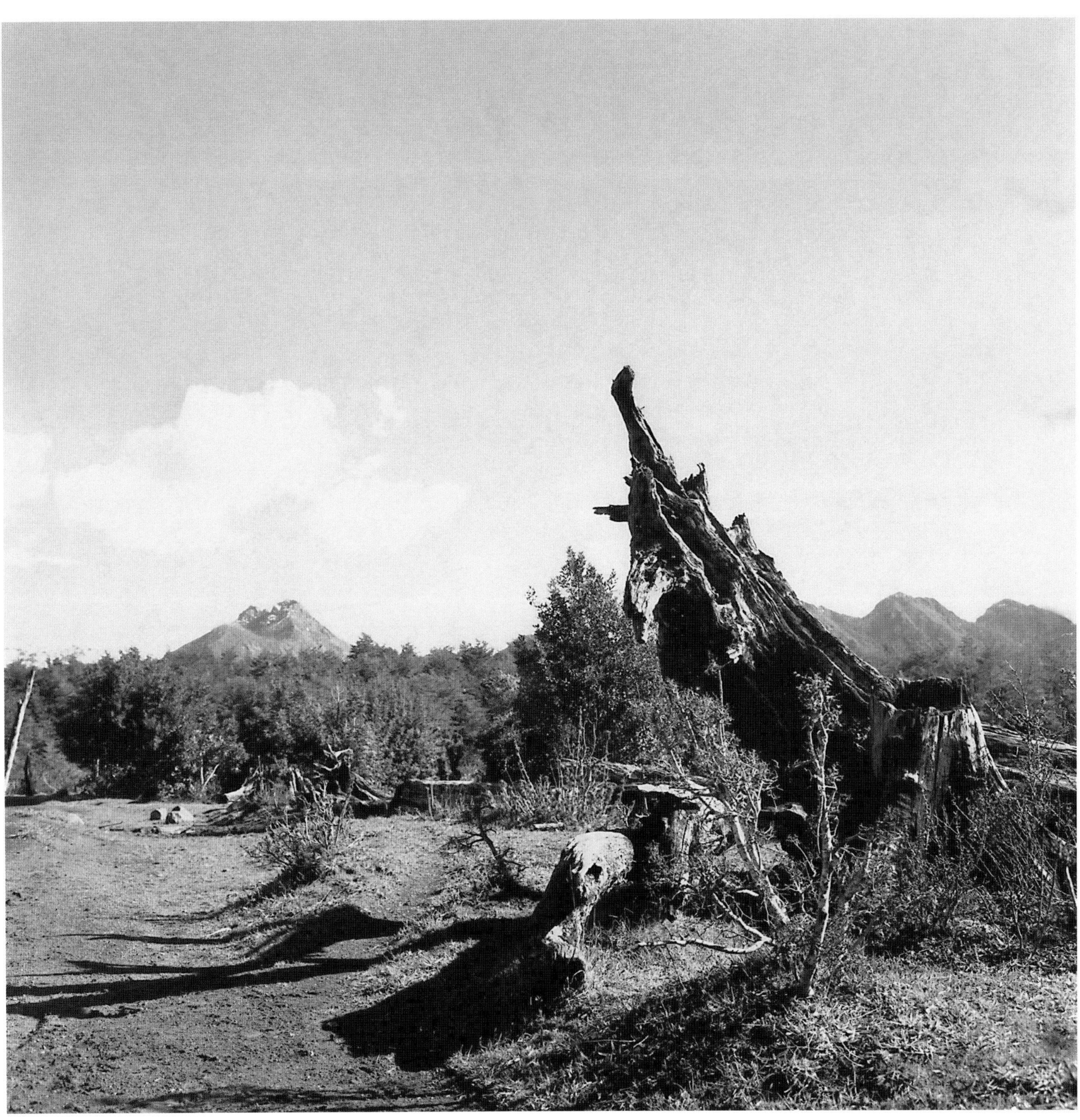

SAGUARO SYMPHONY, 1938

There is perhaps no more enduring symbol of Arizona than the majestic saguaro cactus, which begins its life as a shiny black seed equal in size to the head of a pin and can jut to over fifty feet within a lifespan that can exceed 150 years. At maturity, it can weigh as much as eight tons, granting the saguaro the distinction of being the largest cactus in the United States. A fluted, cylinder shaped column distinguished by long, woody ribs that expand to store moisture for the dry season supports its huge bulk.

Although the exact location of the photograph is unknown, it may be one of many frames Dad captured during his trips to the Saguaro National Park outside Tucson, which was made a national monument in 1933. In November of 1961, President John F. Kennedy, Dad's good friend, signed a bill expanding the original monument to include Tucson Mountain Park. Following a 1975 expansion of an additional 71,400 wilderness acres, Saguaro National Park was formally established on October 14, 1994, with a gross area of 91,446 acres.

Because the photograph proved a favorite among family and friends, Dad experimented widely in its final presentation, including gilding the final print with sepia to further dignify the subtle play of light and shadow that distinguishes its surface.

Negative 847X

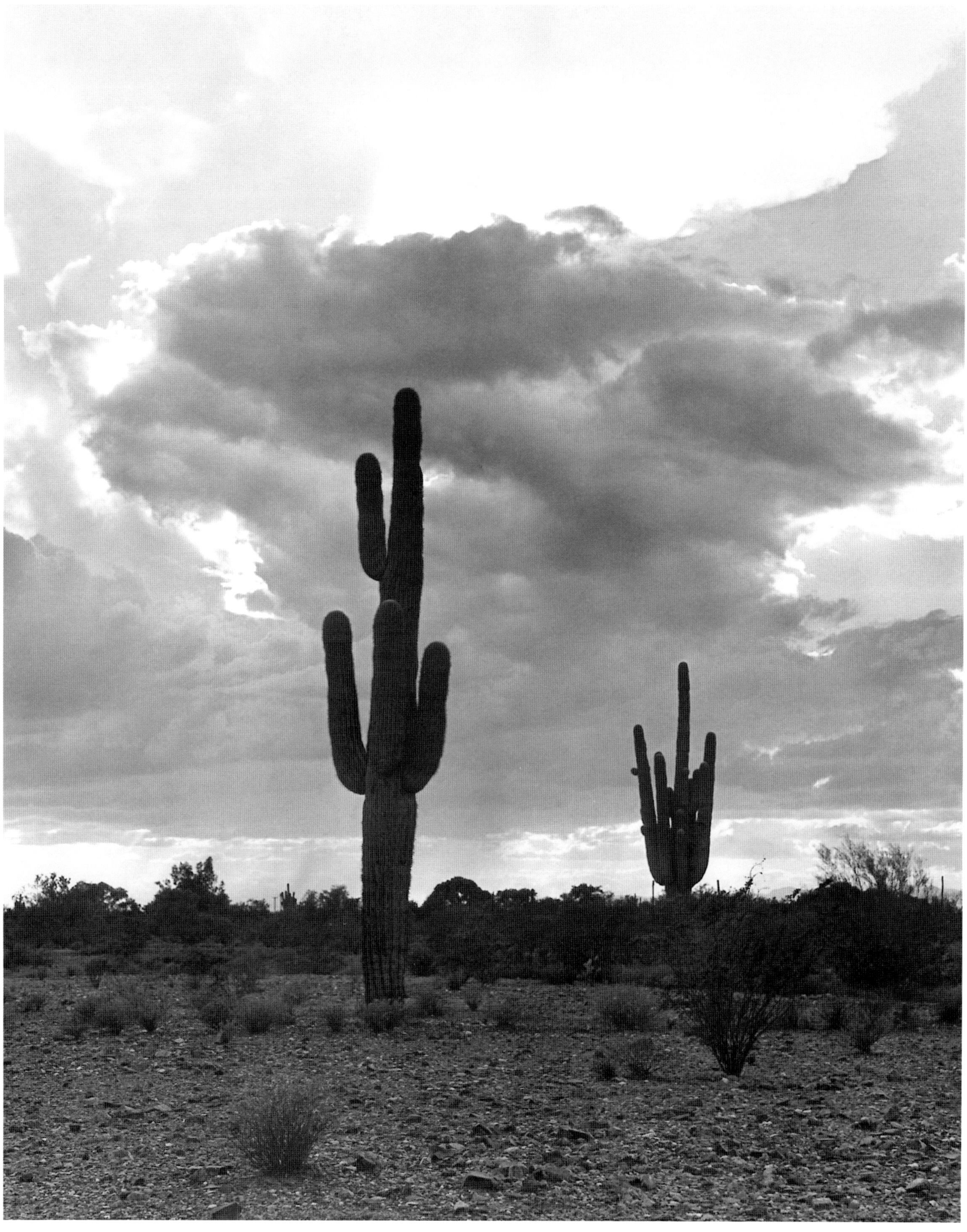

MIDDLE FORK OF THE SALMON RIVER, 1950

The following series of photographs were taken during one of a number of family outings on and along the banks of the Middle Fork of the Salmon River, which stretches between its headwaters in the area around Stanley, Idaho.

During my two trips with my parents, rancher Andy Anderson served as our companion and guide, which made the excursions educational, as well as highly entertaining. These journeys were typically around three days in length and offered some of the best fishing to be found anywhere in the region.

On one early May visit, my parents encountered unseasonably cold temperatures that ended with the bucket holding the fish frozen solid. The related human hardships of the journey tested Mom's patience to the extent that she refused to do a repeat performance until Dad figured out a way to provide her on demand with hot water and the services of a good hairdresser.

Negative 737

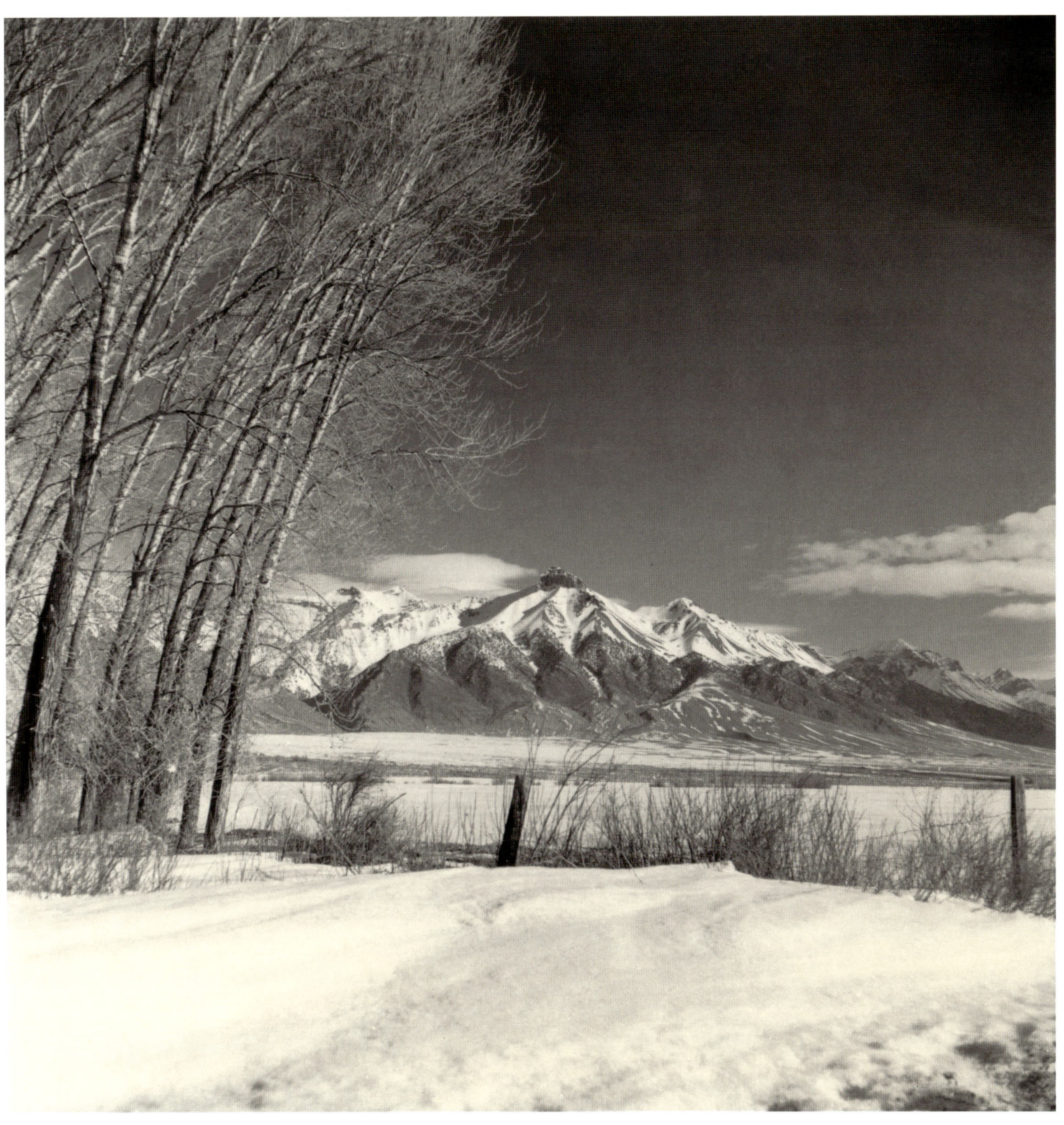

MOUNT BORAH, IDAHO, 1950

This spectral view of Mount Borah reflects both Dad's eye for beauty and his life-long addiction to the majesty peculiar to Mother Nature. The vantage point is south-westerly in the direction of the Birch Springs Road, which leads to a major trailhead approach long favored by hikers and climbers.

Mount Borah is the highest peak in Idaho, jutting a mammoth 12,662 feet in the air from the midst of the Lost River Range, with its alternating mountains, valleys and famed knife edge ridge south of the summit. Located far from any population center, the surrounding terrain is raw, rugged and seasonally riotous.

The bold jewel in Idaho's crown is aptly named in honor of legendary U.S. Senator William A. Borah, whose forceful oratory and shrewd strategizing earned him success as an attorney, politician and practicing ladies man. Born in Illinois at the close of the Civil War, he studied law for two years at the University of Kansas, before being diagnosed with tuberculosis, dropping out of school and reading for the law. After impregnating a Lyons, Kansas woman, he boarded a westbound train at the behest of community leaders and met a gambler who told him about the vast opportunities available in Idaho, then barely three months into statehood.

Borah set up a law practice in Boise and immediately began to dabble in local politics. By 1896, he was the leader of Idaho's Silver Republicans, then turned independent, only to return to the GOP under the progressive banner in 1906, the same year he signed on as chief prosecutor in the trial of labor leader Bill Heywood. The resultant fame oiled the rails to Washington, where he soon emerged a powerful voice in both political and social arenas. Although he earned national recognition for his stalwart opposition to the League of Nations and the Treaty of Versailles, he is perhaps best remembered for his profound and lasting interest in members of the opposite sex, particularly his long and open affair with President Theodore Roosevelt's married daughter and one-time Phoenix newspaper publisher, Alice Roosevelt Longworth, whose unapologetic defiance of social convention earned her the moniker "Aurora Borah Alice."

Negative 857X

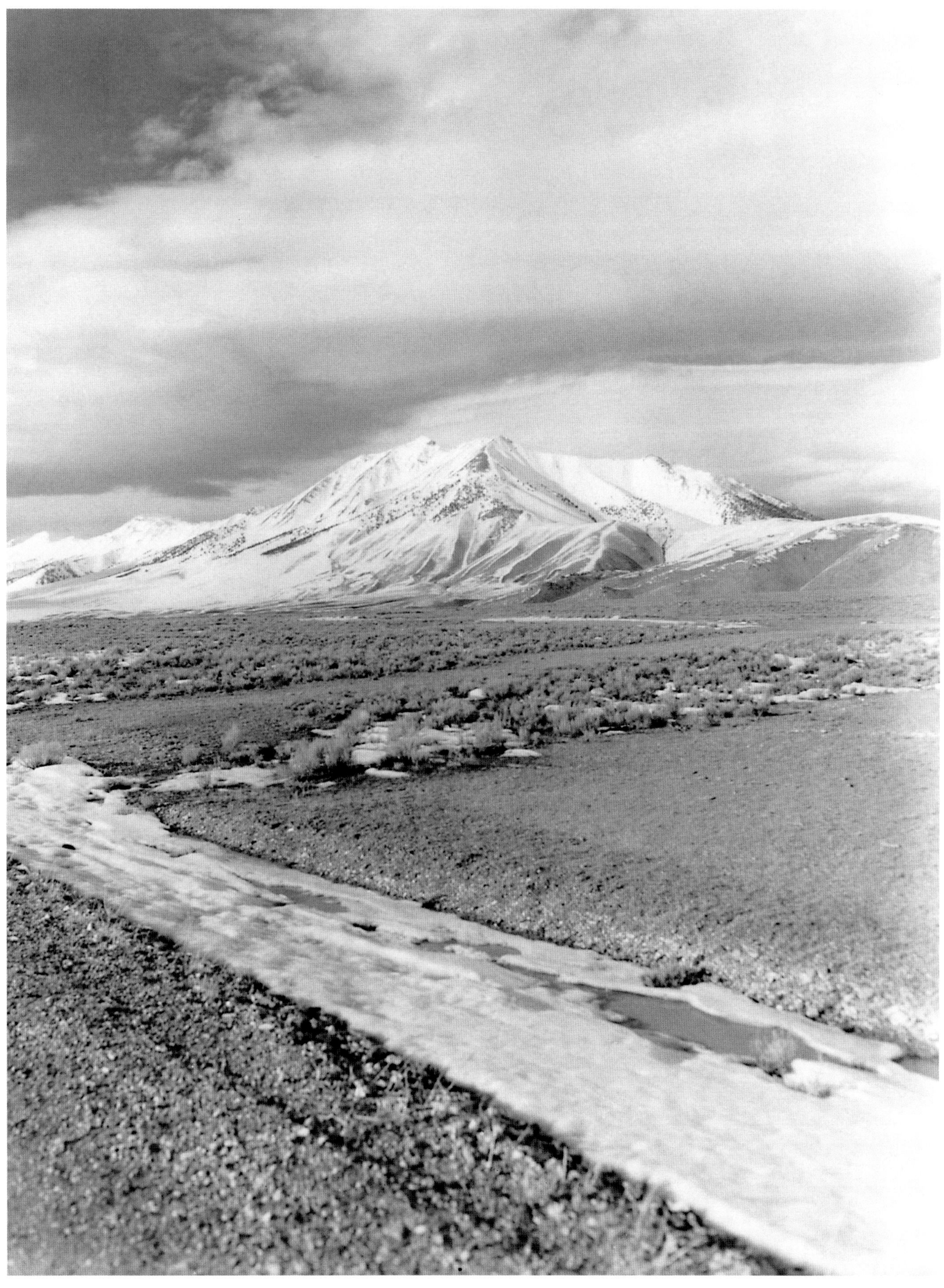

OCEAN, MONTEREY, CALIFORNIA, 1940

Dad's initial exposure to the Pacific Ocean came during his many childhood escapes from the heat engineered by his legendary mother. Santa Monica, California was a favorite destination during the early years, but he later expanded his experiences to include most of the California coastline, including that adjacent to Monterey, California, the historic stomping ground of his self-ascribed photographic mentor Edward Weston, whose stark and straight style he sought to emulate.

Like Weston, Dad was attracted to rocks and other natural shapes cast against their own setting. The combination of fierce waves crashing against stone simultaneously suggests change and permanence in a fashion only Mother Nature can convincingly deliver.

Negative 714-B

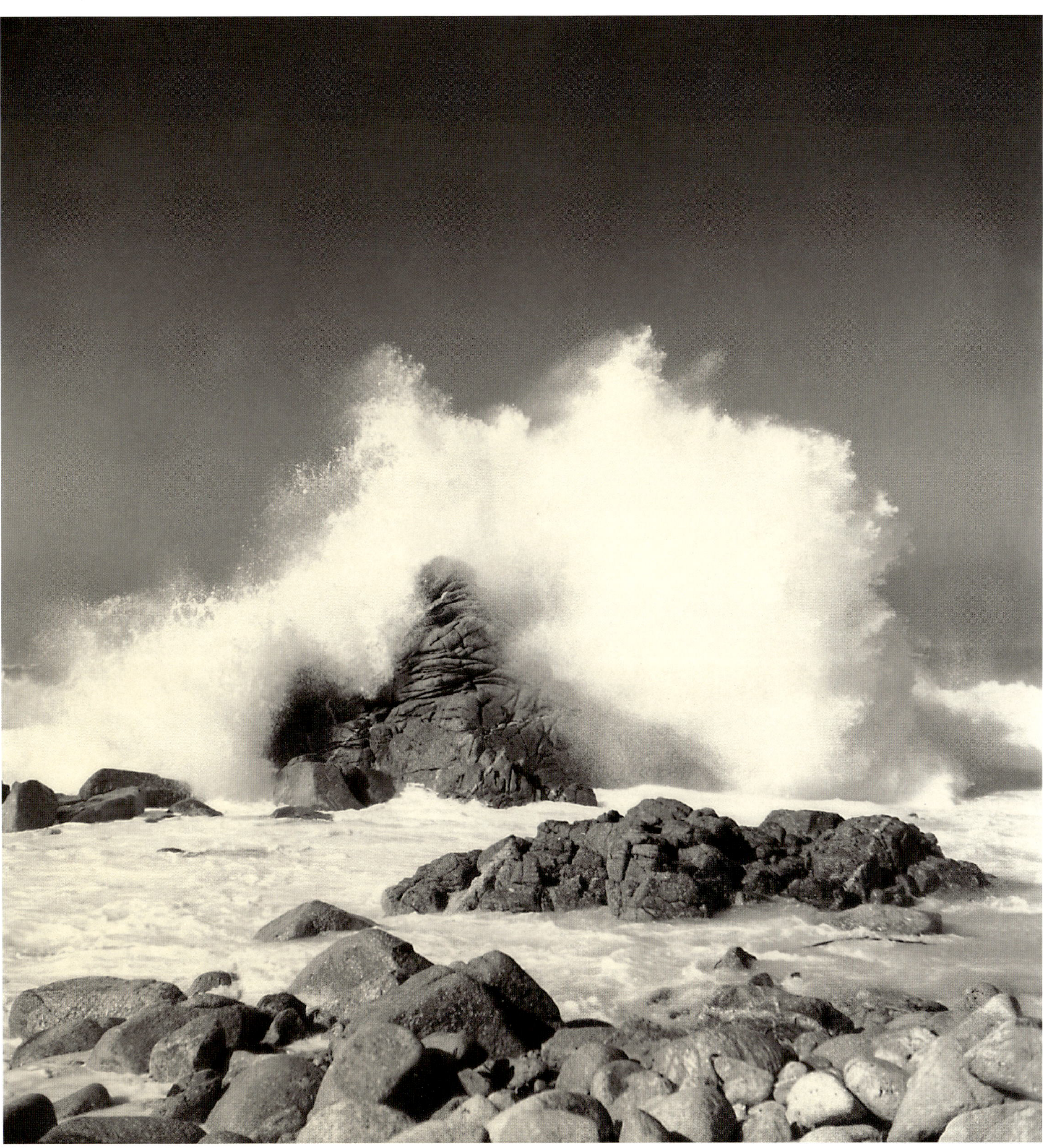

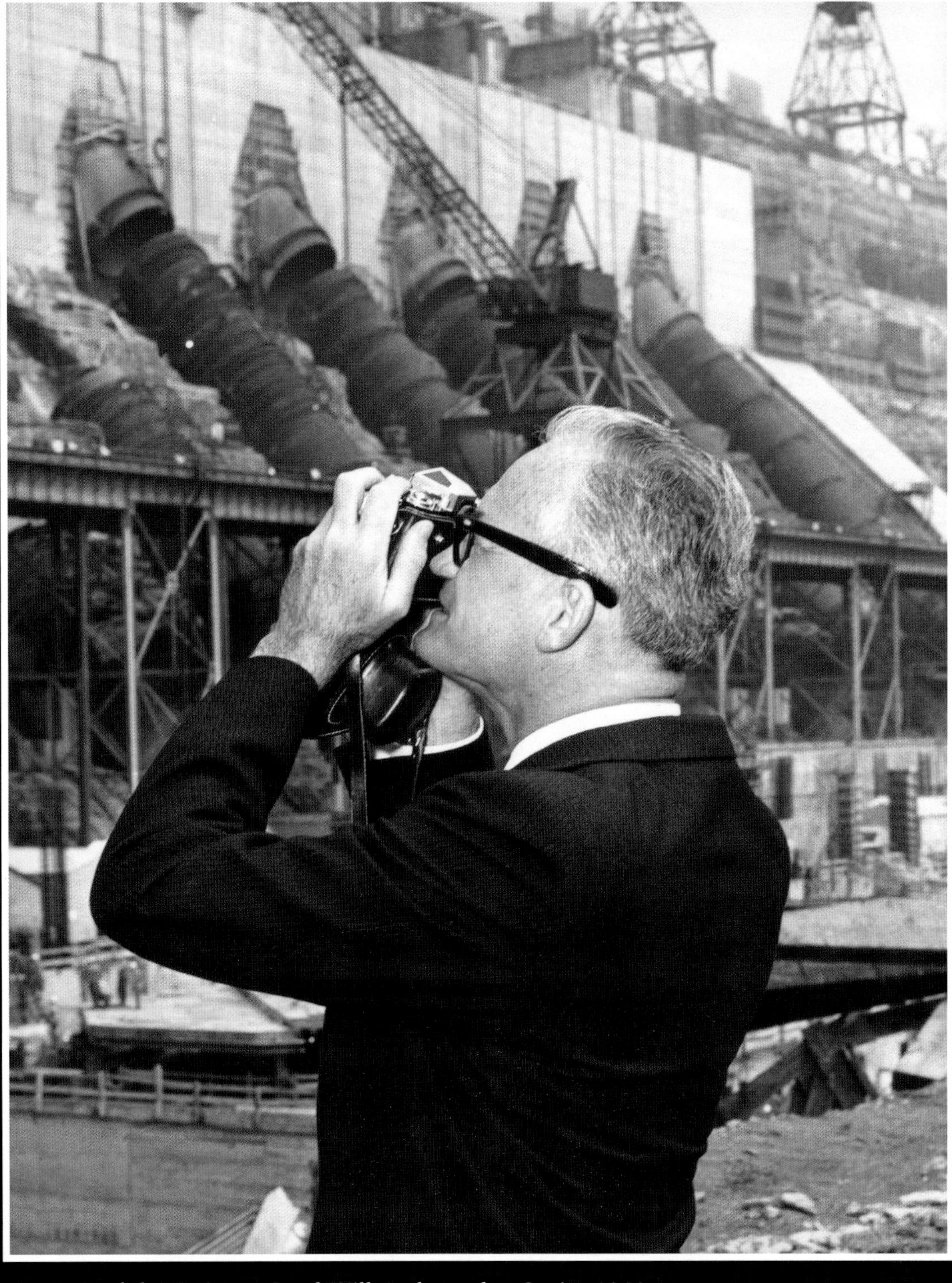

Portrait of the Artist as Good Will Ambassador, Spain, 1966

STATESMAN ABROAD

Peggy and I enjoyed traveling, visiting new countries to see how other people lived. We were always planning trips to someplace where we could walk down a street, stop for a cocktail or a bite to eat without attracting public attention.

Barry M. Goldwater to Evelyn S. Cooper
Spring, 1989

SANTIAGO, c. 1930

There is no more a typical Mexican face than there is a typical face of any people. The Mexican is industrious, kind and a very warm family man whose hogar (hearth) is his citadel, his castle and his life. A Mexican is particularly devoted to his country and will defend it against any slur or attack. Mexicans are loyal and true friends whose word becomes their bond. One doesn't find all of these attributes reflected in any one face, but often a reflection of the dignity born of them comes through.

This man, for example, was a Mexican fisherman with whom I fished the waters of the Gulf of California many years ago. He could be many Mexicans, but not all of them. The sparkle of dignity and pride, however, are common possessions.

Wherever Santiago is today, I wish him buena suerte *(good fortune).*

Barry M. Goldwater
in *People and Places*

Negative 742

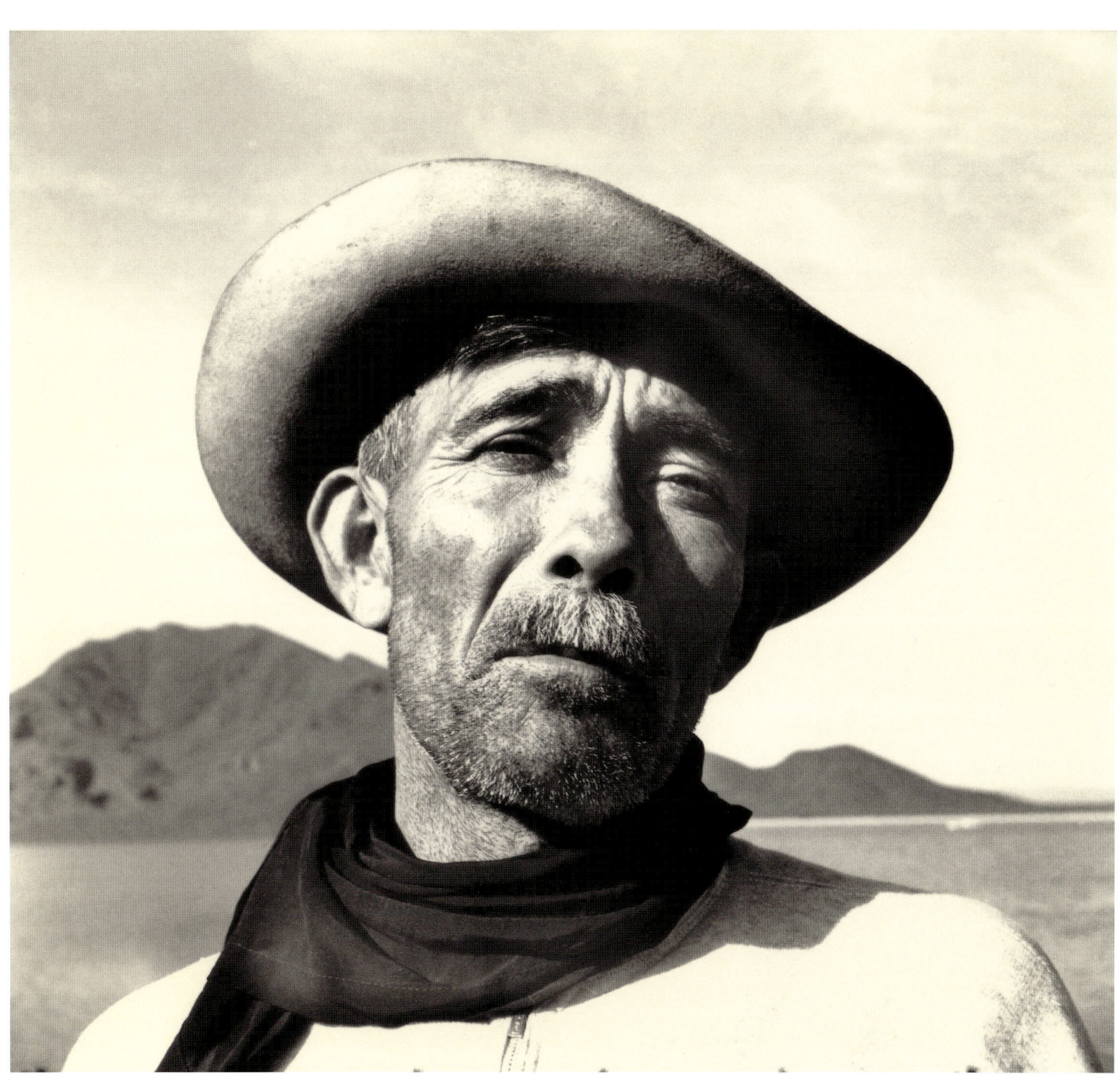

ACAPULCO, 1955

During the years succeeding my parents' marriage, Dad learned a lot about composition from Mom, whose keen eye for fine aesthetics was second to none. She may well have been standing at his side as he turned his lens toward this provocative architectural scene taken during one of their many trips to Acapulco.

The urns lining the steps and the mirror like shadows cast against the opposing wall convey Dad's keen understanding of the variables of timing and light in transforming an ordinary scene into a fine arts photograph.

Negative 2431

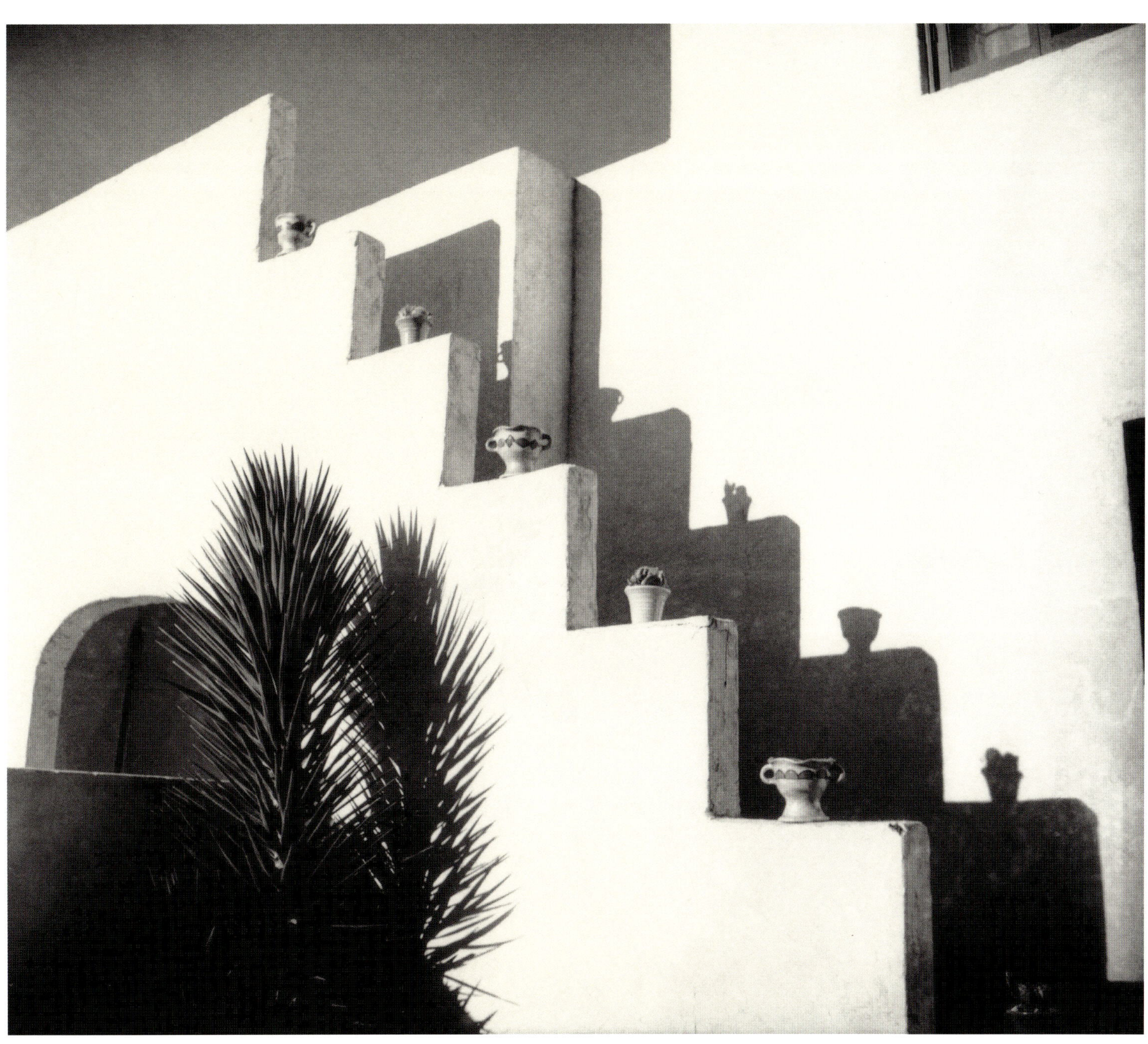

EL VIEJO, MEXICO CITY, 1952

This popular portrait is one of a series of photographs Dad took of the same subject during one of his frequent visits to Mexico. He later explained the time and circumstances surrounding the impromptu sitting:

I initially entitled this one simply 'The Old One.' He was a professional model I met in a park in Mexico City in 1952.

Barry M. Goldwater

Negative 725

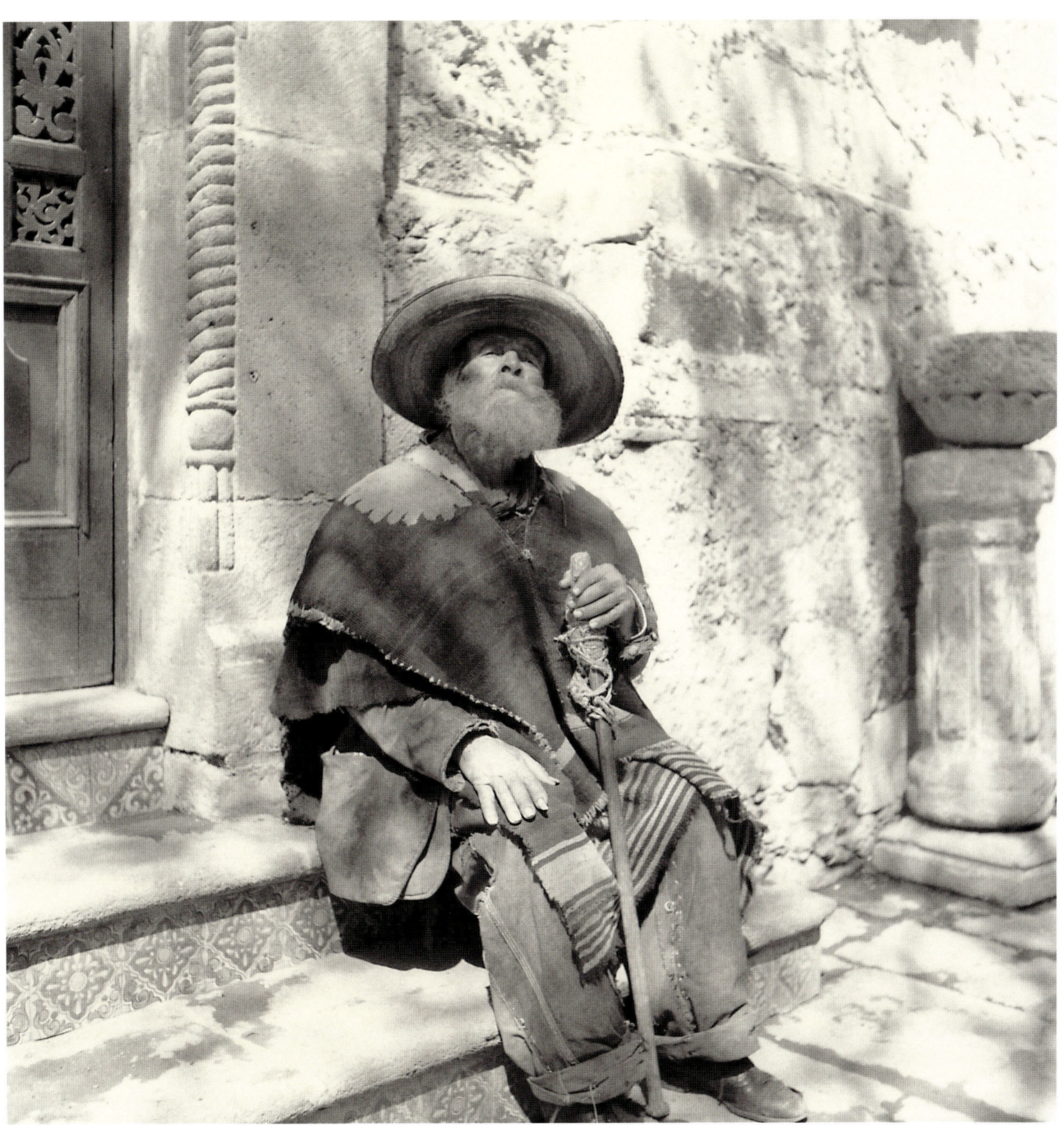

THE NET MENDER, 1952

Through out his eventful life, Dad was never able to resist a face or setting that told its own kind of story. He typically backed the photograph with words designed to send the message to posterity in his own, straight to the point fashion.

That simplicity is evident in his description of the featured image: "This Mexican fisherman is weaving and fixing his nets in the fishing village of Patzcuaro."

Negative 924

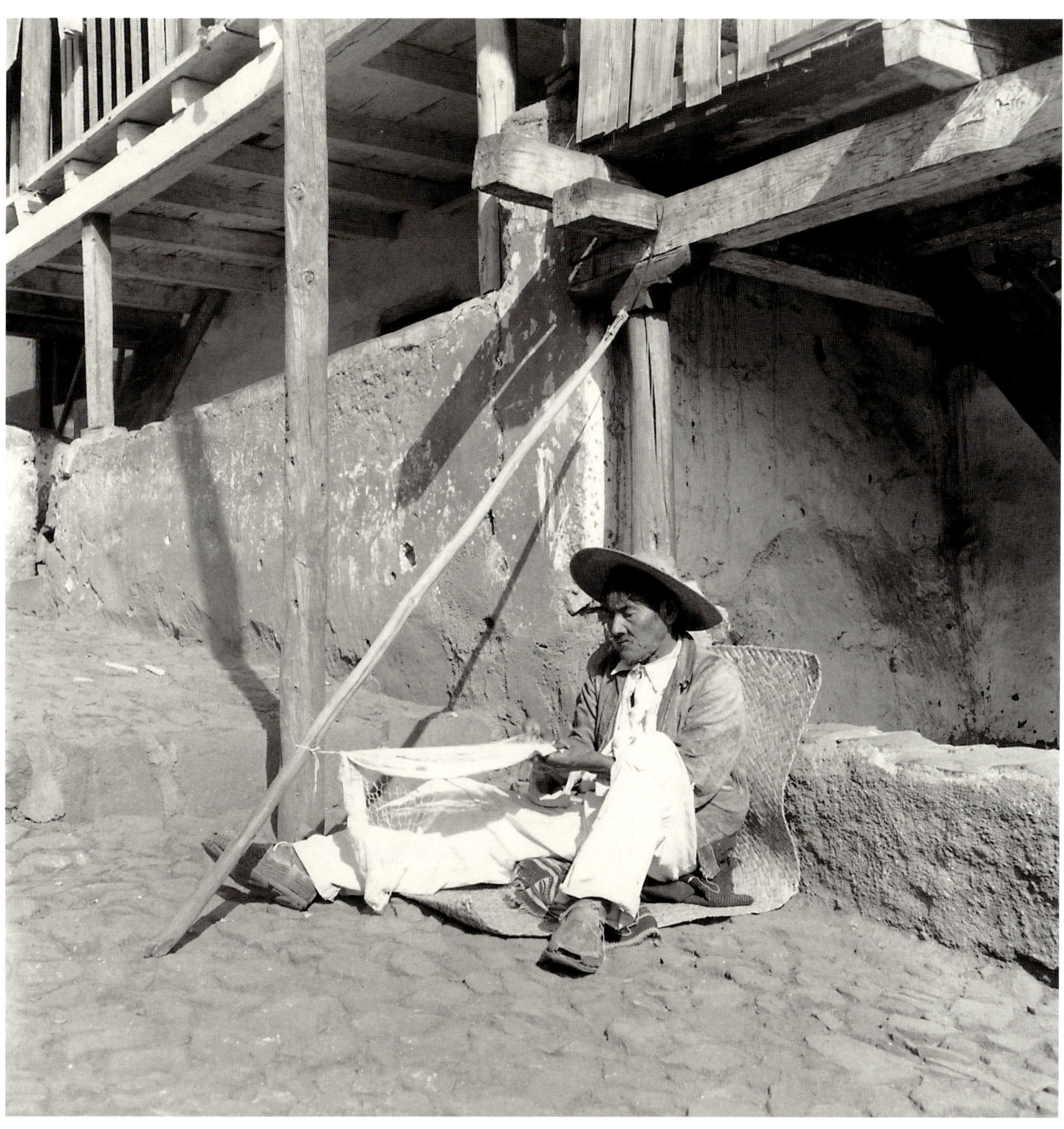

YOUNG GIRL IN SPAIN, 1966

When Dad was initially earning his spurs as a photographer, he developed a fascination for the work of Master Photographer Edward Weston, whose stark, straight style he chose to emulate.

"Young Girl in Spain," with its clever interplay between shadow, light and texture is a another example of the expert homage Dad paid to his mentor, Edward Weston.

Mom and Dad took several trips abroad, including a particularly productive visit to Spain that netted both the present image and the sterling photograph featured on the cover.

Negative 2575

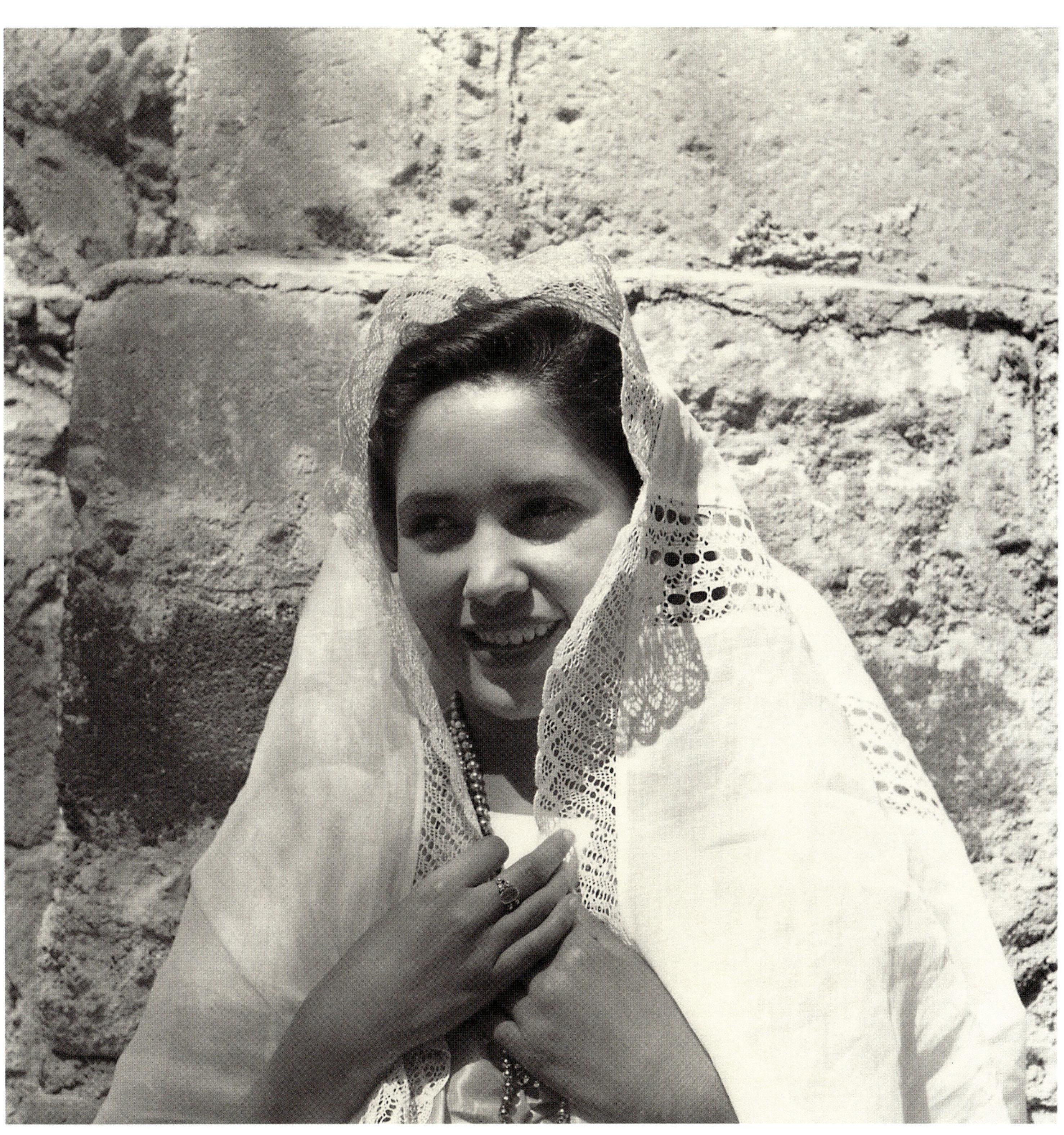

DESERT ARCHITECTURE, 1938

During Spain's nearly three hundred year reign over the American Southwest, she engrafted her language, laws, customs and culture on the region, including traditional architectural styles suited to the temperament of the desert.

The featured architectural view is one of many Dad captured during his trips to Spain as homage to the Old Country prototype that lay all around him at home. Although he opted for a more contemporary American architectural style for *Be-nun-i-kun*, (Navajo for house on the hill), he had a historic appreciation for the stone-tiled roof and high domed style that remains the most dominant motif throughout the southwestern areas once under Spanish control.

Negative 822X

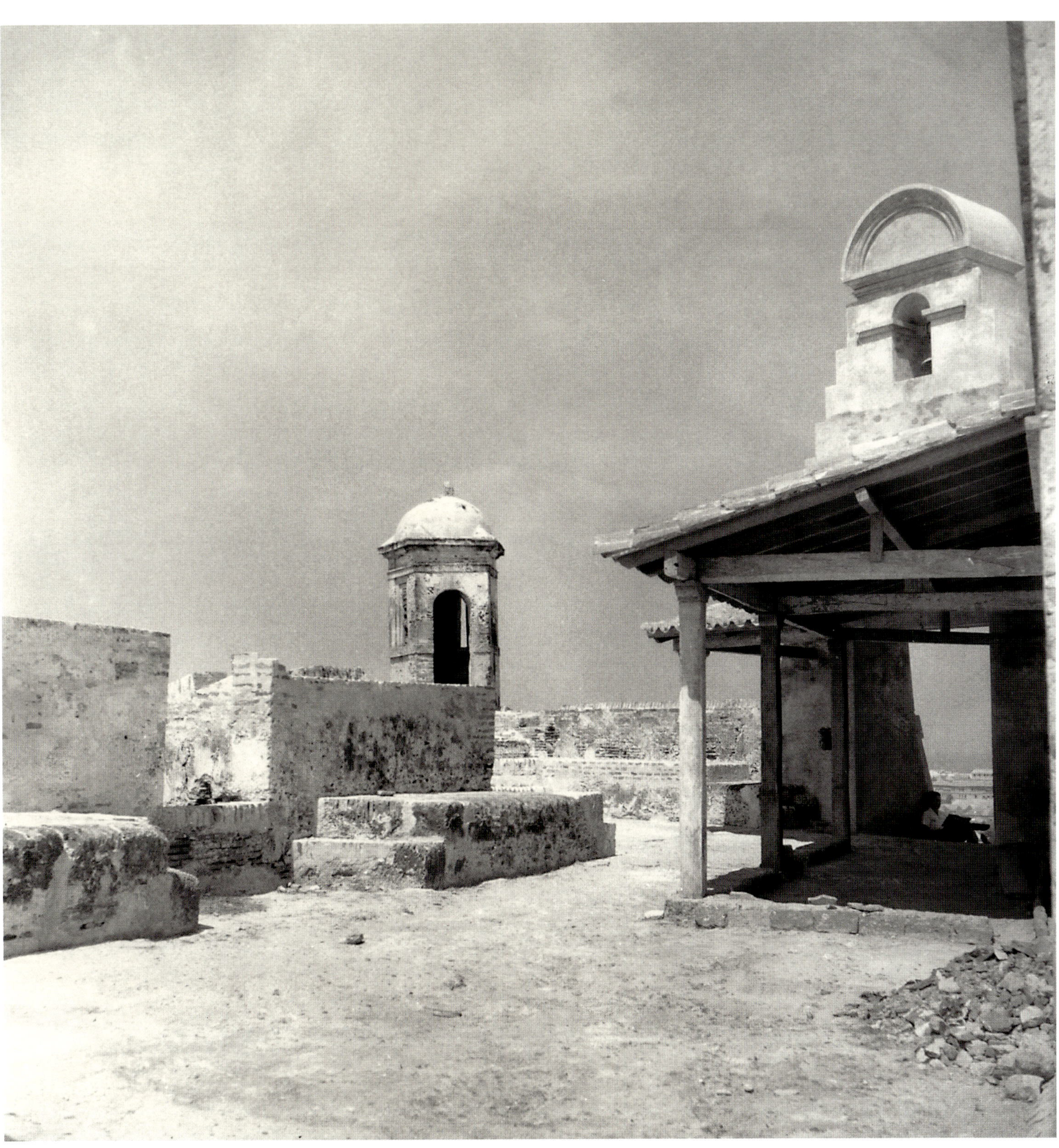

MARCOS DE NIZA MANUSCRIPT, 1964

As a devout student of all things Arizona, Dad could not resist gathering her history at every turn, including the countless hours he spent in Spanish libraries looking for manuscripts and other written documentation of that particular era in southwestern history.

The author, Fray Marcos de Niza was a Franciscan, whom Viceroy Antonio de Mendoza dispatched from Mexico in 1539 to investigate Alvar Nunez Cabeza de Vaca's report on his trek from Texas to northern Sonora, specifically the stories that began to circulate about the mythical Seven Golden Cities situated beyond the northern frontier. Traveling with a Moorish slave, who is alternately referred to in the literature as Estevan or Estanvito, he journeyed down the San Pedro River through eastern Arizona to the Zuni villages in western New Mexico. Estevan or Estanvito was killed there, but Fray Marcos made it back to Mexico, where he alleged to have seen the fabled golden city of Cibola from a distance, thus inspiring additional explorations of the region, including the famed expeditions headed by Francisco Vasquez de Coronado between 1540 and 1542.

Negative 2597

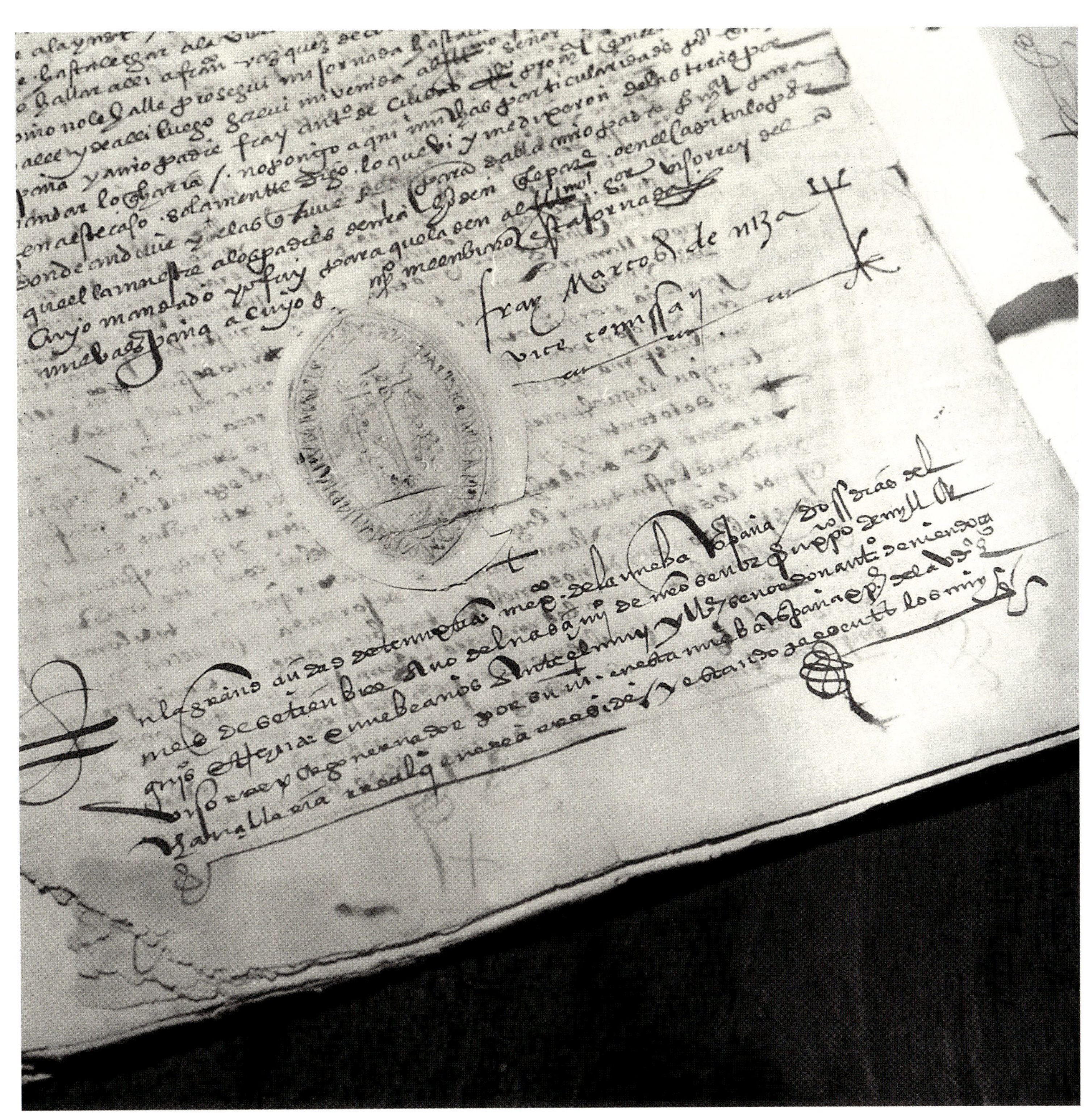

SPANISH MAIDEN, 1965

Like most red blooded, American males, Dad was a sucker for a pretty face and form. Although nothing is known about the female subject shown in an ancient Spanish courtyard, her classic features and riding apparel provide hints about his possible motivation in preserving her likeness on film.

Negative 2575

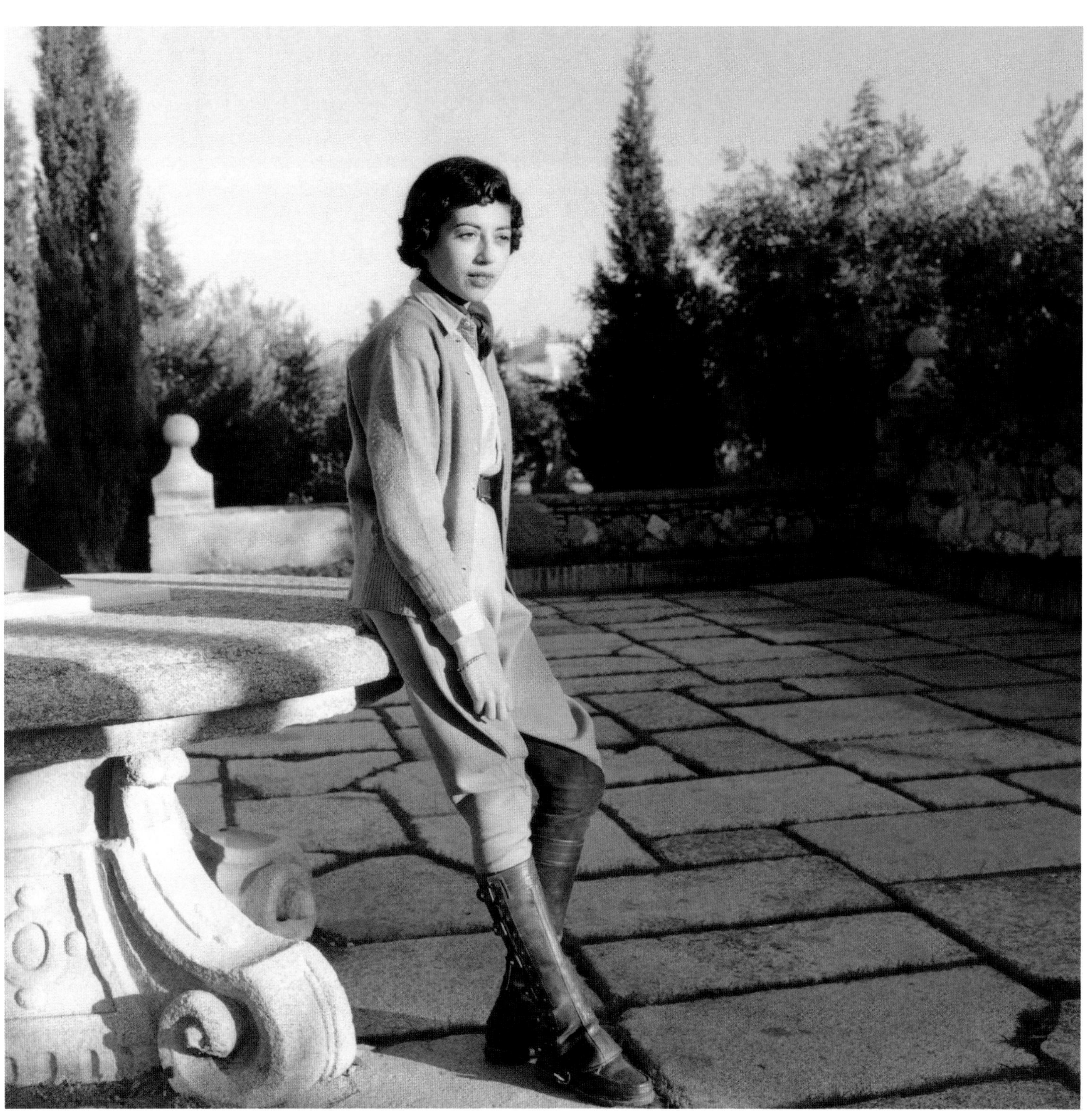

CARIBBEAN, 1960

This classic image of an Old Country courtyard emits a number of characteristics about Dad's growing skill as a photographer. Stylistically, it reflects his aptness as a composer of seemingly disparate elements into a concise and concerted whole. Subject wise, it pays liege to three of his favorite things: cars, architecture and history.

The clock tower in the background may have evoked memories of his own childhood hours spent watching the face of the clock as penalty for not telling his mother the whole truth and nothing but.

Negative 913X

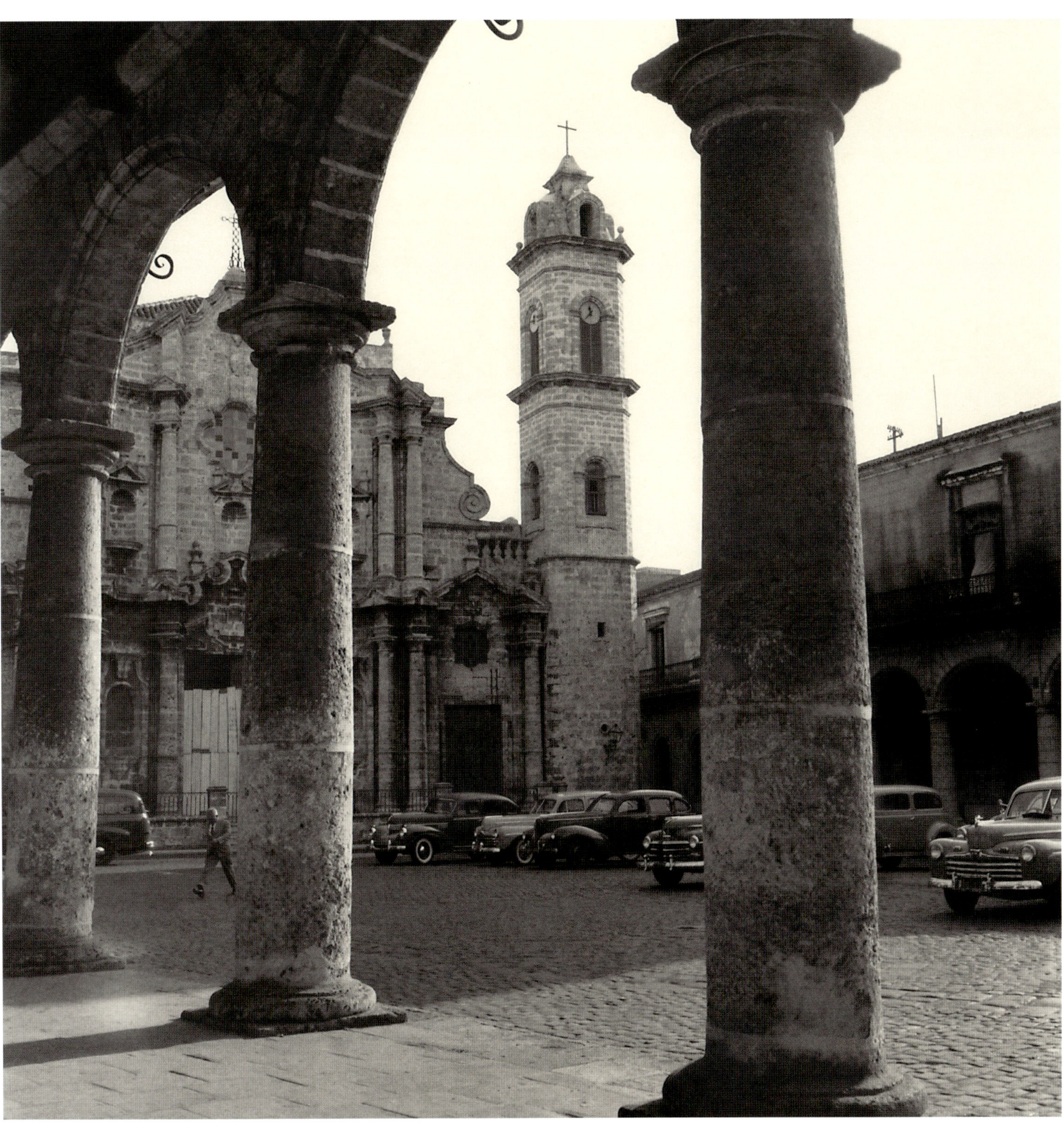

A CARIBBEAN NATIVE, 1960

Dad's intense interest in indigenous beliefs and practices eventually led him to conduct camera studies of the topic worldwide. The present image captures both his respect for tradition and his undying fascination for an interesting face.

Negative 921X

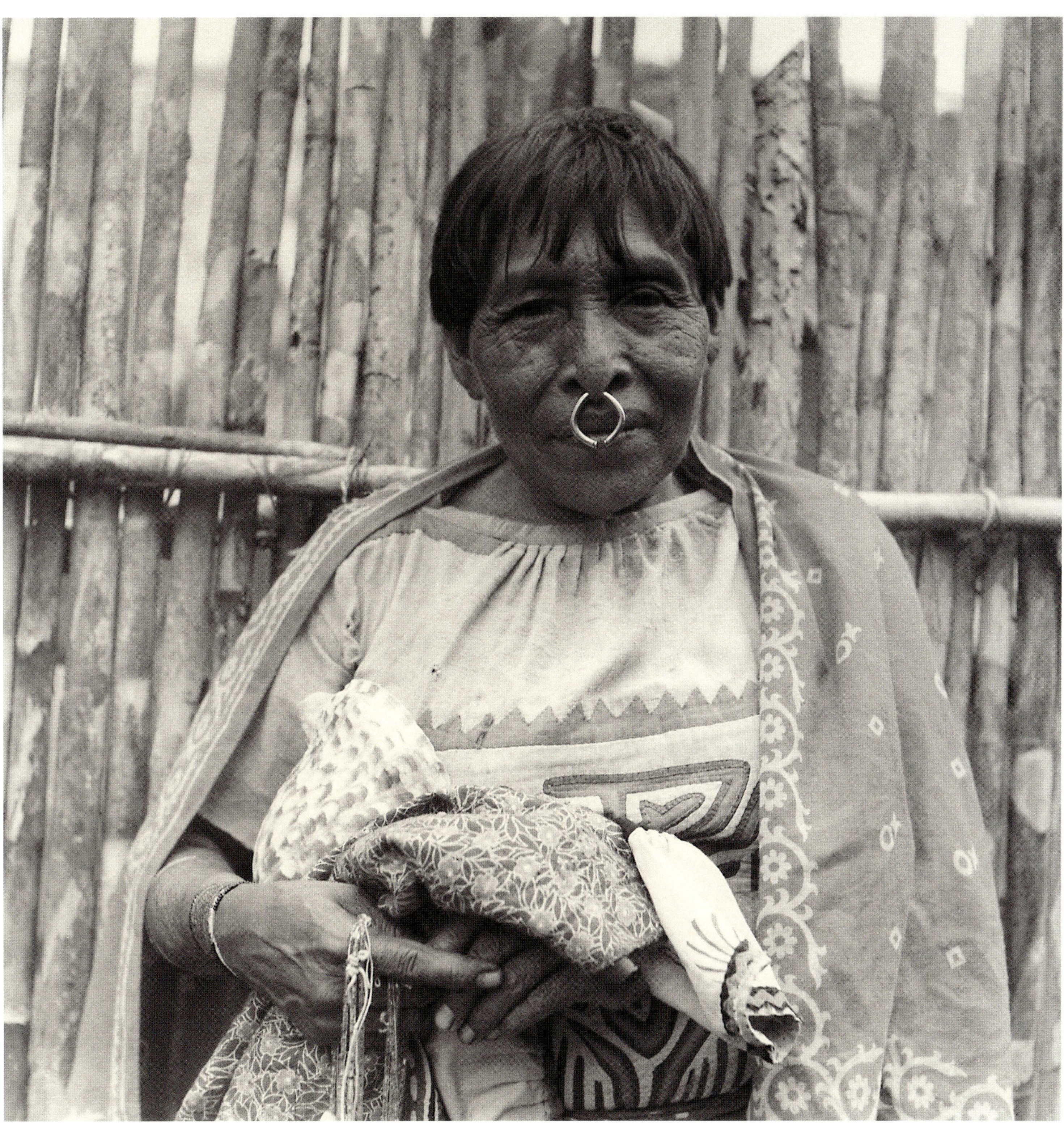

GRASS HUTS, 1960

As a student of history in all of its many manifestations, Dad was particularly interested in the way people lived, from customs to architecture.

This straight-forward, non-judgmental perspective of grass huts was taken during one of my parents' many visits to the Caribbean.

Negative 923X

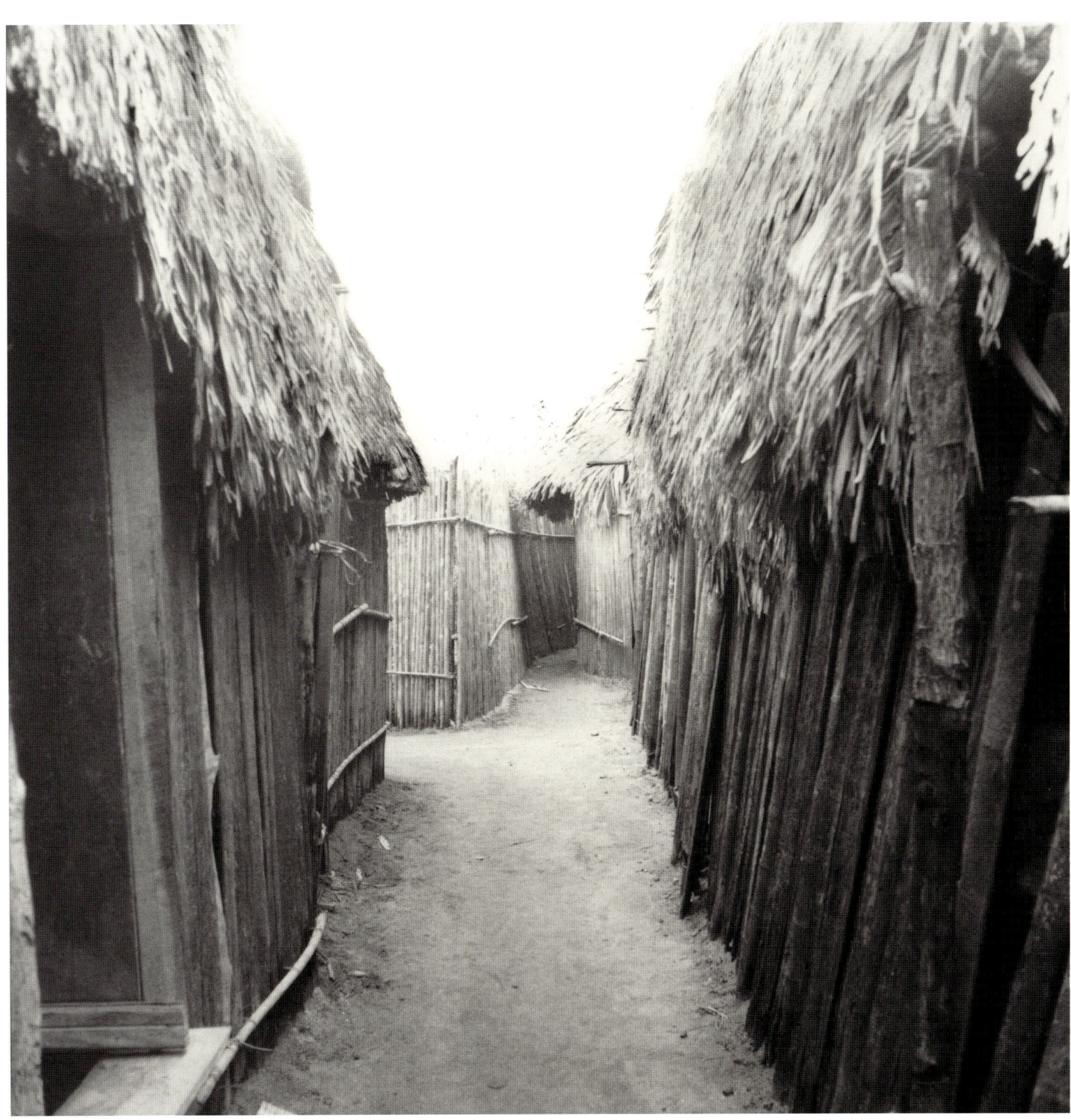

NILE RIVER WASHERWOMEN, 1965

Throughout their many decades together, my parents shared a love for travel that took them to all points of the globe. Each trip netted a new slate of photographs, which eventually found their way into the family album, if not onto the exhibition circuit.

While traveling in Egypt in 1965, Dad photographed these women washing on the bank of the Nile River near Cairo. The stark simplicity of the image is one of many visual testaments of his steadfast belief that there was dignity in all work, regardless of the utilitarian nature of the task.

Negative 863X

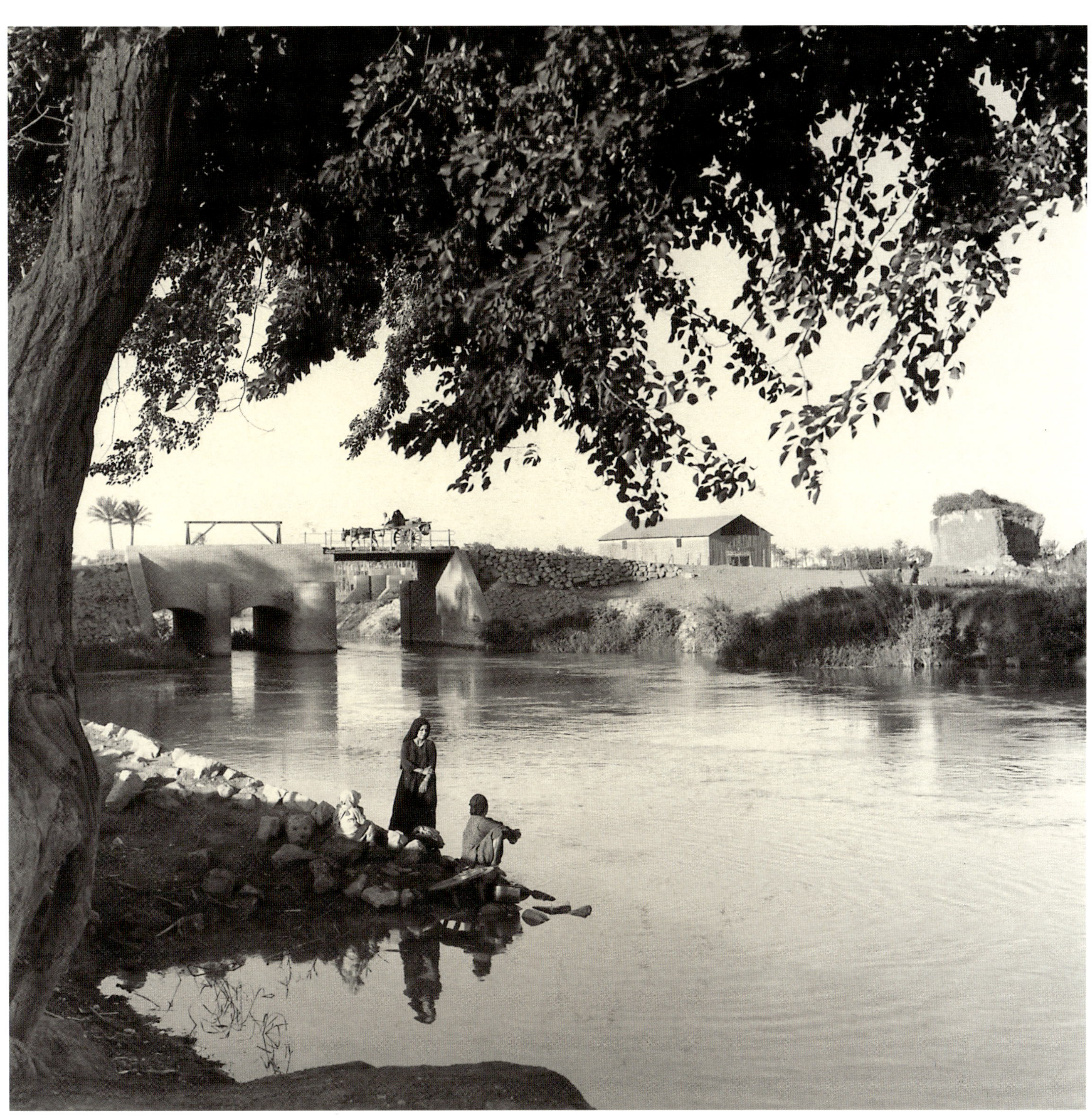

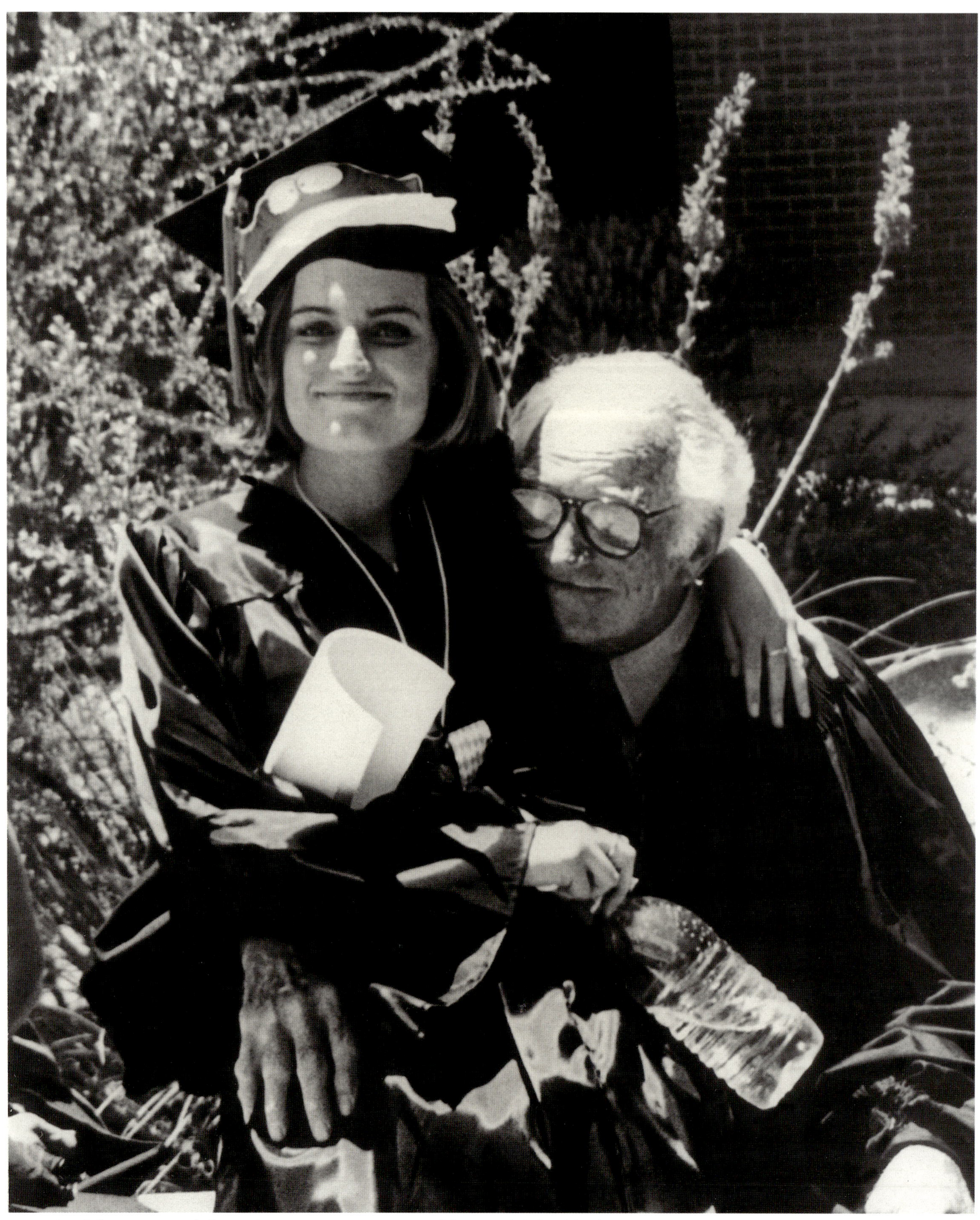

Portrait of the Artist and the Heir. Senator Barry M. Goldwater did double duty as a proud grandfather and graduation speaker, when his granddaughter Anna Rae Goldwater received a degree in fine arts photography from the University of Arizona on May 14, 1994.

AFTERWORD

When we initially approached Arizona's esteemed elder statesman with the idea of doing a book about his photography, he responded with the reluctance natural to one who already had too much to do, too much to think about and too little time left on his ledger to see even a fraction of it through to fruition. He argued lack of public interest and the exorbitant cost of publication. We countered with the only type of argument he ultimately respected—direct action.

We took our case to the community and a glorious cadre of supporters opened their minds, hearts and checkbooks. Because their collective willingness to pick up the tab proved a critical ally in our clumsy attempts to gain a favorable nod from a man who seldom entertained fools gladly, we are honor bound to grant the following visionaries opening act credit: John and Mary Dell Pritzloff, the late Ethel Marley and our fine friends at the Marley Foundation, Newton and Betty Rosenzweig, Merle and Donita Albright, Maggie and Robert W. Goldwater, Sr., Katherine "Kax" Kierland Herberger, Dr. and Mrs. Ross Rice, Hope and John G. Owen, Robert Ross, Nancy Muskin, Sheldon and Paula Silverberg, Patricia Ulzman Tolley and Philip Fountain.

Great men are seldom an easy sell and Barry Morris Goldwater proved no exception. As flattered as he was by the community's warm response, he needed a larger reason than ego to sanction and support another book about his life. The deal clincher was our mutual decision to perpetually reserve all book sale profits for the exclusive benefit of the Arizona Historical Foundation, which was then undergoing an unprecedented expansion that made space and staff shortages loom certain. As its chief financier and fundraiser, he embraced the proposed book as a feasible means of generating revenues to offset the high cost of continued growth and modernization in the cyber age.

In trademark Goldwater fashion, he lent his support to the project on every level. Granddaughter Anna had barely attained a degree in fine arts photography from the University of Arizona, before she was inducted into service in the darkroom. While she selected, sorted and printed the negatives, he shared stories, knowledge, anecdotes and tales about his family and personal history, directed us to documents within his collections at AHF, and introduced us to a seemingly endless list of theories and practices that had long since fallen through the hourglass of history, most often with photographs used as visual references.

His only stipulation was that we keep the tale honest without writing bad reviews of anyone outside his own bloodline. As both a lifelong student of history and a history-maker, he understood the downside of antiseptic accounts that paint mere mortals as minor gods. He believed it was time for Old Arizona to just tell the truth and felt a moral responsibility to lead the charge by sanctioning an account of his own heritage through the prism of pioneer realities.

Although his health began to fail before we could get the project off the ground, the courage and conviction he brought to the early stages set the overall tone for our quest, which was greatly enhanced by the many colorful stories and memories of his sister Carolyn, brother Bob and childhood friend Newton Rosenzweig. Collectively and individually, they added details, dates and descriptions that enabled us to revisit yesteryear with three-dimensional clarity.

By the time Senator Goldwater passed away on May 29, 1998, Anna had completed the dual task of printing the negatives and prioritizing the images on the basis of aesthetic and historic merit. We had a rough draft of the manuscript and a general concept of the scope and theme of the visuals, but grief simply got the best of us. One of us had lost a father, the other a friend. The project close to our hearts became a painful reminder of the vacuum left in the wake of a fallen legend. Idleness set in, the book languished and the guilt proved paralyzing, until we were unceremoniously jolted back on track by a stalwart force named Mary Dell Pritzloff.

As an early and generous supporter of the project, she had a vested interest and she spared no change in letting us know that she expected a return on her investment. As a long-time friend of Senator Goldwater, she was intimately aware of the original priorities, purpose and promises and very pointedly reminded us to cut the excuses and just honor the deal. As a wise and caring witness who is no stranger to the traumas inherent in the life cycle, she helped us realize that honest grief becomes insidious only when it is selfishly permitted to transcend into a crutch.

Mary Dell's role did not end there. Through her adamant insistence that we formulate a plan of work and meet deadlines, *The Eyes of His Soul* quickly became a literary child raised by a village. We dusted off the manuscript, tightened up the prose, narrowed down the selection of photographs, wrote captions and co-opted a set of learned minds to serve as content editors. Judy and Earl Eisenhower read an early draft and provided commentary that filled in critical gaps in the storyline. AHF Board Members William W. Clements, Clarissa Schulte and Joanne Goldwater added a final level of fine-tuning by confirming dates, names and details. Bob Goldwater kept us enthused with a fresh round of stories, while Mary Dell added the befitting touch of a thoughtful and forthright Foreword.

Books are built by many hands and AHF employees Cory Hatch, Sarah Walker and Jared Jackson laid more than their fair share of the bricks. From start to finish, they proved reliable, uncomplaining helpmates who ably shouldered the burden of chasing down facts, organizing visuals, typing labels, scanning photographs, copying and distributing the manuscript and countless other tedious acts ranging from the sublime to the ridiculous. The debt we owe them is equal to an effort much larger than words can adequately convey.

The physical act of transforming loose pages and photographs into an accessible format required the skills of a broad spectrum of talented professionals with whom we enjoy a pleasant and productive history. Eagle-eyed editor Laura O'Bagy brought precision and grammatical accuracy to the manuscript. Designer Nancy Solomon injected style, unity and high aesthetics into every part of the volume from its guts to the dust jacket. Amy Rule, Archivist at the Center for Creative Photography, devised and fine-tuned the Index. The technical savvy and attention to detail we have grown to expect from John Davis, Sheila Johnson and our friends at Arizona Lithographers was further amplified in the present venue by their personal association with Senator Goldwater. A signed copy of a poster featuring his photograph of Betatakin Ruin has long been on permanent display at their heavily trafficked Tucson offices. Michael Roswell, Kristi Nichols and the fine staff of Roswell Bookbinding pledged a similar level of energy to the project for a similar set of reasons. Michael's father was a close Goldwater friend.

Across the various stops and starts of the present volume, we have remained acutely aware that our greatest debt is to the extraordinary man whose crowded resume we herein celebrate. We lay no claim to objectivity, nor do we by any means view our efforts as definitive. Our goal was to shine a light on the man behind the legend by sidestepping the powerful senator and focusing on the various forces that helped shape him into a fearless international champion of the time tested and true American Way.

We found more than we sought and still came away wanting. Photography deserves recognition as a pivot lynchpin, but there is so much more to Barry Morris Goldwater than any of the hobbies, interests, skills, accolades and honors that carry his name. He was a walking history book best likened to a modern day Thomas Jefferson with a soulfully roguish edge. Nature and nurture made him a winner, but that is only the surface. Behind that famous face, voice, and reputation lived a caring and sensitive genius that measured himself and others less by their words and more by their deeds.

We offer the present volume as partial testament of a uniquely personal legacy that is still unfolding. Any errors, omissions and other foolish blunders found within its pages falls exclusively on our heads.

Evelyn S. Cooper
Michael P. Goldwater

A. A. Castaneda Company, 24
A. H. F., *see* Arizona Historical Foundation
Aberdeen, Washington, 27
Acapulco, 1955 (negative 2431), 200–201
Acapulco, Mexico, 200–201
Adams, Ansel, 13, 42
Adler, Nathan, 16
Agassiz Peak, Arizona, 166–67
Agathla (Church Rock), Arizona, 136–37
Alta California (magazine), 20
American Red Cross, 30
Anasazis, 34
Anderson, Andy, 190
Apache Pass, Arizona, 134
Apaches, 21, 34, 134, 182
Arizona Bank, 23
Arizona Biltmore Hotel, Phoenix, 35, 42
Arizona Club, 29
Arizona Development Company, 23
Arizona Highways (magazine), 40, 42, 118
Arizona Historical Foundation (A.H.F.), 46–47, 48, 118
Arizona National Guard, 41
Arizona Pioneer Historical Society, 33
Arizona Portraits (1940), 44
Arizona Republic (newspaper), 118
Arizona State University, 46
Aronson, Peter, 26
Arvizu, Manuela, 25
Ashfork, Arizona, 30
Associated Dry Goods Company, 37
Athapaskans, 34
Aurora Borah Alice, 192

B. Blumenthal and Company, 27
Babbitt Brothers, 41
Baker, C., 132, 164
Bank of Anaheim, 25
Barnett, Aaron, 19
Barry, Jr. Giving Michael a Haircut, Middle Fork of the Salmon River, 1960 (negative 977), 64–65
Barry Goldwater and the Southwest (1976), 47
  excerpts from, 106, 110
Barry M. Goldwater Fine Arts Photography Collection, 53
Barth, Sol, 19
Basalt Cliffs, Arizona, 82
Basaltic Schist, 1965 (negative 942-B), 82–83
Bascom, George, 134
Bate, Claude, 13, 42
Bear Valley, Utah, 84
Bedroom, Dark Canyon, July 18, 1940 (negative FPGD-19), 142–43

Begay, Jegini Yazzie, 170–71
Belle Union Hotel, Los Angeles, 18
Bennett, Fredrick Trotman, 30
Bennitt, E. J., 28
Benson, Arizona, 24, 25
Be-nun-i-kun, 42, 208

Berwin, P., *see* P. Berwin Company
"Best Always, The," 26, 28
Big Country, 1953 (negative 765), 80–81
Big Mike, *see* Goldwater (Goldwasser), Michel
Bill Williams Fork, 104
Biltmore Hotel, *see* Arizona Biltmore Hotel
Birth Control Federation of America, 38
Bisbee, Arizona, 24, 25
Bisbee Massacre, 24
Bluff, Utah, 84
Blumenthal and Company, *see* B. Blumenthal and Company
Borah, William A., 192
Borum, Stanton and Ida Mae, 120
Bosque Redondo, New Mexico, 180
Bowers, E. F., 21
Bowknot Bend, Labyrinth Canyon, July 12, 1940 (negative 776), 146–47
Boys Club of Phoenix, 38
Brigham City, Arizona, 166
Brophy, Frank, 42
Bullock's Department Store, Los Angeles, 37

C. P. Head and Company, 21
Cabeza de Vaca, Alvar Nunez, 210
Cabin at Old Mine in Glen Canyon, July 24, 1940 (negative FPGD-29), 140–41
Camelback Mountain, Arizona, 54
Canyon de Chelly, Arizona, 180
Canyon Snow, 1951 (negative 767), 76–77
Capitan, El, 136–37
Carey, Olive, 94
Caribbean, 214–19
Caribbean, 1960 (negative 913X), 214–15
Caribbean Native, 1960 (negative 921X), 216–17
Carleton, James Henry, 166
Carlson, Raymond, 40, 42, 118
Carson, Kit, 180
Cartier-Bresson, Henry, 49
Castaneda, Jose Miguel, 24, 25
Castaneda Company, *see* A. A. Castaneda Company
Castle Dome Mining District, 23
Cedars of Lebanon Hospital, 25
Century Plant, 1948 (negative 773), 152–53

Chandler, Arizona, 35
Chemehuevi Woman, 1938 (negative 728), 150–51
Chemehuevis, 20, 150–51
Chief, 1948 (negative 79319), 158–59
Chihuahuan Desert, 152
Children on a Hill, 1950 (negative 2136), 98–99
Chiricahua Reservation, 134
Chiricahuas, 134
Church Rock, 1938 (negative 717), 136–37
Civil War, 14, 18
Coal Mine Canyon, Arizona, 52
Cochise, 134
Cochise County, Arizona, 24, 134
Cochise Stronghold, 1965 (negative 991), 134–35
Coconino County, Arizona, 100–101, 132, 164
Cohn, Bernard, 19, 28
Cohn and Goldwater, 19
Cohuilas, 20
Colorado Indian Reservation, 150
Colorado River, 14, 18, 20, 21, 40, 84, 120, 144–45, 150,
    172
Community Chest (United Way), 38
Contention, Arizona, 25
Coronado, Francisco Vásquez de, 210
Crittendon, Arizona, 24

Date Creek, Arizona, 21
Debebekid ("sheep lake"), 128–29
Deer Creek Falls, August 15, 1940 (negative 719), 102–3
Delightful Journey (1970), 47
    excerpts from, 84, 102, 140, 142
Desert Architecture, 1938 (negative 822X), 208–9
Desert Corsage, 1936 (negative 1078), 110–11
Desert Sentinel, 1968 (negative 1066), 90–91
Diné, 120
Dodson, James, 25
Dorothy Grey products, 28
Dos Palmos, Arizona, 20
Dragoon Mountains, Arizona, 134
Driftwood, 1965 (negative 917-B), 122–23
Durham, Homer, 46

Earp Brothers, 24
Egypt, 220–21
Ehrenberg, Arizona, 21, 22, 27, 34
Ehrenberg, Herman, 20
El Paso, Texas, 43
Elizabeth Arden products, 28
Elks Lodge, 29
Elson, Roy, 45
Escalante, Utah, 84
Espejo, Don Antonio de, 104

Face of Arizona (1964), 45–46
Fairbank, Arizona, 24, 25
Fallen Friend, 1965 (negative 959), 124–25
Family Outing [Peggy, Sr., Peggy, Jr., Joanne, Michael,
    Barry, Jr.], 1950 (negative 2375), 66–67
Farfan, 166

Father Garces, 166
Fence, 1967 (negative 1068), 88–89
Fifty-mile Spring, 84
Fisher, John L., 26
Fisher, Sarah "Sallie" Shivers, 26
Flagstaff, Arizona, 41, 112–13
Florence, Arizona, 24
Forest Lake, 1937 (negative 1047), 128–29
Fort Whipple, 21
Fort Yuma, Arizona Territory, 18
Forty-mile Spring, 84
Franciscans, 166, 210
Frank, Abe, 26
Freemasons, 19
Fremont, John Charles, 26
Fremont Peak, Arizona, 166–67

Gadsden Purchase, 34, 182
Gila City, Arizona, 18
Glen Canyon, Arizona, 140–41
Goldwasser, Abraham (great uncle), 19
Goldwasser, Elizabeth (great-grandmother), 15
Goldwasser, Hirsh (great-grandfather), 15
Goldwater (1988), excerpts from, 55, 57, 75
Goldwater, Anna (granddaughter), 45, 162, 222, 223
Goldwater, Baron (father), 20, 21, 26–30, 33–36
Goldwater, Barry Morris:
    Arizona Historical Foundation, 46–47, 48, 53
    Arizona history, interest in, 33–34, 36
    autobiographies, 48
    aviation, 37, 41, 44, 46, 120
    awards and honors, 14, 43, 47
    Be-nun-i-kin, 42, 208
    books by, 44, 45–46, 47, 57, 58
    camera equipment, 12, 13, 39, 42, 45, 50, 52, 53, 54
    Center for Creative Photography, Tucson, 53
    Center Street Gang, 32
    childhood, 31–33
    children, 38, 45, 47, 48, 58, 62–63, 64–65, 66–67,
        68–69, 98–99
    color photography, 42, 53
    community involvement, 38–44
    death of mother, 47
    death of wife, 47
    education, 32–35
    ham radio, 32, 46
    family business, modernization of, 36
    family history, 14–31
    flight instructor, 41
    Grand Canyon, knowledge of, 45, 76
    Heard Museum, 40, 53
    humor of, 45
    Kachina collection, 40, 53
    library, 46
    marriages, 14, 37–38, 48, 58
    military service, 37, 41
    mother, relationship to and importance of, 13, 31, 35,
        47, 214
    motion pictures by, 40, 44, 172–73

Goldwater, Barry Morris (continued):
   Native Americans, friendships with and photographs
     of, 39, 86, 100, 115, 119, 127, 139, 149, 151, 154,
     157, 159, 161, 171, 175, 180
   negatives, 53
   philanthropy, 38, 48
   Phoenix City Council, election to, 44
   photograph collection, 13–14
   photography, attitudes toward, 13, 36, 38–40, 42, 46,
     49–50, 53
   photography, exhibitions, 40, 42, 43, 46, 47, 76, 88,
     92, 98, 106, 114, 138
   photography, introduction to, 31
   political views, 43–45
   portraits of, 12, 52, 54, 56, 74, 196
   Rainbow Lodge and Trading Post, 41–42, 47, 118, 120,
     126, 170
   retirement, 47–48
   scholarly interest in him, 48
   self-portraits, 72–73
   travel outside the United States, 196–221
   United States presidential race, 44, 46, 58
   United States Senate, 44–45, 58
   wilderness, love of, 31–32, 34, 38–39, 45
   wives of, *see* Goldwater, Margaret "Peggy" Johnson;
     Goldwater, Susan McMurray Wechsler
   writings by, 14, 43, 47, 49, 55, 57, 58, 70, 75, 80, 84,
     102, 106, 110, 126, 140, 142, 144, 146, 154, 156, 158,
     160, 174, 197, 198, 202
Goldwater, Barry, Jr. (son), 45, 53
  portraits of, 64–65, 66–67, 68–69, 98–99
Goldwater, Ben (uncle), 20, 27, 29
Goldwater, Carolyn (sister), 30, 31, 35
Goldwater, Carolyn "Carrie" (great aunt), 16, 26
Goldwater, Elizabeth (aunt), 17, 26
Goldwater, Ellen Blackman (great aunt), 21, 25
Goldwater, Harry (cousin), 25
Goldwater, Hattie Josephine "Jo-Jo" Williams (mother),
   29–31, 34–36, 45, 47, 214
Goldwater, Henry (uncle), 18, 26, 27, 29
Goldwater, Joanne (daughter), 38, 144
  portraits of, 60–61, 62–63, 66–67, 68–69
Goldwater (Goldwasser), Joseph (great uncle), 14–26, 34
Goldwater, Julia Kellogg (aunt), 27
Goldwater, Lemuel (cousin), 24, 25
Goldwater, Lenora "Annie" (aunt), 18, 23, 27
Goldwater, Margaret "Peggy" Johnson (first wife), 14,
   37–38, 40, 45, 46, 47, 49, 100, 120, 144, 197, 200, 206,
   218, 220
  photograph by, 52
  portraits of, 58–59, 62–63, 66–67, 70–71, 72–73
Goldwater, Margaret "Peggy" Jr. (daughter), 38
  portraits of, 62–63, 66–67, 68–69
Goldwater, Michael Prescott (son), 38, 45, 53
  portraits of, 64–65, 66–67, 68–69
Goldwater (Goldwasser), Michel "Big Mike" (grandfather), 14–29, 35
Goldwater, Morris (uncle), 16, 20–27, 29, 30, 34, 36, 37,
   47
Goldwater, Robert Williams (brother), 30, 36, 37, 40

Goldwater, Samuel (uncle), 17, 23, 26, 29
Goldwater, Sarah Nathan (grandmother), 15–25, 35
Goldwater, Sarah "Sallie" Shivers Fisher (aunt), 26
Goldwater, Susan McMurray Wechsler (second wife), 48
Goldwater Brothers Mercantile, 20
Goldwater Chair for American Institutions, 46, 48
Goldwater family businesses:
  Cohn and Goldwater, 19
  Goldwater Brothers Mercantile, 20
  J. Goldwater and Bro., 21, 22, 23
  M. Goldwater and Bros., 28, 29
  M. Goldwater and Son, 23
  Goldwater's Inc., 37
Goldwater Girls [Joanne, Peggy, Jr., and Peggy, Sr.], 1948
   (negative 2245), 62–63
Goldwater's Inc., 37
Goulding, Harry and Mike, 78, 178
Goulding's Lodge, 178
Goulding's Museum & Trading Post, 78, 88–89
Grand Canyon, Arizona, 40, 45, 74, 76–77, 82–83, 102–3,
   122, 124, 132, 154, 162, 164
Grand Canyon Hiking, Singing and Loving Club, 94
Grass Huts, 1960 (negative 923X), 218–19
Green River, 130, 146–47
Guanajuato, Mexico, 26
Guindani, Joseph, 24, 25

Hall, J. L., 24
Hamblin, Jacob, 116
Hamilton, Alexander, 34
Hamlin, William "Gunlock Bill," 116
Hayden, Carl, 46
Hayden Library, Tempe, 46–47
Hayes, Rutherford B., 26
Head, C. P., *see* C. P. Head and Company
Heard Museum, Phoenix, 40, 53
Hebrew Benevolent Society of Tuolumne County, 19
Helena Rubenstein products, 28
Hell Roaring Canyon, July 12, 1940 (negative 872X),
   130–31
Heywood, Bill, 192
Hohokams, 34
Hole in the Rock, 1938 (negative 1113), 84–85
Holiday, "Doc," 24
Hopi, 1949 (negative 858X), 174–75
Hopi Child, 1959 (negative 859X), 154–55
Hopis, 40, 148, 154–55, 166, 170, 174–75
Howells, Arizona, 27
Hualapais, 126–27
Humphreys Peak, Arizona, 166–67

Indians, *see* Anasazis, Apaches, Athapaskans,
   Chemehuevis, Chiricahuas, Cohuilas, Hohokams, Hopis,
   Hualapais, Maricopas, Mohaves, Navajos, Paiutes,
   Pimas, Zunis
Impromptu Family Portrait [Joanne, Peggy, Jr., Barry, Jr.,
   and Mike], 1948 (negative 2271), 68–69
Iron Springs Outing Club, 29
Irving Kravitz School of Flying, 37

J. Goldwater and Bro., 21, 22, 23
Jefferson, Thomas, 34
Jegini Yazzie Begay, 1949 (negative 876X), 170–71
Joanne Goldwater, 1939 (negative 2071), 60–61
Jones, Wilson W., 18, 19, 21, 22
*Journey Down the Green and Colorado Rivers: From the
  Diary of Barry M. Goldwater* (1941), 44
*Journey's End, Separation Canyon at the Head of Lake
  Mead,* August 22, 1940 (negative FPGD-90), 144–45
Julien, Denis, 146

Kachinas, 40, 174
Kanab, Arizona, 176
Karsh, Yousuf, 53
Kellogg, Julia, 27
Kelly, Charles, 146
Kenilworth School, 32
Kennedy, John F., 188
Knee, Maurice and Rosemary, 178–79
Korrick's Department Store, Phoenix, 30

La Jolla, California, 60–61
La Paz, Arizona, 14, 19, 27
Labyrinth Canyon, Arizona, 130, 146–47
Lake Mary, Arizona, 168
Lake Mead, Arizona, 144–45
Lake Powell, Arizona, 84–85
Landscape, 1959 (negative 843X), 186–87
Lava Falls, Arizona, 82
Leavitt, Dudley, 116
Leon Sylvester Wholesale House, 19
Leroux, Antoine, 104
Life (magazine), 53
Long Walk, 120
Longworth, Alice Roosevelt, 192
Los Angeles, California, 17–20, 26, 27, 28, 37
Lost Dutchman's Mine, 182
Lost River Range, 192–93

M. Goldwater and Bros., 28
M. Goldwater and Son, 23
Marcos de Niza Manuscript, 1964 (negative 2597), 210–11
Margaret Arch, White Mesa, 1954 (negative 768), 100–101
Maricopa County, Arizona, 43
Maricopa Wells, Arizona, 22
Maricopas, 150
Maurice and Rosemary Knee, Informal Portrait, 1967
  (negative 1033), 178–79
McIntyre, Robert, 116
McNary, Arizona, 80–81
Mendoza, Antonio de, 210
Mexicans, 198, 204–5
Mexico, 200–05
Middle Fork of the Salmon River, 1950 (negative 737),
  190–91
Mitten, 1967 (negative 1058), 92–93
Mitten Peak, Arizona, 92–93
Mohave Desert, 26, 150
Mohaves, 20, 21, 150
Mohawk Valley Canal Project, 26

Monterey, California, 194
Monument Valley, Arizona, 78–79, 86–87, 88–89, 90–91,
  92–93, 94–95, 136–37, 178–79
Mormon Lake, Arizona, 166–67
Mormons, 84, 116, 142
Mother's Health Clinic, Phoenix, 38
Mount Borah, Idaho, 192–93
Mount Borah, Idaho, 1950 (negative 857X), 192–93
Mount Lemmon, 12
Mummy Mountain, Arizona, 54

Nathan, Hannah, 15
Nathan, Moses, 15
Nathan, Sarah, *see* Goldwater, Sarah Nathan
Navajo, 1938 (negative 1999), 114–15
Navajo County, 128–29
Navajo Elder, 1967 (negative 1088), 148–49
Navajo Maidens, 1956 (negative 53), 160–61
Navajo Mountain, Arizona, 41–42, 120, 158
Navajo Man at Spring, 1959 (negative 807), 180–1
Navajo Pony, c. 1938 (negative 932), 108–9
Navajos, 34, 100, 114–15, 118–19, 120, 138–39, 148–49,
  158–59, 160–61, 166, 170–71, 180
Net Mender, 1952 (negative 924), 204–5
Neville Expedition, 144–45, 146–47, 172
New York, 28, 29, 30
Nicaragua, 16
Nile River Washerwomen, 1965 (negative 863X), 220–21
Nixon, Richard, 44
Niza, Marcos de, 210
Nogales, Arizona, 25

Ocean, Monterey, California, 1940 (negative 714-B),
  194–95
*Odyssey of the Green and Colorado Rivers: The Intimate
  Journal of Three Boats and Nine People on a Trip Down
  Two Rivers* (1941), 44
Old Hualapai Indian Scout, 1938 (negative 867-X),
  126–27
Old One, 1938 (negative 782), 138–39
Old Williamson Valley Road, Arizona, 106
O'Neill, Buckey, 26
Oñate, Juan de, 104
Oraibi, Arizona, 40, 166

P. Berwin Company, 21
Pacific Ocean, 194
Paiute Strip, 78
Paiutes, 116
Palmer, E. Payne, 30
Panguitch, Utah, 84
Paradise Valley, Arizona, 54
Parker, Arizona, 22, 27, 150
Parowan, Utah, 84
Patzcuaro, Mexico, 204–5
Peach Springs, Arizona, 39
Pearl Harbor, 40
Peggy, 1941 (negative 2228), 58–59
Peggy G (P-47 Thunderbolt), 41
Peggy the Fisherwoman, Middle Fork of the Salmon River,
  1950 (negative 1057), 70–71

People and Places (1967), 46, 80, 198
Pfeiffer, Albert, 180
Peters, Dave, 98–99
Phoenix, Arizona, 13, 22, 27, 28, 29, 30, 34, 37, 42–43, 53, 68–69, 156, 184
Phoenix Chamber of Commerce, 29, 38, 44
Phoenix Country Club Manor, 38
Phoenix Indian School, 39, 126, 156
Phoenix Union High School, 32
Photographic Society of America, 43
Pimas, 182
Pinal County, 186
Pipe Springs, Wolf Hole, 1938 (negative 2443-C), 116–17
Pipe Springs National Monument, 116, 176–77
Portrait of the Artist as a Good Will Ambassador, [n.d.], 196
Portrait of the Artist as a Married Man, Coal Mine Canyon between Tuba City and Third Mesa, c. 1935, 52
Portrait of the Artist as a Young Man, Mt. Lemmon near Tucson, 1925, 12
Portrait of the Artist Mid-Stride, Camelback Mountain with Mummy Mountain and Paradise Valley in the Background, c. 1970, 54
Portrait of the Artist on His Mission, Grand Canyon, c. 1945, 74
Portrait of the Artist With His Family, on the Occasion of his 50th Wedding Anniversary, September, 1985, 56
Poston, Charles D., 150
Potato, Charlie, 114–15
Potter, 154
Powell, John Wesley, 40, 130, 132, 146, 164, 176
Power of Advertising, 1948 (negative 1338X), 172–73
Prager, Lenora "Annie" Goldwater, 18, 23, 27
Prager, Ralph, 27
Prager, Ruth, 27
Prescott, Arizona, 19, 21, 22, 23, 26, 27, 29, 30, 37, 42, 106
Prescott and Central Arizona Railroad, 26
Professional Photographers of America, 14
Pulliam, Eugene, 44
Pyle, Howard, 44

Quesade, 166

Rainbow Bridge Trail, 42
Rainbow Lodge and Trading Post, Arizona, 41–42, 47, 118, 120, 126, 170
Rainbow Natural Bridge, Arizona, 120
Redbud Pass, Arizona, 120
Redondo, Jose Maria, 23
Richardson, Hubert, 120
Richardson, S. I., 41, 120
Richmond, California, 27
Ridley, Alonzo, 18
Rio de los Reyes, 104
Rio Sacramento, 104
Rio San Francisco, 104
Road to Rainbow, 1938 (negative 715), 120–21
Robidoux Expedition, 146
Roosevelt, Alice, *see* Longworth, Alice Roosevelt
Roosevelt, Theodore, 184, 192

Roosevelt Dam, 1936 (negative 134), 184–85
Roosevelt Dam, Arizona, 184–85
Rosenzweig, Harry, 31, 32, 35, 44, 46
Rosenzweig, Isaac, 35
Rosenzweig, Newton, 31, 32, 35
Royal Order of Thunderbirds, 38
Royal Photographic Society, 14, 43, 48

Saguaro National Park, 188
Saguaro Symphony, 1938 (negative 847X), 188–89
Saint Francis of Assisi, 166
Saint Joseph, Arizona, 166
Salmon River, 64–65, 70–71, 190–91
Salt River, 184
Salt River Valley Water Users' Association, 184
San Diego, California, 22
San Francisco, 16–25, 29, 58
San Francisco Peaks, 166–67, 168–69
San Francisco Peaks from Mormon Lake, 1967 (negative 1096), 166–67
San Juan River, 84
San Pedro River, 210
Sanger, Margaret, 38
Santa Monica, California, 194
Santiago, c. 1930 (negative 742), 198–99
Self-Portrait, 1948 (negative 2383), 72–73
Sevier River, 84
Shasta, California, 17
Shepherdess, 1946 (negative 762), 118–19
Sherman, William Tecumseh, 26
Show Low, Arizona, 30
Sierra Cienega, 166
Sierra de la Espuma, 182
Sierra de los Cosninos, 166
Sierra Napoc, 166
Sierra Nevada (ship), 16
Sierra Sinagua, 166
Silver Republicans, 192
Skull Valley, Arizona, 21
Smith P. W., 24
Smoki Clan, 38
Snow Fence Near Flagstaff, 1936 (negative 1080), 112–13
Snowbank, 1965 (negative 985), 96–97
Snowfall, San Francisco Peaks, 1957 (negative MPG-01), 168–69
Sonora, California, 16
Sonora, Mexico, 210
Sonoran Desert, 26, 152
Spain, frontispiece, 49, 206, 208–9, 212–13
Spanish Maiden, 1965 (negative 2575), 212–13
Spires, White Mesa, 1936 (negative 1079), 132–33
Springerville, Arizona, 80–81
Stanford University, 36
Stanley, Idaho, 190
St. Joseph, *see* Saint Joseph
Staunton Military Academy, Virginia, 32–34, 64
Street Sweeper, Spain, 1966, frontispiece, 49
Strole, Henry, 132, 164
Sun Angel Foundation, 46
Sundust, Sally, 156–57

Sundust Family Portrait, 1959 (negative 1097), 156–57
Sunnyslope, Arizona, 30
Sunset, Arizona, 166
Superstition Mountains, Arizona, 182–83
Swilling, Jack, 34
Tapeats Creek, Arizona, 162–63
Tash, Esther, 16
Tash, Marcos, 16
Taylor, John, 84
Texas, 210
Thunderbolt (airplane), 41
Tombstone, Arizona, 24, 25
Tonalea, Arizona, 108–9
Totem Pole and Yei-Be-Chai, 1967 (negative 1067), 86–87
Tovar, El, 154
Treaty of Guadalupe Hidalgo, 34
Truman, Harry, 44
Tse bii ndisgaii (Monument Valley), 78–79
Tuba City, Arizona, 156
Tucson, Arizona, 22, 23, 188
Tucson Mountain Park, 188
Tweed, H. K., 24

United States Cavalry, 134, 182
United States Military Academy, West Point, 34
United Way, *see* Community Chest
University of Arizona, 35, 45
Utah Historical Quarterly, 146

Valley, 1967 (negative 733), 78–79
Valley of the Monuments, 1967 (negative 1036), 94–95
Venture [magazine], 78, 86, 88, 90, 92, 94
Verde, 1951 (negative 855X), 104–5
Verde River, Arizona, 104–5
Viejo, Mexico City, 1952 (negative 725), 202–3
Vietnam War, 46
Vulture Mine, 19–20, 182

Waltz, Jacob, 182
Warnekos, Paul B., 24
Warner Gear Company, 14
Washington, D.C., 45, 53

Waterway, 1954 (negative 775), 162–63
Wayne, John, 94
Weaver, Pauline, 182
Weaver's Needle, Superstition Mountains, 1938
    (negative 2438A), 182–83
Webb, Del, 41, 120
West Point, *see* United States Military Academy, West
    Point
Weston, Edward, 13, 36, 42, 53, 122, 194, 206
Westward Ho, c. 1938 (negative 929), 106–7
Whipple, Amiel W., 104
White, James, 132, 164
White Mesa, 1967 (negative 1084), 164–65
White Mesa, Arizona, 100–101, 132–33, 164–65
White Mountains, Arizona, 80–81, 96–97
Whitmore, James M., 116
Wickenburg, Arizona, 172, 182
Wickenburg, Henry, 19
Williams, Hattie Josephine, 29
Wilson, Sam, 41, 120
Wilson, William W. "Bill" and Katherine, 41, 120
Windmill, 1938 (negative 2443-A), 176–77
Window Rock, Arizona, 114
Winkler, Nita, 27
Winsor, B. P., 116
Winsor Cattle Livestock Growers Association, 116
With No Apologies (1979), excerpts from, 58, 174
Wolf Hole, Arizona, 176–77
World War I, 30, 37
World War II, 41, 62

Y.M.C.A., 38, 98
Yei-Be-Chai, 86–87
Yellow Rock Spring, 116
Young, Brigham, 84
Young Girl in Spain, 1966 (negative 2575), 206–7
Young Men's Christian Association, *see* Y.M.C.A.
Yuma, Arizona, 22, 24, 26
Yuma County, 23

Zunis, 210

About the Author

Evelyn S. Cooper holds a PhD in American history, specializing in the trans-Mississippi West. She is the author of two previous books, *The Buehman Studio Tucson in Focus* and *Arizona's Hal Empie, His Life, His Times and His Art*, as well as numerous monographs, articles, stories and essays.

About the Photo Editor

Michael Prescott Goldwater managed political campaigns for both his father and older brother, before pursuing a career in construction, initially an independent contractor in northern California and currently as Registrar of Contractors for the State of Arizona, a gubernatorial appointment he has held since 1991. An inveterate wilderness addict and seasoned river runner, he is active in a broad array of charitable organizations devoted to quality of life issues.

DESIGN: Nancy Solomon

TYPE: Adobe Slimbach

PRINTING: Arizona Lithographers

BINDING: Roswell Bookbinding